WOMEN
OF THE
FOREIGN
OFFICE

WOMEN OF THE FOREIGN OFFICE

BRITAIN'S FIRST FEMALE AMBASSADORS

ELIZABETH WARBURTON AND RICHARD WARBURTON

The
History
Press

First published 2021

The History Press
97 George's Place, Cheltenham,
Gloucestershire, GL50 3QB
www.thehistorypress.co.uk

British Library Cataloguing in Publication Data.
A catalogue record for this book is available from the British Library.

ISBN 978 0 7509 9300 5

Typesetting and origination by The History Press
Printed and bound in Great Britain by TJ Books Limited, Padstow, Cornwall.

Trees for Life

CONTENTS

ACKNOWLEDGEMENTS

The authors would like to thank the help and generosity of the many people who gave their time to assist us, and without whom this book would not have been possible, especially the late Rt Hon. The Lord (Paddy) Ashdown of Norton-sub-Hamdon GCMG CH KBE PC, Juliet Campbell CMG, Dame Denise Holt, Rosamund Huebener, Dame Rosemary Spencer and Joyce Zachariah.

LIST OF ABBREVIATIONS

BBC	British Broadcasting Corporation
BIOT	British Indian Ocean Territory
CBE	Commander of the [Most Excellent Order of the] British Empire
CMG	Companion of the Order of St Michael and St George
CSSB	Civil Service Selection Board
CVO	Commander of the Royal Victorian Order
DBE	Dame Commander of the [Most Excellent Order of the] British Empire
DCMG	Dame Commander of the Most Distinguished Order of Saint Michael and Saint George
DCVO	Dame Commander of the Royal Victorian Order
ECOSOC	United Nations Economic and Social Council
EEO	Equal Employment Office
EU	European Union
FCDO	Foreign, Commonwealth and Development Office
FCO	Foreign and Commonwealth Office
FO	Foreign Office

GIPD	Guidance and Information Policy department, FCO
HM	Her/His Majesty
HRH	Her/His Royal Highness
ICTR	International Criminal Tribunal for Rwanda
ICTY	International Criminal Tribunal for the former Yugoslavia
ILO	International Labour Organization
JP	Justice of the Peace
MP	Member of Parliament
NATO	North Atlantic Treaty Organization
OBE	Order of the British Empire
PPE	Politics, philosophy and economics
PUS	Permanent under-secretary
PWE	Political Warfare Executive
SIS	Secret Intelligence Service
SMS	Senior management structure
SOE	Special Operations Executive
UK	United Kingdom
UN	United Nations
US	United States of America
USSR	Union of Soviet Socialist Republics

INTRODUCTION

The Civil Service was all but civil to women in the nineteenth and twentieth centuries. Many obstacles lay between a capable, educated woman and the fulfilment of her potential. Neither did women's roles within the Foreign Office evolve in line with women's rights in society in general. This book endeavours to lay out the multiple layers of resistance that lay between capable women and their careers as civil servants, and more interestingly to focus on those who successfully broke through the constraints of convention, prejudice and law, and why.

The discussion specifically focuses on the progress of women within the foreign service departments of the United States and Great Britain over the last 200 years. Our approach is to look at those developments in relation to concurrent external changes in Western society and in the context of historical events of the day. We will consider what was happening in other government departments and in other countries where progress was more evident. The research was fascinating and helped us appreciate the societal blocks to equal opportunities, and how society 'norms' of the day often provided adequate excuses for an effective resistance in furthering women's careers within the establishment.

The first female employee of the British Foreign Office was a typist called Sophie Fulcher, who was hired in 1894. It took another fifty-two years for a female diplomat to be officially inducted through the Civil Service Selection Board (Monica Milne in 1946); and another thirty years passed before the first female ambassador took up a posting: Dame Anne Warburton in Copenhagen in 1976. During this particular span of eighty-two years there were two world wars and the women's suffrage movement, both of which catalysed positive changes including equal pay, equal admission rates and improving equality at senior levels for women in the Foreign Office.

So where did diplomacy start, and when were women first recorded as having a significant role to play? The first part of that question is unanswerable, but we do have evidence of the application of diplomacy through the writings of an ancient Egyptian vizier, known as *The Maxims of Ptahhotep* (Ptahhotep, 2375–50 BC).[1] He wrote a series of maxims designed to instil wisdom into his son and other young men of society and to equip them with a set of virtues and behaviours that would guide them to living a good life in harmony with their neighbouring kingdoms. The main themes Ptahhotep focuses on are silence, timing, truthfulness, relationships and manners, i.e. the essence of diplomacy and good relations: 'Be a craftsman in speech that thou mayest be strong, for the strength of one is the tongue, and speech is mightier than all fighting.'

Diplomacy has been an aspect of state leadership since civilised cultures have formed, and whenever negotiation, rather than warring, has been the preferred method of resolving issues. Those issues range from national supremacy to local trade, from statements of identity to competition. Diplomacy, often as the hand of democracy, has been the most effective and cheapest method of progress throughout civilisation.

Long before Whitehall became the established power base of the United Kingdom diplomacy was a way of life, and women have always played a part. At the heart of diplomacy lies communication. Even in this modern era where communication is near-instantaneous, the sheer task of conveying the requirements and/or demands of an entire nation to another is a task of enormous delicacy and responsibility. There have been many women leaders in history who have undertaken high-profile diplomacy with great skill and authority who are certainly worth mentioning briefly, but our study is predominantly of women in modern history.

Also, in order to understand why it took so long for women to be valued and permitted equal opportunities in the workplace, it is important to review what was happening across the population. Today's 'Me Too' generation take up arms and noisily name and shame those who practise any form of prejudice against women. With the sword of social media they can slice through the mystery of any closed men's room and crack open injustices. However, 200 years ago there were few organised bodies to represent working women and they therefore mostly suffered in isolated silence. The excuses for discrimination lay in historical developments and religious and social customs; very often, resistance to change was born out of a fear of the unknown. A significant advance in women's rights was the granting of suffrage to women, but one of the major groups of antagonists to change were also female.

The unequal status of men versus women was partly based on a sincere belief that men and women were designed to have different roles in society, as ordained by God. Many people thought that blending the roles would weaken the family unit, resulting in a widespread deterioration of moral values and a degradation of society. In an age without welfare, this risk was too daunting for even the most desperate of the oppressed. Women's rights, like most social trends, are prone to cultural shifts and progress that mutually influence one another. Emancipation and suffrage were successful in the early twentieth century because they were collective, co-ordinated movements, with multi-national conferences for women's rights advocates being called to spread a common gospel. In part, they resulted from the spread of shared ideologies. This is comparable to today's trends towards the constitutional acceptance of same-sex marriage in an ever-increasing number of countries across the Western world.

In the following chapters, we shall examine these developments, and the lack of them, from within the Civil Service both in the United Kingdom and in the United States, and we shall cast a glance at what was happening elsewhere. An important factor in the development of women's opportunities within the Foreign Office was the arrival of outstanding individuals who demonstrated an ability to perform as well as, or better than, their male counterparts. On the diplomatic front, we have given more attention to the careers of the first three women to reach ambassadorial level. These 'first' women also carried the huge responsibility of being successful; any other outcome would have probably closed doors to their successors and narrowed opportunities and progress all too quickly.

The goal in these chapters is to provide an historically accurate description of the development of women's rights in the Foreign Office leading up to the present day. Researching and writing this book has been both an education and an inspiration for the authors, and we hope that we have been able to convey our admiration for the women involved, and what they accomplished.

Richard Warburton and Elizabeth Warburton

1

WOMEN AS LEADERS, RULERS AND DIPLOMATIC CONSIDERATION

Diplomacy is the art of letting somebody else have your way.

David Frost[1]

In exploring the varied and changing role of women in the diplomatic field we found powerful historical female leaders, princesses dispatched with the purpose of marrying a monarch they had never met, through to today's highly skilled career diplomats and politicians. The modern-day diplomatic service has been operational for only 200 years, and before that diplomacy existed but lacked protocols and consistency, and was not backed up by a scaffold of defined international laws, as it is today. The appointment of officials tended to be chosen by the ruling council (male) and appointees were therefore male, designated to deliver dispatches to overseas rulers and governments (also usually male). Due to the social status of women in Europe, even if they were involved in diplomatic relations they were silent, invisible and unaccountable, but exceptions did exist and there are examples of women leaders who demonstrated fine diplomatic skills. Most of these women were rulers and masters of their own thoughts and words. These historical figures demonstrated the ability of women to lead, reason and negotiate with outstanding success even under the pressures of male-dominated societies.

Where there was a dispute or contract or proposal between civilisations, negotiation has been, and remains, the preferred solution. Today that is the defined, refined and well-practised skill and profession of diplomacy. All modern nations recognise that the alternative to diplomacy is war, which is costly, painful and usually much less productive. The *Encyclopedia Britannica*'s definition of diplomacy is as follows:

> Diplomacy is the principal substitute for the use of force or underhanded means in statecraft; it is how comprehensive national power is applied to the peaceful adjustment of differences between states. It may be coercive (i.e., backed by the threat to apply punitive measures or to use force) but is overtly nonviolent. Its primary tools are international dialogue and negotiation, primarily conducted by accredited envoys (a term derived from the French envoyé, meaning 'one who is sent') and other political leaders.[2]

The popular notion of a diplomat is that of some genius who can use words to twist others to his or her will. As Winston Churchill is reported to have said, 'Diplomacy is the ability to tell someone to go to hell in such a way that they look forward to the trip.'[3]

But there is nothing in the above definition or quote that would suggest it is exclusively the domain of male diplomats. In addition to strategy, negotiations often take place as face-to-face discussions, and so the personality of the individual also matters. Until modern technology allowed for secure communications, most international negotiations were conducted via letters which were bound in vellum, tied with cord and sealed with a waxed coat of arms, and carried in a locked diplomatic bag that was personally escorted by the vetted king's messenger. Dispatches might also be conveyed by proxy by the personal representative of one ruler visiting the leader of the other country. Only in the cases of very close relationships would leaders meet, due to the risks involved in being a guest in another country and of travelling outside one's own borders.

Women were mostly excluded from all these roles, unless they held power as rulers by right (by birth or inheritance), by influence as regents, or as brides providing contractual consideration to seal treaties between countries. Women in most societies around the world have historically been viewed as wives and mothers, whose task is to take care of the home and leave the matters of governing to men. For example, in medieval England through to the nineteenth century, producing children was considered the most important function of women in society, but also one of the most dangerous, since childbirth was the leading cause of death among young women.

Societal expectations became ingrained norms, which were then assumed to be true by male legislators, who incorporated them into the laws, thereby disabling even the few women who might have had independent means to forge their own paths. Many women did not hold power in their own right, but they did wield great influence through their ruling husbands.

Historically, the most common way for a woman to become a ruler was as a regent. There were, however, many cases where the regent decided to stay in power. A prime example is Empress Wu Zetian who, as consort, ruled over China's Tang Dynasty. She married Emperor Gaozong in 655; however, when he suffered a debilitating stroke five years later, she became the Administrator of the court until his death in 683 and went on to rule for another twenty-two years. Initially this was as regent in place of her son,

Emperor Zhongzong, but she then deposed him in favour of his younger brother. But that was not the end: after 690, Wu Zetian assumed control again and ruled in her own right, the only woman to do so, thereby establishing the Zhou dynasty as a short break within the Tang Dynasty.[4]

In medieval France, Catherine de Medici also ruled for several years as the Regent for her young sons.[5] She was born in the Republic of Florence in 1519, the daughter of Lorenzo de Medici, Duke of Urbino. To improve relations between Florence and France her uncle, Pope Clement VII, arranged for the 14-year-old Catherine to marry the Duke of Orleans, the younger son of the King of France. Ten years later, Catherine gave birth to their first child, the first of seven children to survive infancy, and in 1547 her husband became King of France. He died only five years later, leaving the 15-year-old Dauphin, Francis, to inherit the throne. Catherine served as regent, expecting to hand over the reins when Francis was old enough, but tragedy struck when he succumbed to illness in 1560 and was succeeded by his 10-year-old brother, Charles. Catherine continued as the regent while the young king, known as Charles IX, matured. When Charles came of age, her experience, wisdom and power was valued, and she continued to rule through him. Charles died of an illness on 30 May 1574 at the age of 23 and was succeeded by his brother Henry III.

During that period Catherine dealt with a myriad of state affairs, including ongoing civil and religious wars, with strength and intelligence. She died in 1589 and was buried next to her husband. Sadly, only eight months later Henry III was assassinated, and Henry of Navarre became King Henry IV of France. Clearly impressed by the late regent's accomplishments, he declared:

> I ask you, what could a woman do, left by the death of her husband with five little children on her arms, and two families of

France who were thinking of grasping the crown – our own [the Bourbons] and the Guises? Was she not compelled to play strange parts to deceive first one and then the other, in order to guard, as she did, her sons, who successively reigned through the wise conduct of that shrewd woman? I am surprised that she never did worse.

Painting of Catherine de Medici by an unknown artist, between 1547 and 1559. (Uffizi Gallery, Florence, Italy)

The laws of royal succession in Europe (and most countries that have or had monarchies) gave the right of inheritance to the eldest male, followed by younger males and, only in their absence, to females. Perhaps the most famous and colourful female leader in history was Cleopatra, the last active pharaoh of Egypt (her son Ptolemy Caesar, though formally pharoah, did not rule). When her father, Ptolemy XII (Auletes), died in 51 BC, Cleopatra and her 10-year-old brother, Ptolemy XIII, became co-rulers. However, her brother's advisors acted against her and she had to flee to Syria. In exile Cleopatra raised an army of mercenaries and returned to defeat her brother's forces the following year. (At least, they were nominally his forces, but since he was so young, it would have been his advisors who were behind them.) During the dispute both parties welcomed Caesar from Rome, but Cleopatra, aware of the advantages of such an ally, convinced the visitor to side with her and after several months of battling, Ptolemy XIII was defeated; he fled and died soon after.

Cleopatra and her next younger brother, Ptolemy XIV, were then made co-rulers. Caesar stayed on with Cleopatra and in 47 BC they had a son, Ptolemy Caesar (Caesarion). When Caesar returned to Rome, he was famously assassinated at the Senate, causing Rome to split into two factions: one led by the military general Mark Antony and politicians Octavian and Lepidus, and the other by politicians Brutus and Cassius. Both sides vied for Egypt and Cleopatra's alliance, and eventually she gave her allegiance to Mark Anthony, who then defeated Brutus. Mark Anthony and Octavian divided Rome between them, and Mark Anthony travelled to Egypt to establish the alliance. The relationship went better than probably either imagined, as he and Cleopatra spent the entire winter in Egypt, leaving Anthony's wife Octavia (Octavius's sister) back in Rome. The relationship was somewhat sealed when Cleopatra gave birth to twins, Alexander

Helios (sun) and Cleopatra Selene (moon), in 40 BC. Four years later, after Mark Anthony had spent more time in Egypt, Cleopatra gave birth to another son, Ptolemy Philadelphos.

Later, after a falling-out between Octavius and Mark Anthony over Octavia and power, the latter pronounced Caesarion as Caesar's son, thus declaring Octavian an imposter. Failing diplomacy, both sides gathered their forces for battle and Mark Anthony and Cleopatra's combined forces were defeated by Octavius at the battle of Actium in 31 BC. They fled to Egypt, where in true Romeo and Juliet fashion, Mark Anthony heard that Cleopatra had killed herself and so fell on his sword, surviving just long enough to hear that the message was incorrect. Cleopatra then took her own life, supposedly by clasping an asp (a venemous snake) to her bosom, though how she actually died is not known.

Egypt was wealthy but much weaker than the neighbouring Roman Empire, and only survived during Cleopatra's time due to her nimble negotiating. As a leader, Cleopatra was obviously very astute, with a good grasp of military issues. She knew how to rule a nation (control the currency, suppress insurrection and alleviate famine), and she skilfully assessed who could assist to her greatest advantage. Rome, however, was going through a period of internal turmoil and successive civil wars, and Cleopatra knew it was not enough to be friends with Rome: she had to befriend the most powerful Roman leader of that day. She deployed all her feminine charms in developing strong relationships with those leaders, creating advantageous relations for her nation, albeit giving her a reputation for seduction. Despite what her critics may say about her methods, Cleopatra successfully negotiated the shifting sands of Roman politics for twenty years.

Another queen who came to power as the eldest daughter with no surviving male siblings was Maria Theresa of Austria. She was the only surviving child of Emperor Charles VI, who ruled over an extensive empire including Austria, Hungary, Croatia, Bohemia, Transylvania and Mantua. Maria Theresa came to the throne in 1740 upon her father's death as Archduchess of Austria and Queen of Hungary and Croatia. Despite Charles's efforts to secure the succession to Maria Theresa, many disputed her claim, especially when the alternatives were in their favour. Frederick II of Prussia was one of these and he expressed his viewpoint by invading soon after her ascension. After the War of the Austrian Succession (1740–48), most of the territory initially lost to the Prussians had been recovered, but Prussia succeeded in keeping the wealthy province of Silesia.

Maria Theresa came to the throne with the treasury empty, an army weak and under-resourced, and with her citizens deprived and

Marble bust of Cleopatra circa 40–30 BC, made during the time of her visit to Rome. (Photograph by Louis le Grand, Berliner Museumsinsel)

discontented. She worked hard to improve Austria's international standing, revamped the army, promoted commerce and agriculture and filled the treasury coffers. However, her dislike of Protestants and Jews gave her a reputation for intolerance. The Seven Years' War, which began in 1756, was a power struggle between Britain, Prussia and Portugal on one side, against France, the Austrian-led Holy Roman Empire, Russia, Spain, Saxony and Sweden on the other side. Maria Theresa sent forth her revamped army, but despite a valiant effort, they failed to win back Silesia.[6]

The underlying cause of the Seven Years' War was a shifting balance of power across Europe. Great Britain had previously allied with Austria as a counterweight against French power, but as Austria's power weakened after the War of the Austrian Succession, the British started courting smaller German states instead and agreed with Prussia that it would not support Austria in a conflict over Silesia in the Westminster Convention of 1756. Therefore, needing powerful allies, Maria Theresa started to court France as an ally by sending her trusted foreign policy minister, Count Wenzel Anton von Kaunitz, to Paris. Maria Theresa also started building up an anti-Prussian alliance, but Prussia responded by invading Saxony, which angered the Russians who then attacked and thus began the Seven Years' War.

For political reasons Maria Theresa had married Francis Stephen, Duke of Lorraine, in 1736, and the marriage had been fruitful, with ten of their sixteen children surviving to adulthood. The Archduchess had promised the Duke an equal share in the government when they came to the throne, but she ultimately decided to remain as the absolute queen of her realm. However, he was not left lacking a kingdom, since he was elected Holy Roman Emperor in 1745, making her also a Holy Roman Empress. Maria Theresa managed many complex diplomatic relations for Austria, through Count Wenzel Anton von Kaunitz, with great skill; and

Portrait of Empress Maria Theresa by Martin van Meytens, 1759. (Academy of Fine Arts, Vienna)

in doing so she reversed Austria's fortunes. Events often happen beyond the control of leaders and greatness is often measured with how they respond to those events.

While the female leaders discussed earlier were either queens in their own right or ruled as regents, some women seized power for themselves without the pretence of being a regent. The prime example is Catherine the Great of Russia, who started out as the German Princess Sophie Friederike Auguste von Anhalt-Zerbst-Dornburg. She was sent to Russia to marry the 16-year-old Grand Duke Peter (later Tsar Peter III), as an arranged marriage. Peter was Prussian, did not speak much Russian and was generally unpopular. Catherine, presumably, was also unimpressed with Peter, since she organised a coup d'état that resulted in his death under suspicious circumstances. Catherine then proclaimed herself sole ruler of Russia, and during her reign of thirty-four years Russia grew to become a major power of Europe.

These women were remarkable in what they achieved, ruling their respective lands competently, reaching the pinnacle of power, holding positions that traditionally were the reserve of men and which demanded skills that were generally thought of as masculine.

Countries cannot afford to remain insular (even those which are islands); they need to interact with other counties to settle disputes and promote their individual and joint interests. As former US Ambassador Wendy Sherman explains:

> Every country puts its own interests first, but the interests that we have don't just stay inside of our country, whether it is concerns about terrorism or climate or the movement of people. All of these things cross borders, so you have to build alliances. You have to understand other people's interests.[7]

Another remarkable female leader was Queen Elizabeth I (1533–1603), who adroitly managed her international relations over forty-five years. Her ascension to the throne came in the wake of the Reformation in England started by her father Henry VIII. In particular, Mary, Queen of Scots, Elizabeth's Catholic cousin, posed a threat and there was an ongoing war in France.

Elizabeth was under great pressure to marry in order to bear a successor to shore up the Protestant throne, but she resisted marriage, believing that it would dilute her power as a queen if a man were to share the throne. She clearly viewed her role of queen regnant as very different from a queen consort, whose primary goal was to produce a male heir, as was the case for her mother, Anne Boleyn, and the rest of Henry VIII's wives. Elizabeth, however, was actively engaged in talks with other sovereigns and leaders, and she would use courtship rituals in those negotiations, with for example Francis, Duke of Anjou. It has been debated whether these courtship overtures were genuine but were unable to be completed, or if they were just posturing with no intention on her part of going through with them. Historian Natalie Mears wrote 'Elizabeth was shrewd enough to see that rules framed for chivalrous lovemaking might very aptly be applied to diplomatic purposes, and very probably for that reason she always liked to mingle an element of lovemaking in her diplomacy.'[8]

Elizabeth's use of flirtation in diplomacy showed much less personal commitment than Cleopatra, who forged a much more intimate relationship with Roman leaders whose help she needed. Without such support, it is unlikely that Cleopatra would have held the throne for as long as she did, whereas Elizabeth – though facing many challenges herself – ruled without a husband for nearly forty-five years but used the possibility of marriage as a diplomatic tool. Later, in 1559, Elizabeth famously declared to the House of Commons, in response to a delegation exerting pressure on her to marry, 'And, in the end, this shall be for me sufficient, that a marble stone shall declare that a queen, having reigned such a time, lived and died a virgin.'[9]

At the start of her reign, England (and Wales) was a weak country in relation to the powerhouses of Catholic Spain and neighbouring France. But Elizabeth was able to reverse those fortunes through her shrewd diplomatic relations, largely limiting foreign wars until the defeat of the Spanish Armada in 1588. By the end of her rule, her kingdom had become one of the most powerful countries in Europe and Elizabeth one of the most successful rulers.

Elizabeth's declaration of virginity was her mark of resolute authority, and by removing the fertility issue she also removed the gender issue. She rejected the advice of her brother-in-law Philip of Spain that she should 'take a consort who might relieve her of those labours which are only fit for men', and by staying unmarried maintained her individual right to rule as queen regnant.[10] In contrast, nearly a century later Mary II shared the throne with her husband, William of Orange (William III). The downside of remaining single was that without marriage there were no heirs and the Tudor line died out with Elizabeth in 1603. Elizabeth was succeeded by James VI of Scotland (son of Mary, Queen of Scots), who became James I of England, thus uniting these two kingdoms.

Marriage had been a key method of diplomacy since ancient times. These so-called marriages of state successfully sealed bonds of kinship that tended to promote or restrain aggression between nations. The hand of a princess might be part of the consideration for the treaty, along with a sizeable dowry and/or some power sharing. Marriages driven by treaty or economics rarely made for love matches, and so mistresses and lovers outside of marriage were much more acceptable for royalty than they are today.

The political nature of royal marriage meant that it was considered very carefully, not only the immediate issues at hand but also across future generations, such as whether the union might result in lands passing to the ruling dynasty of another country. Often rulers worked hard to prevent this from happening if adverse to their interests, typically in the form of requiring the daughter to renounce her claim to the throne or drafting special marriage contracts that dictated inheritance rights. These contracts were essentially treaties negotiated between the countries. For example, the Treaty of Perpetual Peace, signed in 1502 between England and Scotland, was sealed by the marriage of James IV of Scotland and Margaret Tudor, the daughter of Henry VII of England. While the treaty itself was broken when James IV invaded England, it did eventually unify the countries three generations later, when in 1603 James VI of Scotland became King of England.

The story of Catherine of Aragon is well known for its tragic ending but her role as the teenager vehicle of diplomacy was initially a success. At the age of 3 Catherine was betrothed to Arthur, Prince of Wales, the oldest son of Henry VII of England. They married in 1501 when she was 16 and he 15 years old, but he died of illness five months after their wedding. Two years later, Catherine's parents and Henry VII arranged for Catherine to marry Arthur's younger brother Henry (aged 11), with a treaty and betrothal in 1503. Henry was not keen on the idea and rejected Catherine when he was 14. Her father wanted Catherine to stay in England and appointed her as ambassador from the Aragonese Crown to the court of Henry VII in 1507. Catherine thus became the first female ambassador in European history and her presence greatly stabilised relations between the two countries.

There was also a reluctance of monarchs to have their off-spring marry commoners, since that would reduce opportunities for valuable alliances and erode the power of the throne. In Great Britain, the rules of royal marriage were formalised in the Royal Marriages Act of 1772, which limited the ability of the descendants of George II to marry without the express permission of the sovereign. This act was only repealed with the Succession to the Crown Act 2013.

The young Princess Victoria became queen after her father's elder brother William IV died in 1837 when she was only 18 years old. Her father, Prince Edward, Duke of Kent, the fourth son of

King George III, had died in 1820. Victoria married Prince Albert in 1840, three years after she came to the throne. Thus arose the dichotomy of the Queen of Britain and its Empire: Victoria ruled the Empire and theoretically owned all its properties, and yet, as a married woman, she could not legally own property in her own right. Queen Victoria was a constitutional monarch, so the actual power of government lay in the hands of the Prime Minister of the day, though she was actively involved in discussions and political decisions. After the destruction of Europe in the wake of the Napoleonic Wars, the Queen and Prince Albert looked for ways to bring stability to Europe and they set about interlinking the remaining royal families through marriage. Queen Victoria and Prince Albert had nine children, four boys and five girls born between 1840 and 1857, and they believed that it was important for them to project the image of a respectable, close-knit and loving family. This image of respectability and the ideal family presented a distinctly domestic, perhaps even feminine, difference from many of the prior monarchs, with their public affection for their mistresses and illegitimate but acknowledged children. In the end, eight of Victoria and Albert's children were married into the royal families of Europe.[11] Her and Albert's creation of royal ties encouraged future strong relations but differed from such marriages in the past where the hand of a princess was part of the consideration of a treaty between the countries.

2

A BRIEF HISTORY OF DIPLOMACY AND DIPLOMATS

Because I am a woman, I must make unusual efforts to succeed. If I fail, no one will say, 'She doesn't have what it takes.' They will say, 'Women don't have what it takes.'

Clare Boothe Luce

During the Middle Ages and the Tudor era, negotiations between ruling parties were conducted by envoys and letters. Elizabeth I never left the shores of England nor crossed the borders into Scotland or Wales.[1] Away from the security of the royal court, monarchs were vulnerable to attack and, with poor communications, it was difficult to leave the national helm for lengthy periods. The envoys of old are the forerunners to today's diplomatic service. This chapter will give a very brief history of their role and service, the establishment of modern diplomatic services, and the rules that governed them.

There have been envoys or emissaries since before there were city states and the Bible, for example, describes several instances where emissaries are sent from one kingdom to another in both the Old and New Testament:

> After all this, when Josiah had prepared the temple, Necho king of Egypt came up to fight against Charchemish by Euphrates: and Josiah went out against him. But he sent ambassadors to him, saying, What have I to do with thee, thou king of Judah?[2]

And:

> Or what king, going to make war against another king, sitteth not down first, and consulteth whether he be able with ten thousand to meet him that cometh against him with twenty thousand? Or else, while the other is yet a great way off, he sendeth an ambassage, and desireth conditions of peace.[3]

In some primitive societies women would commonly be the peacemakers,[4] perhaps as they were less combative than men or less threatening and would therefore be afforded a more peaceful reception from the potential enemy.[5]

The Chinese had an established system of diplomacy with resident envoys during the warring states period (*c.* 800 BC), where the envoys would also serve as hostages to their hosts if their home nation behaved unethically. This system fell into disuse once China was unified by the Qin Emperor in 221 BC. For the Greeks, with their many city states, diplomacy was similarly important. Short-term visitors were dispatched to address a particular matter. The Greeks believed that envoys were protected by the gods, especially Hermes, the messenger of the gods, who became associated with diplomacy. The Greeks developed rules for international diplomatic conduct, negotiating many truces, including neutrality, commercial, treaties, and alliance agreements, and they even kept archives of their work.[6]

The Romans inherited the Greek traditions and often sent an envoy (*nuntius*) abroad with written instructions or a larger party (a *legatio*) of ten to twelve leading citizens who were skilled at oratory. Like the Greeks, they considered envoys inviolable, and they also developed sophisticated archives with professional archivists. The Roman Catholic Church adopted many of its practices from the Roman State, and Roman law became the basis for canon law.

As envoys were needed by secular leaders in Europe, they followed the practice of the Church and the term 'ambassador' (from the Latin *ambactiare*, meaning 'to go on a mission') came to be commonly used from the twelfth century. By the fifteenth century this term was commonly used for secular envoys, though the Church continued to use the Latin names *legates* and *nuncii*. Emissaries were typically sent to deliver a message or perhaps negotiate a particular matter. Over time, it was found beneficial to both sides to retain a permanent representative in foreign royal courts and so countries started to build permanent embassies, especially in Italy with its many city states. Niccolò Machiavelli (1469–1527), from Florence, is probably the best-known sixteenth-century diplomat. He immodestly defined his talents: 'An envoy needs integrity, reliability, and honesty, along with tact and skill in the use of occasional equivocation and selective abridgement of aspects of the truth unfavourable to his cause.'[7]

This philosophy has been adopted by almost every politician from then to modern times. The role of ambassador was becoming more formalised, as Machiavelli's description indicates. There were almost no female ambassadors at this time (Catherine of Aragon being the noted exception), primarily because women's roles were generally seen to be keeping the home and raising children. The Church, of course, had no leadership role for women outside of convents and with few exceptions women did not have many leadership roles in civil society either. The exceptions were the few queens regnant, professional writers such as Christine de Pizan (1364–*c.* 1430) who provided advice for women[8] and of course the truly remarkable Joan of Arc (1412–31), who helped drive the English out of France.

England's first resident ambassador was John Sherwood, who was posted to the Vatican in 1479. Henry VII understood the need for improved diplomacy, and so adopted much of the Italian system for secular relationships. England's first secular resident ambassador was John Stile, who was posted to Spain by Henry VII.[9] Catherine of Aragon was one of the first resident ambassadors posted to England when she was appointed in 1507. By 1520 the English diplomatic service had been established under Cardinal Thomas Wolsey. Initially most diplomats were selected from the royal court, but by the mid 1500s royal secretaries were also appointed to this role. Ambassadors had to be trustworthy and reliable, since travel and communications were slow, requiring considerable patience and discretion on their part. In addition to selecting suitable diplomats, communications had to be improved and England established the first modern courier system to enable private diplomatic communications.

During the Elizabethan period diplomats became much more professional. While some came into the field with foreign expertise, many rose up through the ranks of the diplomatic service, starting as assistants and eventually rising to become ambassadors. Diplomacy was also a good career path for men, with a large proportion of ambassadors going on to become members of Parliament, ministers and significant men of the government.[10]

As embassies spread across Europe, it was not unknown for squabbles to erupt over who held the highest-ranking order. In London in 1661 a dispute escalated dangerously between the

French and Spanish ambassadors about whose carriage should go first. At that time the centre for European diplomacy was the court of Louis XIV in Paris, which only admitted aristocratic emissaries, which also gave the diplomatic corps a certain decadent style. Since many of the diplomatic corps were independently wealthy, it was common for ambassadors to choose and pay for their own staff, furniture and entertaining, a tradition that placed a burden on later generations of would-be diplomats who were of lesser means. It also meant that Latin gave way to French as the official language of diplomacy, until English became the dominant language in the twentieth century.

Two hundred years later, on 9 June 1815, following the Napoleonic War, the Congress of Vienna had rearranged Europe to the victors' benefit and among other things, the seventeenth and final treaty signed was the Regulation on the Precedence of Diplomatic Agents. The text is as follows:[11]

> ACT No XVII Regulation concerning the Precedence of Diplomatic Agents
>
> Article I Diplomatic characters are divided into three classes That of Ambassadors Legates or Nuncios That of Envoys Ministers or other persons accredited to That of Chargé d Affaires accredited only to the Ministers Foreign Affairs
>
> […]
>
> Article IV Diplomatic Characters shall rank in their classes according to the date of the official notification of arrival

Article 4 took care of the competition between ambassadors for precedence; rank now depended on their longevity as appointees to that court. Distinction was made between great powers and 'powers with limited interests' since only the former exchanged ambassadors, and the others appointed ministers, and it was not until 1893 that the United States appointed ambassadors. Even though the number of signatories was small, comprising the eight powers at the time, these norms were still adopted worldwide. The United States adopted these norms since their major trading partners were using them, and during the period of decolonisation of the nineteenth (mainly South America) and the twentieth century, the newly created countries also adopted them.[12]

There is a long tradition of not harming emissaries, since they are the agents of peaceful interaction between states. For the most part emissaries were received with respect, even when they brought bad news. However, there were exceptions, for example in 491 BC when the Persian Emperor Darius I sought to expand his empire to include the Greek city states; he sent emissaries to each state asking them to send a token gift of earth and water to signify acceptance of their subjugation by the much larger Persian Empire. Most of the Greek city states complied, but Athenians threw the emissaries into a pit, killing them, and the Spartans threw the Persian emissaries down a well.[13] The Spartans later regretted this action, fearing retribution not from Darius but from the gods; they sent two Spartan men to the Persians to be executed in exchange for the emissaries. The ancient Greeks considered that emissaries were protected by the gods and if they were harmed, it was considered similar to directly insulting the gods themselves and incurring their wrath. It was not just the Greeks who held this view; when the Persian Emperor Xerxes received the two sacrificial men from Sparta, he responded, 'You violate the laws of all humans by killing heralds, but I will not do that for which I censure you, nor by putting you to death in turn will I set the Lacedaimonians [Spartans] free from this guilt.'[14] The Athenians were not so accommodating, and so the Persians sent an army which greatly outnumbered theirs, which the Athenians, to everyone's surprise, defeated in the Battle of Marathon in 490 BC.

This tradition of protection of official envoys goes back much further. For example, in the eleventh century BC, during the reign of Ramesses XI, an Egyptian envoy named Wen Amun was charged with stealing silver from some merchants in the Syrian port of Byblos, which he had done to replace silver that had been stolen from him. The Prince of Byblos declared that since Wen Amun was an official envoy, he was immune from arrest.[15]

The same tradition was followed in Tudor England. In 1584 the Spanish ambassador to England, Bernardino de Mendoza, was implicated in a plot to assassinate Elizabeth I as part of a conspiracy by Francis Throckmorton to bring Mary, Queen of Scots, to the throne. Throckmorton was tried and executed, and there were calls from members of the Privy Council for the ambassador to be tried for treason. However, the Privy Council sought advice from two well-respected experts in international law, Alberico Gentili and Jean Hotman, who both said the law was clear: ambassadors, even ambassadors who committed criminal acts, were protected by diplomatic immunity 'infallibly within the sanctuarie of the Lawe of Nations',[16] and so the ambassador was deported.

Diplomatic immunity was only formalised under British law with the passage of the Diplomatic Privileges Act of 1708, following the arrest and mistreatment of the Russian ambassador Andrej Matveyev because he owed money. The Russians at that time were not to be trifled with; Matveyev received apologies from the Queen, and Parliament formalised the immunity to temper the anger of Tsar Peter the Great.[17]

In the mid-eighteenth century, well-respected international lawyer Emmerich De Vattel wrote his very influential treatise, which still underlies much of modern treatment of diplomats:

94. How he may be punished. 1. For ordinary transgressions.

Should an ambassador forget the duties of his station – should he render himself disagreeable and dangerous – should he form cabals and schemes prejudicial to the peace of the citizens, or to the state or prince to whom he is sent – there are various modes of punishing him, proportionate to the nature and degree of his offence. If he maltreats the subjects of the state – if he commits any acts of injustice or violence against them – the injured subjects are not to seek redress from the ordinary magistrates, since the ambassador is wholly independent of their jurisdiction: and, for the same reason, those magistrates cannot proceed directly against him. On such occasions, therefore, me plaintiffs are to make application to their sovereign, who demands justice from the ambassador's master, and, in case of a refusal, may order the insolent minister to quit his domains.[18]

The law of diplomacy and diplomatic missions has since been codified by international treaty, initially the Congress of Vienna in 1815 (discussed earlier), modified in 1928 by the Convention Regarding Diplomatic Officers.[19] The current rules for diplomatic immunity are covered by the Vienna Convention on Diplomatic Relations (1961).[20]

The world of diplomacy is still not without its dangers. In the last sixty years there have been several cases where diplomats have been seized, injured or killed by host governments or mobs with the encouragement of the government. These include the sacking of the British Embassy in Jakarta by a mob in 1963 with the tacit support of the Indonesian government following a dispute over Malaysian independence. The British Embassy in Beijing was taken and gutted in 1967 during the Cultural Revolution in China, and in 1979 Iranian students ransacked the US Embassy in Tehran and kidnapped and held over 50 staff hostage for 444 days with the active support of the newly established Islamic Republic.[21]

Up until the twentieth century the British Foreign Office was an all-male affair, in large part because government (with the exception of the monarchy) was an all-male affair. Society was not ready for female government officials, let alone female diplomats, but as the nineteenth century progressed, British society started changing. The Foreign Office generally reflected a more conservative side of British society and so the acceptance of professional women took longer. Through the nineteenth and twentieth centuries, including two world wars, international society radically progressed; there were changes in law and policy, and women were finally permitted to apply for the Foreign Service and to represent their nations.

While the idea of women diplomats may have been unimaginable to the Foreign Office officials of the late nineteenth century, several women had served in these roles in the past. For example, Bartholda van Swieten (also known as Bartholda de Swieten or Miss T'Serclaes) was a Dutch noblewoman who successfully negotiated with the Archduke of Austria, Albert VII, the return of family properties that had been seized by the Spanish Netherlands in 1609. The Spanish Netherlands consisted of what is now most of Belgium, Luxembourg and parts of northern France and Germany. These lands were inherited by the Spanish Habsburgs upon the abdication of the Holy Roman Emperor Charles V in 1558.[22] For eighty years the largely Protestant northern seven provinces of the Low Countries rebelled against the rule of the Roman Catholic King Philip II of Spain, eventually separating in 1581 and formally becoming an independent state (the United Provinces of the Netherlands) in 1648.[23] After her husband died in 1612, van Swieten continued to travel to the southern Netherlands to see her daughter and to serve as an informal messenger and negotiator between the two sides.[24] By 1621 she was formally appointed by the Archduke as an official negotiator and was welcomed in that capacity by the Spanish King. Her role continued for several years and in 1629 she negotiated a swap of prisoners.[25]

Another female diplomat was Catharina Stopia, who in 1620 married Johan Möller. He was accredited as Sweden's ambassador to Moscow in 1630. The Russian army had attacked and laid siege to the Polish–Lithuanian city of Smolensk, but the city held out for about a year until the Polish king could organise a relief force, and during this time Möller was reporting news back to the Swedish king. Möller died in 1632 and Catharina took over his position; she was officially credited by the Riksråd (the Swedish equivalent of the Privy Council) to continue with the work of her husband and serve as ambassador, which she continued to do until 1634.[26]

Another example of female diplomacy in the seventeenth century was Isabelle-Angelique de Montmorency-Bouteville (1627–95). She was the wife of Christian von Mecklenburgh, who was a diplomat for the French Ministry of Foreign Affairs. Isabelle used her large network of friends to also perform parallel diplomacy for the French Government, which she described as 'visits to friends'. Her activities became so significant that she became more active than the official French Ambassador.[27]

One of the more common arguments against women diplomats in the British Foreign Office before 1946 was that women would be unable to perform the functions of a consul. These issues included having to deal with drunken British sailors in foreign ports and concern that foreign governments, particularly Muslim ones, would not accept female diplomats.[28] Perhaps the speakers should have remembered the story of Mrs Jean White, acting consul in Tripoli 1763–67.

One of the toughest places to serve as British Consul in the eighteenth century was in the states forming the Barbary coast of north Africa. One of the main economic engines of this region was raiding merchant and other ships. The cargoes were sold, the ships seized and the crew were also sold in the North African slave markets. The more wealthy captives would be freed upon payment of a ransom, captured women ended up as concubines. The remaining slaves spent the rest of their lives performing hard labour. The Barbary States felt justified in these actions because they believed that the Qur'an instructed them that it was acceptable to enslave non-believers such as Christians.[29] The Barbary states were formerly part of the Ottoman Empire, but by the eighteenth century they were largely ruled by their local bashaw, dey, aga or divan.

It was not just merchant ships that were targeted: the Barbary States' corsairs (pirate ships) had been pillaging shipping and raiding European coastlines (including Britain) for slaves since the early Middle Ages. Back in 1675 the matter had been settled for British shipping when Rear Admiral Sir John Narbough brazenly sailed his gunboats into the Tripoli harbour at night and set fire to or sank most of the Dey's ships. The resulting treaty of 1676 included promises that British shipping would no longer be molested.[30]

Nearly a century later the piracy problem continued, and negotiating the release of captives was one of the roles of the consul. The treaty was renegotiated by British Consul, Robert White, in 1751.[31] Robert had married Jean Mackenzie before they were posted to Tripoli, and when he died there in November 1763, Jean was left in a precarious situation.[32] However she took up the mantle and served as the Consul for over a year until a replacement was sent from London and she was able to return home in 1765. Her role as consul was approved by the Bashaw[33] (well before it was believed that Muslim countries would not accept female diplomats) and the British government, though not formally appointing Jean to this role, kept her on the payroll.[34] If a female consul could deal with the difficulties of eighteenth-century Tripoli and liberating British subjects from the slave markets, then her counterparts should have no difficulties dealing with a few drunken British sailors in more friendly ports around the world.

As a postscript, Robert and Jean's son, who was also called Robert, was appointed British Consul to Tripoli in 1775.[35] The piracy/corsairy continued against weaker states such as the United States, including the well-publicised capture of the US merchant ships the *Maria* and *Dauphin* in 1785. These attacks prompted the newly formed United States to create the US Navy, which took on the pirates in the Barbary wars of 1803 and 1815, essentially ending the activities of the Barbary corsairs.[36]

In Britain, the Electric Telegraph Company began hiring women as telegraph operators in the 1850s. Male and female telegraphic operators were separated; male operators worked in the Foreign Gallery providing communications abroad, and the female operators worked in the Great Gallery for telegraphic communications within the UK:

> The male and female telegraphists have separate staircases to gain their respective offices: that for the men leads from the principal staircase. The female clerks have a private staircase, leading from their large room direct to the street-door of the premises. By this staircase also they descend to a dining-hall and cloak-room, which are provided exclusively for them.[37]

The nationalisation of the Telegraph Companies (under the Telegraph Act of 1869) meant that its staff became employees of the Post Office and, therefore, the female employees, by default, became the first female civil servants in Great Britain. The Postmaster General found that women not only worked well, but were cheaper than men and so he hired more women as telegraph operators for the Clearing House branch of the General Post Office (GPO). In 1871 he spoke of his findings:

They have in an eminent degree a quickness of eye and ear and a delicacy of touch, which are essential qualifications of a good operator.

[Women] are more patient during long confinement to one place.

The wages offered will attract male operators from an inferior class of the community and will attract females from a superior class.

The superior class women will write and spell better than the inferior men, and where the staff is mixed, will raise the tone of the whole staff.

Women are less disposed to get together to extort higher wages.

Women will not require increases related to length of service as they will retire for the purpose of getting married as soon as they get the chance.

There will also be fewer women than men on the pension list.[38]

Two years later, in 1873, a woman was appointed directly to a civil service position as an inspector for the education of girls in pauper schools and workhouses, as opposed to being an imported employee of a nationalised company. The appointment of Mrs Senior as the first female civil servant was an 'unpopular innovation' and considered 'unendurable' to the male civil servants at the time.[39] Mrs Jane (Jeanie) Nassau Senior (1828–77) was a person of remarkable talents, who spent her life promoting the interests of poor girls and women and believed in the application of direct material assistance where it was needed.

The Civil Service has always been a conservative organisation, but following a large influx of women into the clerical streams, the question of female employees was then examined in detail by the Playfair Commission.[40] The Commission reported in 1874/5:

We have taken evidence regarding the employment of female clerks. The experience of the Post Office ... shows that women are well qualified for clerical work of a less important character and are satisfied with a lower rate of pay than is expected by men similarly employed. We, therefore see no reason why the employment of female clerks should not be extended to other departments where the circumstances will admit of it. In the Telegraph Office, male and female clerks are employed in the same rooms without inconvenience. But, as regards the ordinary clerical work of an office, we are not prepared to recommend the employment of women unless they can be placed in separate rooms, under proper female supervision.

In 1875 the Savings Bank, a subsidiary of the Post Office, engaged forty young women. The opinion of the traditionalists on hiring them was voiced by the Bank's Controller who argued that:

There are grievous dangers both moral and official in employing women, and one clerk gave evidence to the Playfair Commission saying that some women would be able to do some of the lighter office work, but that they would be unable to wield the 'heavy pressure', using very hard pens and carbon paper required for the job.

The experiment was presumably considered a success since in 1880 the Postmaster General, a progressive Mr Fawcell (husband of Dame Millicent Fawcett, who campaigned for women's suffrage), opened up applications to public competition by examination, and so allowed women to apply in direct competition with men.

The Foreign Office had employed women since its founding in 1782, but their function was only that of cleaners and housekeeping, so-called 'necessary women', and their employment was only on a casual basis.[41] As women clerks became a common sight in offices across the land, even the conservative Foreign Office hired its first female employee in 1889.[42] Sophia Fulcher was a typist who was certified as 'qualified' for this position in 1894. She was followed soon after by Ethel Gunton.[43] More women were hired and by 1914 there were eleven female typists on staff.

Sophia Isabella Wright was born in January 1857 at Limehouse, East London. She married James Fulcher in 1882 and they had three children, but James died around 1891 and Sophia became the breadwinner for her young family, taking up employment with the Foreign Office. In 1907 Fulcher and eight other typists petitioned the Treasury for a pay rise, arguing that their meagre salary was barely a living wage. They were supported in their request by Sir Edward Grey, then the Foreign Secretary, who wrote that:

> [He had] pleasure in testifying to the excellent work which is performed by these typists under the able guidance of their Superintendant Typist. The work comprises the transcription of a considerable amount of French manuscript which is often difficult to decipher, as well as the reproduction of documents emanating from foreign countries and written by persons imperfectly acquainted with the English Language. … [It] is very desirable to grant adequate renumeration to such persons for the valuable services which they are able to render.[44]

The secretaries received their pay increase, and by 1911 Fulcher had risen to the rank of superintendant typist.

The Royal Commission on the Civil Service of 1912 reviewed how women should be hired. They took as their guiding principle that 'the object should be not to provide employment for women as such, but to secure for the State the advantage of the services of women whenever those services will best promote its interests'.[45]

The Commission had the following points to make:

The responsibilities of married life are normally incompatible with the devotion of a woman's whole-time and unimpaired energy to the Public Services.

The salaries of women should be fixed on a lower scale than those of men.

Female clerks where employed should be accommodated separately from male clerks.

There were significant reservations from some committee members to this report. The differences of opinion centred on recruitment of women and their salaries. The majority recommended open recruitment by separate examination with a minority suggesting that there should be a limited number of places for women using the Class 1 examination. As for salary, the majority requested a Treasury enquiry into removing the inequalities of salary, and that women should be paid the same as men for the same work. The minority opinion was that a 'scale, adequate for men, was excessive for women because, after all, women did not have families to keep'. There was also a minority opinion that favoured the extension of the employment of women into the upper ranks of the Civil Service, but to a lesser extent than the lower ranks. These differences of opinion suggest that ideas about women's employment were beginning to change.[46]

The most important debate on women's rights in the early twentieth century concerned women's suffrage. People in favour of suffrage argued on the basis of fairness and equality, whereas those opposed to suffrage argued that men and women had different roles in society, and that women's roles were to keep house and raise children and not to be involved in national politics.

In 1914 the McDonnell Commission was tasked with considering the many issues concerning the employment of women in the

Civil Service, but it was unable to come to a unanimous conclusion. There were those who recognised that valuable experience was lost when a woman retired on marriage, especially in the higher grades where a specialist's knowledge was significant. However, the overriding conclusion was determined by consideration of a woman's role in the family and the belief that the responsibilities of married life were normally incompatible with public service. The Commission also recommended continuing with a segregated workforce.[47] To place the conclusions of the Commission into a social context, it was the 'norm' in the early twentieth century for a wife to leave her employment to care for the family, and therefore render herself wholly financially dependent on her husband.

The First World War profoundly affected many aspects of society, and brought about unprecedented changes in traditional gender roles, and yet, several decades passed before Westminster caught up. The war also intervened on the road to women's rights and the suffragette campaigns were temporarily set aside. However, 'man-power' shortages gave opportunities for women to take on many of the roles that had traditionally belonged to men, and for the most part, they were as competent as their male counterparts. Between 1914 and 1918 the number of women employed in agriculture increased by about 44,500 and the number in industry increased from 3.3 to 4.9 million.[48]

Meanwhile, the Foreign Office was showing no inclination to change its admission policy, until there arose a sudden requirement for a person of the right credentials to fulfill a role in Stockholm. Bertha Phillpots (1877–1932), a Cambridge-educated expert on Scandinavia, was visiting her somewhat inept brother, the Commercial Attaché at the Stockholm Legation, in 1916 when he suddenly left and she stepped into the breach, most capably. The Head of the Legation implored her to stay on, which she did, serving as his Private Secretary, despite not receiving a proper salary until 1917.[49] After the war, she returned to the UK and became the Principal of Westfield College for Women and later Mistress of her alma mater, Girton College, Cambridge. Bertha Phillpots, later Dame Bertha, was therefore one of the earliest women to be hired by the Foreign Office in a prominent role, even if somewhat unofficially.

Gertrude Bell was another exceptional woman who was in the right place at the right time.[50] She had trained at Oxford as a linguist and made her mark in the early 1900s as a remarkable adventurer and writer of the Middle East. She successfully published *The Desert and the Sown*[51] based on her extensive, and usually solo, travels through modern-day Palestine, Syria and the desert city of Hayyil, befriending the leaders of local Arabic tribesmen. At one point, she was held prisoner for eleven days, which led to her receiving the Royal Geographical Society's Gold Medal. It was through these special relationships with the local tribesmen and chiefs that she was able to procure valuable intelligence for the British government. In 1914 the War Office contracted Bell to write a memo forecasting how the Arabs might respond in the event of a British offensive against the Turks, which she did, with considerable accuracy.

A year later Bell was running the Red Cross's Wounded and Missing Enquiry Department in London. Already known to the Foreign Office as an 'asset', in June 1915 David Hogarth (another British academic drafted in to assist with Middle Eastern affairs) invited Bell to join the fledgling Arab Bureau of the Foreign Office in Cairo. Her first task was to produce a comprehensive handbook on the tribes of Arabia based on her extensive knowledge of the region and personalities. She was accordingly made an assistant political officer, and later her position was regularised as an officer of the Indian Expeditionary Force D, with the title 'Oriental Secretary', for which she was paid a regular salary. Despite some misgivings from the top brass, Bell played a key role in

Photograph of Gertrude Bell. (Alamy)

liaising with the pre-united Arab tribes following the expulsion of the Turks from Mesopotamia (modern day Iraq). She also wrote the 'Review of the Civil Administration of Mesopotamia',[52] an analysis on the proposed establishment of an Arab government, which was published by the British government as a white paper. Bell retained her position after the implementation of that government and the coronation of her friend, Faisal bin Abdulaziz Al Saud, who became King of the Arab Kingdom of Greater Syria in 1920, and King of Iraq from 1921 to 1933.

It is unlikely that any other person could have achieved as much as Bell did in that region. For a woman to achieve so much, and to be recognised in her own time, was remarkable. It is therefore surprising that Bell was overtly hostile to the feminist movement and strongly opposed to the women's suffrage movement before the war.

As the war was winding down, the question of women's suffrage came up again and in 1918 the Representation of the People Act gave the vote to women over the age of 30 who owned property. It would be another ten years before women had parity with men, with the passage of the Representation of the People (Equal Franchise) Act of 1928 which gave all adults over the age of 21 the right to vote.

Following the end of the First World War, the role of women in the workplace again became a focus for discussion and this time, Parliament confidently passed the Sex Disqualification (Removal) Act of 1919.[53] The law essentially made sex discrimination in the Civil Service illegal, except for where the government wanted to retain it. This statute, and an order of the Council of 22 July 1920, obliged the Civil Service commissioners to develop regulations for the admission of women to the Civil Service. The Foreign Office was, however, considered a special case, and on 23 August 1921 the Civil Service commissioners gave notice that:

> On behalf of the Secretary of State for Foreign Affairs, all posts in the Diplomatic Service and in the Consular Service are reserved to men. […]
> 4) on behalf of the Secretary of State for Foreign Affairs and the President of the Board of Trade, all posts in the Commercial Diplomatic Service and the Trade Commissioner Service are reserved to men, provided that this reservation is not applicable to the post of Chief Clerk in the respective Offices of His Majesty's Trade Commissioners.

The law was a profession that also held an attraction to educated women, but the Inns of Courts had refused entry and clung tightly to their privileges for decades, until the Sex Disqualification (Removal) Act forced them to open their doors. The Act, importantly, also gave women eligibility for jury duty. Once women were admitted, it was found that the system worked; society did not collapse, and the initial resentments were soon overcome and largely forgotten about.[54]

The Sex Disqualification (Removal) Act also opened up many new occupations previously denied to women, but there were some notable exceptions. Women were still barred from direct entry into the administrative grades of the Civil Service, whereupon this resistance became the focus of pressure from women's movements. It was obvious that once the government accepted female employees, then most other employers would be expected to follow suit, except for the Church, of course.

In 1920 Major John Hills (MP for Ripon) secured a debate and significantly obtained a vote for equal opportunity of employment (although the equal pay provision was watered down). Despite this support for women from Parliament, the Treasury and other departments created multi-layered delays and obstructions and did their best to evade the plain meaning of Parliament's revised laws. In August 1921 the government held a second successful vote, and this time pledged that every grade of the Civil Service would be open to women who could apply through the same competitive examinations. These changes actually took effect with the introduction of the 1925 Civil Service Entrance Examinations.[55]

The first three women who passed the entry exam to become 'administrative cadets' were Alix Kilroy, Enid Russell-Smith and Mary Smeiton. Each one would later be bestowed the title of DBE. Other women had reached the administrative grade through promotion from the executive grades before the 1925 entrance exam. For example, Beryl Power rose up through the ranks of the Board of Trade and later served in the Ministry of Labour.

Although women were now permitted to take the administrative grade entrance exam, very few actually reached the upper levels (only fifteen passed the exam between 1925 and 1939). It is likely that many suitable candidates were deterred by the marriage bar. Several departments considered it inadvisable to hire women (Defence, Mines, Overseas Territories, and the Foreign Service), so women in these divisions were still subjected to significant discrimination. For example, the First Civil Service Commissioner, Sir Stanley Leathes, is reported to have said:[56]

> I cannot tell whether, under combined open competitive examination, women will get more than their share or less than their share of appointments. I cannot tell whether, under open competition, the right women or the wrong women will be selected. I am afraid it might turn out to the latter.

However, progress was being made elsewhere for women in society: Ada Jane Summers was elected Mayor of Stalybridge, and as such was *ex officio* a Justice of the Peace (JP), and she was sworn in as the first female JP on 31 December 1919, only a week after the Sex Disqualification (Removal) Act came into force. In October 1920 she was appointed a JP in her own right; again, the first woman in Britain to be so.

The Women's Police Service was founded in 1914 by Nina Boyle and Margaret Damer Dawson and, in August 1915, Edith Smith was appointed the first female constable with full powers of arrest.[57] The existence of women police officers was a shocking reality for those men who only a few years before had been concerned about having to report to a female boss, and now they could be arrested by a woman and called before a female jurist. The tide was turning.

In 1919 the Paris Peace Conference was held with the intention of preventing another war from occurring, which led to the formation of the League of Nations and other organisations including the International Labour Organization (ILO).[58] The League of Nations' founding charter included a clause saying that men and women were equally eligible for all positions in the secretariat and there were no bars on married women, and both the League and the ILO provided paid maternity leave to female employees between the wars. These organisations were remarkably progressive for their time, though there were still relatively few women in the senior leadership. The ILO was the only organisation in the League whose mission was, in part, to further women's rights, as the preamble to its constitution called for the 'protection of children, young persons and women' world-wide in its stated objectives.[59] The ILO remains active to this day.

While the senior fellows at the London Foreign Office were still debating whether women were capable of functioning within the diplomatic service, other countries were already appointing them. One of the world's first female diplomats was Diana Abgar (1859–1937), a respected Armenian writer and diplomat.[60] Abgar (née Agabeg) was born in Burma (now Myanmar) and grew up in Calcutta. She married fellow Armenian Michael Abgar, and they moved to Japan in 1891. She was appointed ambassador to Japan of the newly created but short-lived First Republic of Armenia in 1918, which became part of the Soviet Union in 1920. Abgar stayed in Japan, where she continued her humanitarian work until she died in 1937, and was buried in Yokohama. She is generally considered as one of the first female diplomats even though Armenia was not recognised by most other countries at that time.[61] Abgar went on to write extensively about the Armenian Massacre in Adana of 1909,[62] and the attempts by the Russians, Germans and Turks to exterminate the Armenians during and after the First World War.[63]

Around the same time, Rosika (Rózsa) Bédy-Schwimmer (1911–48) was appointed by the Hungarian Government as Ambassador to Switzerland in 1918.[64] Schwimmer was born in Budapest (Austria-Hungary) to a Jewish family and started life

Photograph of Diana Abgar, Armenian ambassador to Japan, January 1920.
(Photographer not known)

as a bookkeeper. She married Paul Bédy, a journalist, in 1911 but they divorced two years later and she became the corresponding Secretary of the International Women's Suffrage Alliance. In 1914 she moved to London where she helped to found the Women's Peace Party. Once the war had ended, and Hungary became an independent state, Prime Minister Mihály Károlyi appointed Schwimmer as ambassador to Switzerland. However, her appointment was short lived, since she was strongly opposed to the Communists who took control of Hungary in 1919. Schwimmer moved to Vienna and then to the US, where she lived for the rest of her life, promoting her feminist and pacifist agenda despite a continued anti-Semitic and xenophobic backlash. She received the World Peace Prize in 1937 and was nominated for the Nobel Peace Prize in 1947, but no award was given that year.[65]

Rosika Schwimmer, *c.* 1910 to *c.*1915. (Bain News Service, Library of Congress Reproduction Number: LC-DIG-ggbain-18633)

Schwimmer's place on the diplomatic circuit was followed soon after by Alexandra Kollontai (1872–1952), a Russian Bolshevik who was posted to Oslo in 1922 as Head of Mission by Joseph Stalin.[66] She was next posted to Mexico in 1926, and later returned to Sweden as the Ambassador.[67] Kollontai was in Stockholm when the Winter War between Russia and Finland broke out, and she used her influence to ensure that Sweden remained neutral. Kollantai was a significant figure on the Russian political scene and spoke out for women's rights throughout her life, and she is the subject of several books and the 1939 film *Ninotchka*, starring Greta Garbo. When she died in Moscow in 1952, less than a month away from her 80th birthday, she was one of only two members of the Bolsheviks' Central Committee that had led the October Revolution who managed to live into the 1950s, other than Stalin himself.

Alexandra Kollontai, 1927. (Bain News Service, Library of Congress
Reproduction Number: LC-DIG-ggbain-25077)

The US Department of State, like its British counterpart, was
reluctant see women in the diplomatic ranks. Their justifica-
tions included:

A woman's well-known inability to keep a secret;
   The physical risks presented by the profession that a woman
could not be called upon to face;
   Giving offence to foreign officials who might not like the US
being represented by a woman;
   Women's inability to cultivate the necessary social ties (in the
men-only clubs); and
   Women were too emotional.[68]

Fortunately, the US government's angst did not last as long as it did in Britain, when in 1922 Lucile Atcherson became the first woman to join the officer class of the US Department of Foreign Affairs (similar to the administrative grade of the Foreign, Commonwealth and Development Office (FCDO)).

In her early 20s Atcherson had volunteered as a nursing aide and was an activist in the women's suffrage movement of Ohio. During the First World War she joined the staff of the American Fund for the French Wounded, which led to her being transfered to Paris where she became the Director of Personnel. For her efforts, she was awarded the Medaille de la Reconnaissance Francaise in 1919 by the French government. This medal was awarded only to civilians who had voluntarily come to the aid of injured or disabled refugees, or who had demonstrated exceptional dedication in the presence of the enemy during the First World War.

In 1920, with the ratification of the Nineteenth Amendment to the US Constitution, American women won the right to vote, and Atcherson, therefore, became eligible to take the Foreign Service test. Eligibility was based on citizenship and, prior to obtaining the vote, women were not considered full citizens. Atcherson was the first to apply for the test having been nominated by President Warren G. Harding in 1922. However, the US Senate refused to approve her appointment since they considered it inappropriate for a young single woman to travel overseas as a diplomat. Atcherson was instead appointed to the State Department's division of Latin American Affairs in Washington DC, which the Senate confirmed on 4 December 1922.[69] Atcherson's many supporters in the women's suffrage movement then swamped the Senate Committee on Foreign Relations with letters of protest. Eventually she was recommended for an overseas posting, which was accordingly approved by the full Senate in 1923. Atcherson was appointed as Third Secretary to the Legation in Bern, Switzerland, but it was

Lucile Atcherson Curtis, 1 January 1922. (US Department of State)

not a comfortable situation as many of her male colleagues would not accept her, and she was passed over for promotion. Atcherson met her future husband while in Bern; however, being ambitious she still accepted a transfer to Panama in 1927, which was an equally uncomfortable assignment for her.

Atcherson decided to marry in January 1928, whereupon she was forced to resign due to the US State Department's marriage bar. While she was no doubt somewhat fatigued with the systemic chauvinism, Atcherson had successfully broken through a significant glass ceiling, forging a pathway for other women to follow in her footsteps. Pattie Field was the second woman to pass the entrance test for the State Department, in 1925, followed by four more women over the next five years.[70]

Around the same time in London, Margaret Bondfield (1873–1953) was elected to Parliament and became the Minister for Labour, the country's first female government minister. Unfortunately for her, she lost her seat in the general election the following year.[71] She regained it in a bye-election in 1926 and was re-appointed Minister for Labour in 1929, the first female cabinet minister in Ramsey MacDonald's second administration.

However, Bondfield was again defeated in the 1931 election.[72] By that time a second woman, Dame Katherine M. Stewart-Murray (Duchess of Atholl), was appointed as Parliamentary Secretary to the Board of Education in 1924. The next minister was Susan Lawrence, who was appointed in 1929 as Parliamentary Secretary of Health.[73]

Across the Atlantic, the first female cabinet member, Frances Coralie Perkins (1880–1965), was appointed as Secretary of Labor

Margaret Grace Bondfield, August 1919. (Library of Congress Reproduction Number: LC-USZ62-85157)

by President Franklin Delano Roosevelt in 1933 and she remained in that position until 1945.[74]

There was tangible progress for women in other areas too, for example, in 1926, Gertrude Ederle (an American competitive swimmer, Olympic champion, and former world record-holder in five events) was the first woman (and fourth person) to swim across the English Channel,[75] under horrendous conditions, beating the records of the men who had previously made the swim from 1875 to 1923. She made a memorable contribution in an age when many found it difficult to take female athletes seriously.[76]

The 1920s were an exciting time with women achieving full suffrage, becoming MPs and cabinet ministers, and with individuals, such as Ederle, breaking until-then male-only records. The advances of women in the outside world gave the government further

Frances Perkins, 1932. (Library of Congress Reproduction Number: LC-USZ62-1132)

impetus to re-examine its employment policies. The Royal Commission on the Civil Service, 1929–31, chaired by Lord Tomlin, reviewed the structure, pay grades and status of female employees. After the 1919 Sex Disqualification (Removal) Act women were technically permitted to all ranks of the Civil Service, but the Commission found that very few were actually employed in positions of responsibility. The Ministry of Defence, for instance, employed no women other than as typists, and the Post Office channelled all female employees into a separate, more poorly paid, Women's Branch. It appeared that there was no way that the Civil Service was going to have a woman giving orders to a man.[77] The Commission did, however, find that most positions should be open to both men and women:

> 397 We refer in paragraph 381 in the view of the McDonnell Commission that, in connection with the employment of women, the object should be to secure for the State the advantage of the services of women wherever those services will promote its interests.
>
> 398 Speaking generally we do hold that the best course is to adopt what has been called the policy of 'a fair field and no favour.' We think that so far as possible all posts in the Service should be open to men and women. We are however, agreed that it is neither practical nor desirable to abolish all the existing reservations of posts to men or women and that the 'fair field and no favour' must be subject to modification in regard to those areas of the Service in which the reservation of certain posts to men or to women is demanded in the public interest, or where it is necessary to employ a minimum proportion of men or of women in each grade.
>
> 399 The adoption of the policy of 'a fair field and no favour' is sometimes opposed on the ground which admittedly exists that men are likely to prove more suitable than women for

certain posts and vice versa. In present circumstances, and until men and women have had opportunities of working side by side, we do not think that in regard to many occupations anyone can forecast the posts for which a man or woman is likely to prove better suited. This is a matter which can only be decided in the light of experience to be gained by employing men and women together.[78]

The Commission additionally recommended equal pay within ten years. However, that was where the intention to foster equality ended, as it recommended maintaining the marriage bar, which was the most significant obstacle to any women with aspirations for a career and a married life:

436 The view held by the majority may be stated as follows:
(i) The main argument against the retention of the marriage bar is that it may result in the loss to the Service of experienced workers. This argument no doubt has weight as regards officers in the higher grades. On the other hand, in regard to certain classes such as the writing assistant class, retirement on marriage results in securing a rapid turn-over of staff employed on routine duties. This is an advantage. [since it keeps wages lower]
(ii) On balance, in considering the question of the marriage bar as it affects the Service as whole, at the present time the disadvantages which would result from the removal of the bar outweigh the disadvantages which result from its retention. The retention, however, of the marriage bar as a general rule can be combined with some provision framed to meet the objections referred to as the loss to the Service of experienced workers.[79]

By the 1930s British women had the vote, they sat in Parliament and in the Cabinet, but the higher levels of the Civil Service, for all practical purposes, remained a single-sex affair. The Foreign Office was, perhaps, the most conservative corner of the Civil Service, and the world of diplomacy was not considered a suitable place for women, and vice versa. Proponents of female diplomats at that time could point out that women were already undertaking diplomatic negotiations with no detriment to the country.[80] For example, when tariffs were introduced in the 1930s, the negotiations with Sweden were successfully handled by Alix Kilroy (see below) from the Board of Trade.[81] Despite evidence to the contrary, the traditionalists prevailed.

Across the Channel, in February 1928, France announced that the entrance examination for the Ministry for Foreign Affairs would be open to female applicants, and the first to pass was Suzanne Borel

Dame Alix Hester Marie Kilroy (Lady Meynell) by Walter Bird, July 1958. (National Portrait Gallery, London)

(1904–95) in 1930. Borel became France's first female diplomat, working at the bureau until the outbreak of the Second World War, whereupon she joined the Resistance. She was highly active, taking many risks, until she caught the attention of the Gestapo, which forced her to go into hiding. After the war, Borel married the French Foreign Minister, Georges Bidault.[82]

US State Department heads of mission were, and still are, mainly political appointees selected by the President, and therefore candidates do not need to rise through the ranks of the State Departments. In the 1930s the US diplomatic mission to Denmark was ranked as a legation, and therefore the head of mission was a minister.[83] The first female Minister was Ruth Bryan Owen, who was posted to Denmark from 1933 to 1936.[84]

Ruth Bryan Owen, c.1910 to c.1915. (Bain News Service, Library of Congress Reproduction Number: LC-DIG-ggbain-19661)

Owen, a democratic politician who served two terms in Congress as Florida's Representative (1929–33), lost the primary in 1932. She campaigned vigorously for Franklin D. Roosevelt and when he won, she was rewarded with the offer of a posting as Head of Mission to Copenhagen, which she readily accepted. Denmark might have been selected since it was a friendly country but not a major power, and was progressive on women's issues (women having had the vote there since 1915). Owen learned to speak Danish, which was rare among diplomats and endeared her to the Danes. In August 1936 she married Borge Rohde, a captain of the Danish Life Guards, which under Danish law made her a Danish citizen, and since she also became a duel citizen she resigned her post.

This was not the first time that Owens had to deal with a question about her citizenship. Born to a prominent American family, Owens had lost her citizenship when she married Reginald Owen, a British army officer, in 1910, and had consequently lost her US citizenship under the Expatriation Act of 1907 which automatically stripped women (but not men) of their citizenship when they married a foreigner. Congress reversed this law with the passage of the Cable Act in 1922, but it was not retroactive and so Owens had to go through the nationalisation process, reclaiming her US citizenship in 1925. British women also lost their citizenship if they married a foreigner, and it was not until the 1948 Nationality Act that the law was changed.[85] Both countries also had a marriage bar, which would remain for another quarter of a century.

When Owens won her seat in the House of Representatives in 1928 as Florida's leading female activist, her opponent claimed she was ineligible since she had not been a citizen for seven years, as required by the US constitution, never mind that she had been a citizen for twenty-eight years prior to her marriage. Owens discussed her case as an example of the discrimination against women, and after a House vote she was allowed to take her seat.[86] Reginald Owen died in 1928.

Following Owen's success, Roosevelt appointed Florence Jaffray 'Daisy' Harriman as Head of Mission to Norway in 1937. Then in 1949, with the Second World War over, Roosevelt appointed Perle Mesta as Minister to Luxembourg.[87]

The first US female career diplomat to reach ambassador status was Frances Elizabeth Willis (1899–1983). With a PhD in political science, she taught political science at Gardner College and Vassar College until she decided to switch careers. She passed the Foreign Service exam in 1927, rose quickly through the ranks, and held positions in Chile, Sweden, Great Britain, Belgium, Spain and Finland. In 1953, President Dwight Eisenhower appointed her Ambassador to Switzerland, and she later served as the Ambassador to Norway (1957–61) and Ceylon (now Sri Lanka) (1962–64).[88] Further details of her life can be found in her biography by Nicholas J. Willis.[89]

Between the First and Second World Wars, the British government appointed another committee to consider the admission of women into the Foreign Office. Sir Claud Schuster,[90] Permanent Secretary to the Lord Chancellor's Office, chaired the Inter-Departmental Committee on the Admission of Women to the Diplomatic and Consular Services, which met on ten occasions and heard statements from over forty individuals. The Schuster Report was published in 1936;[91] it summarised the arguments for and against admitting women to the Foreign Office. There were strong feelings about the subject on both sides. In 1934 Sir Robert Vansittart, while Permanent Under-Secretary for Foreign Affairs, wrote a memo to the Schuster Committee stating that the admittance of women would be a mistake.[92] His main arguments were that foreigners would not treat women equally to men and that women could not be sent to hazardous postings, thus putting

Frances Willis, US Ambassador to Switzerland, 1951. (US Department of State, photographer Whit Keith Jr)

an unfair burden on male diplomats. He also asked, what would happen to the husband of a diplomat?

He concluded saying that admitting women to the Service would 'incontestably affect the prestige of His Majesty's Government abroad and the respect which the opinions and influence of His Majesty's Government at present command in international relations'.

There were nine members on the Committee, led by Howard Smith, Assistant Under-Secretary of State for the Foreign Office. The Committee gave the following reasons as to why women should be admitted:

The general policy of Parliament and successive governments as embodied in the Sex Disqualification (Removal) Act was a policy of 'fair field and no favour', i.e. a person should not be disqualified from being appointed to or holding any civil office unless those who desire to make such a reservation should show good cause for making it.

Women have successfully performed duties analogous to those discharged by the Diplomatic Service, e.g. work performed at the League of Nations.

Broadening the pool from which candidates are drawn will improve the quality of the Service.

Women's concerns and women's viewpoints need to be considered and risk being overlooked if there are no women in the Service.

Some foreign governments have women in diplomatic positions and at least some of them have proven to be successful.

Most of the objections are due to prejudice, and the first few women posted may encounter obstacles, but in time these obstacles will pass.

The committee gave the following reasons for not allowing women to join the diplomatic service:

Women may not be as efficient as men abroad because of social habits, political conceptions and religious beliefs such that women are not sufficiently regarded to make it possible for them to be employed as diplomatic officers.

If the ambassador was a woman, her position might be regarded as ridiculous, and foreign governments may resent her, or her single status might excite 'undesirable comment'.

It would be awkward working with a woman diplomat in the close confines of a Chancery abroad, and the buildings and accommodations are not set up for women.

Women are not as capable as men of working in the heat and high altitude of many foreign missions.

If women were sent to the nicer posts, then it would be unfair to the men, who necessarily must have a greater probability of going to the less desirable posts.

Diplomatic wives contribute significant free labour towards social and philanthropic duties, which benefits the Service with no additional cost to the State.

Initially adding women will cause disruption and at least at first the numbers will be small and the disruption not worth the gain.

The members of the Committee were unable to agree on a single resolution and instead split into three groups.

Sir Ronald Graham, Sir Roderick Meiklejohn, Mr Howard Smith and Mr D.T. Dunlop found the arguments against the admission of women persuasive and recommended no change to existing positions. The two female members of the committee, Miss Hilda Martindale and Miss Muriel Ritson, recommended that women should be eligible for admission into the diplomatic service.[93] Two remaining members, Sir Claud Schuster and Sir James Rae were in favour of admitting women for a limited period as an experimental measure.

Since the members of the committee could not agree, the report to Parliament essentially concluded that while women had been employed successfully in the Home Office, the diplomatic service was a very different situation. With the above factors in mind, the majority of the committee decided to keep the status quo.[94] Anthony Eden brought the matter out into the open again by publishing the report as a White Paper on 28 April 1936. This duly recorded the government's view that they:

Do not consider that any injustice is being done to women by their continued exclusion from the Diplomatic Service, and that they were convinced that the time has not arrived when women could be employed either in the Consular Service or in the Diplomatic Service with advantage to the State or with profit to women.[95]

The topic of civil service reform came up again five years later, in 1941, in a statement to the House of Commons on 11 June when the Secretary of State for Foreign Affairs announced the intention of the government to introduce a series of reforms. These were wide ranging and included separating the Foreign Office from the Home Civil Service, and combining the Foreign Office and diplomatic services with the Commercial Diplomatic Service and the Consular Service. One of the proposed reforms was the admission of women, but the issue was again punted until after the war:

> Women are not at present eligible for posts in the administrative branch of the Foreign Office or in the Diplomatic, Commercial Diplomatic or Consular Services. For the duration of the War, all regular entry into the Service has been suspended. The Secretary of State for Foreign Affairs has, however, already announced his readiness to regard the report of the Committee which in 1934, examined the question of the admission of women into the Foreign Service, as no longer necessarily being the last word on the subject, and to consider, after the War, the appointment of a Committee, which will not be confined in its composition to members of the Civil Service, to review the question again in light of the existing circumstances. In the subordinate branches of the Service, women will continue to be employed as at present.[96]

Due to labour shortages, the Foreign Office, under orders from Foreign Secretary Sir Anthony Eden, announced that temporary appointments should be open to women and promised the MP

Thelma Cazalet that a new committee would review the question of women's eligibility for diplomatic posts once the war was over.[97]

At that time, mid Second World War, any capable ex-military man was called up for service in the forces and auxiliary services, and women were also required to register for work; unmarried women between the ages of 20 and 30 attended compulsory national service. On the home front, in the Civil Service, not everyone was pleased with women taking over men's functions, as this quote from 1945 shows: 'To us, married women have been, to quote the Treasury – "a perfect nuisance" – and I very much doubt whether we have got more than 50% attendance out of them compared with the attendance of the pre-war permanent Civil Servant.'[98]

Another reference from the same inquiry was also less than positive:

Naturally, their home comes first with them, and if their husbands or children are ill, they regard it as their duty to remain home and look after them, especially in these days when nurses and domestic help are almost unobtainable. In addition to remaining at home to look after and nurse members of their own household, it is not uncommon for them to have special leave to nurse parents or sisters etc. Obviously before the War our big permanent staff of women must have had similar responsibilities with regard to mothers and sisters, but very little time off was taken in order to look after them. Possibly pre-war leave was more generous, and this sort of attention was given out of Annual Leave, but his does not explain it all.[99]

In the debates about whether women should be allowed to join the diplomatic service, Sir Harold Nicholson, the famous author, diplomat and politician, commented that diplomats should be 'impartial, imperturbable and a trifle inhuman', qualities that he ascribed only to being male.[100] Although it should be noted that these negative comments appear to be rare exceptions.

With the demobilisation of troops women were encouraged to step down from these occupations to free up jobs for the return-ing troops and to return to more appropriate female work.[101] The female civil servants were particularly irritated because the direc-tive assumed that the men had a family to support and the women did not, regardless of the individual circumstances of the men or women.[102] However, after six years in the workforce, holding the fort, the arguments that women were either unsuited or incapable were largely no longer credible.

In 1942 Mary McGeachy (1901–91)[103] became the first British woman to be granted diplomatic status. She held a temporary position in Washington DC as part of the effort to project British viewpoints to the Americans. It was, however, only a temporary appointment and she was told emphatically that she would 'make no further advancement in the Diplomatic Service'.

One of the weightier questions at the time was whether to lift the marriage bar, a condition of employment that required women (only) to resign from their positions upon their marriage. The British government sought advice from various parties, includ-ing other governments such as that of the United States, to see what their policy was. In September 1945, the British Embassy in Washington asked the US State Department five questions (the answers below are greatly condensed):

1. Are married women employed (in normal conditions and not merely in war-time) either regularly or exceptionally in the public services of the United States?
   There were no restrictions on the employment of women in the US.

Mary Craig McGeachy, First Secretary, British Embassy, 15 December 1942, Washington DC. (Yousuf Karsh / Library and Archives Canada / PA-212296, Item No. 3599691, Library and Archives Canada)

2. If the normal rules forbid the employment of married women, is there any provision for exceptions, and if so in what terms?

Not applicable to US civil service.

3. If married women are employed, what advantages and disadvantages have they been found to possess as employees?

No specific studies have been conducted but married women have been widely employed in governmental service.

4. Is there any system of paying gratuities or 'dowries' to women who resign on marriage, compulsorily or voluntarily, as the case may be?

No.

5. If married women are employed in normal conditions and not merely in war-time, what arrangements are made for leave of absence for childbirth?

There are no maternity leave provisions, and the amount of sick/annual leave varies with job position.[104]

This exchange shows that the UK government was not making decisions blindly, but was seeking advice from other countries who were facing many of the same issues. In 1946 the decision was finally made to remove the marriage bar from the UK-based Civil Service departments:

The following Question stood upon the Order Paper:
75. Mr. JOHN EDWARDS. – To ask the Chancellor of the Exchequer whether any decision has yet been reached on the abolition of the marriage bar in the Civil Service.

The Chancellor of the Exchequer (Mr. Dalton) Might I, Mr Speaker, with the leave of the House, be allowed to give a reply to a Question which I know is of considerable public interest and which was not reached, namely. Question No. 75? The answer is: Yes, Sir. His Majesty's Government have decided that the marriage bar in the Home Civil Service shall henceforth be abolished. I am circulating in the OFFICIAL REPORT a statement on certain points of detail arising out of this decision.[105]

The *Spectator* aired the pros and cons though its publication, reflecting public opinion at the time, and came down on the side arguing for the marriage bar to be dispensed with for the home Civil Service.[106] However, the question still remained as to whether the marriage bar should now be lifted in the Foreign Office.

3

WOMEN'S RIGHTS IN THE FOREIGN OFFICE AFTER 1946

In the 1940s it was openly claimed that women were too emotional, too sentimental and too lacking in natural authority to be entrusted with safeguarding British interests overseas.[1] However, the arguments rang hollow since there had been female spies for many years who had shown extraordinary bravery under fire and in tense situations, and who had been highly effective.

While there had undoubtedly been many forms of espionage, for the sake of national security and defence, only in July 1909 did British Prime Minister Herbert Asquith order the formation of a Secret Service Bureau in response to concerns about German spying operations. Since then Britain's Secret Service Bureau[2] has had women on the payroll as agents and handlers, many of whom were deployed behind enemy lines during wartime. These roles required a cool head and better guardianship of secrets than most Civil Service positions. In 1920, the name of the organisation was changed to its present name, the Secret Intelligence Service (SIS). It is also unofficially known as MI6, a nickname left over from the Second World War.

Women have been involved with spying operations since ancient times and female spies have participated in every war of the last few centuries and probably most of the major conflicts before that. Kathleen Maria Margaret (Jane) Sissmore, MBE (1898-1982) became the first female officer in the Security Service (MI5) in 1929. During the Second World War the SIS ran networks of agents behind enemy lines in Europe. One of the largest was the 'Alliance' Network in Occupied France, with over 145 agents, led by Marie-Madeleine Fourcade, who took over leadership of the French Resistance after the former leader, Georges Loustaunau-Lacau, was arrested. As discussed later in this book the SIS worked in parallel with another clandestine organisation, the Special Operations Executive (SOE), which also operated behind enemy lines. After the war the SOE merged into the SIS.[3]

There were many very brave and resourceful female agents during the Second World War. For example, an operation called 'La Dame Blanche', which employed both male and female agents in German-occupied Belgium, provided valuable information on German troop movements. One method to convey messages involved a midwife, whose job allowed her to cross military lines, and so she carried reports wrapped around the whalebones of her corset.

The first British agent to work behind enemy lines (and Winston Churchill's favourite spy) was Christine Granville, a Polish countess born Krystyna Skarbek, who delivered British propaganda to Nazi-occupied Poland. When she first approached British Intelligence, the SIS rejected her because she was female, but the SOE welcomed her aboard. She survived using her wits; for example, once, when arrested, she bit her own tongue to fake tuberculosis. Another time in France she saved two SOE agents from execution by threatening to kill the German officer responsible. Another agent was Nancy Wake, a New Zealander whom the Gestapo called 'The White Mouse' for her ability to avoid capture. She led a force of 7,000 guerrilla fighters and helped hundreds of Allied soldiers escape. She is also reputed to have killed an SS guard with her bare hands. Another British-American agent was Betty Pack, codename Cynthia, who used her stunning good looks to seduce Count Michael Lubienski, the chief aide to the Polish foreign minister, and she provided information that helped crack the Enigma code. She later described her work: 'Our meetings were very fruitful, and I let him make love to me as often as he wanted, since this guaranteed the smooth flow of political information I needed.'

Other successful assignments using the same skills included the procurement of the Italian naval codes, the Vichy France naval cyphers, and smuggling Spanish nationalists to safety. She commented, 'Ashamed? Not in the least, my superiors told me that the results of my work saved thousands of British and American lives […] It involved me in situations from which "respectable" women draw back – but mine was total commitment. Wars are not won by respectable methods.' When she died in 1963, *Time* magazine wrote that she 'used the bedroom like Bond uses a Beretta'.[4]

Another remarkable spy was Daphne Park (1921–2010),[5] who was born in Surrey, although much of the first few years of her life were spent in humble circumstances in a mud hut without running water or electricity, with her gold-prospecting parents John Alexander and Doreen Park outside of Dar-es-Salaam, Tanzania. At aged 11 she was returned to London to live with her great-aunt in Clapham in order to attend school. From there she went up to Oxford with a special grant from Surrey County Council. When the Second World War broke out she joined the SOE, serving primarily in Europe. Once the war was over she was invited to join the SIS, whereupon she learned Russian, travelled extensively across the Soviet Union and worked on many Cold War issues, as well as serving in various African countries, Vietnam and Mongolia. Later she was asked if she had ever been discriminated against because of her gender, to which she replied, 'The only time I ever experienced sexism was when an African chief gave me a special gift of a hoe, instead of a spear.'

She was appointed Controller, Western Hemisphere, in 1975, the first woman to hold this position. She retired from the SIS in 1979 to become the Principal of Somerville College, Oxford. Then in 1989 she was elevated to the House of Lords as a life peer, becoming the Baroness Park of Monmouth.

After Labour's victory in 1945, Ernest Bevin, the new Foreign Secretary, authorised another review of the employment of women in the diplomatic service, led by Sir Ernest Gowers, and therefore known as the Gowers Committee. Despite the tremendous war efforts and a considerable change in societal opinion, not everyone was supportive of women serving in the Foreign Office. For example, during a debate in the House of Commons in June 1945, MP Captain McEwen declared, 'Will my Right Honourable friend bear in mind always, that this is an entirely unsuitable occupation for women?'[6]

However, compared to earlier reviews, women had by now been visibly involved in diplomacy in various ways during the war. Gertrude Bell, Freya Stark (Iraq and Italy) and Nancy Lambton (Persia), female agents and assets in the SIS and the public diplomacy of women such as Caroline Haslett and Winifred Cullis, who helped improve Britain's image in the US and Commonwealth, had raised the profile of women. By 1945, at least 108 women graduates were known to have been appointed to temporary administrative posts in the diplomatic service; of these, thirty-one served at assistant principal level and sixteen served overseas as first, second and third secretaries, as vice-consuls and as press attachés.

In addition, women had played key roles in the establishment of the League of Nations, such as Dame Rachel Crowdy who had a leading position in the League's Secretariat from 1919 to 1931. As previously discussed, Article 7 of the league had made all positions open to both sexes and had also provided League Officials with diplomatic privileges and immunities.[7]

The Gowers Committee report, published in January 1946, recommended that 'women should be equally eligible for admission to the Foreign Service as men' but their numbers should be limited to 10 per cent of recruitment during the period of reconstruction after the war. There remained the problem of what to do if they married. The Committee recommended that women still be required to resign upon their marriage. The Labour Cabinet agreed with the Committee and, henceforth, women were admitted to the diplomatic service but remained subject to the marriage bar:

His Majesty's Government have agreed to accept the Report and, on the assumption that a general marriage bar will be imposed, which I shall have the power to waive in exceptional circumstances, we have accepted the Committee's recommendation that women shall be equally eligible with men for admission to the Foreign Service.[8]

The Committee, however, recommend that during the reconstruction period that the numbers of women to be recruited should be limited to a maximum of 10 per cent Reconstruction Competition as a whole. We have accepted the Committee's recommendation that when making appointments to posts abroad women should be eligible equally with men for appointment to both diplomatic and consular posts. The necessary arrangements are being made by the Civil Service Commissioners to give effect to these recommendations.

Progress was coming slowly and now there was a crack in the open door. Admittance required passing the same gruelling examination as the male candidates. Initially, only a handful of eligible women applied, and the number who passed the examination were fewer still, but those who did were remarkable individuals.

The first woman to succeed and be appointed to A-Branch was Monica May Milne on 7 October 1946.[9] Born in 1917, the daughter of a London surgeon,[10] Monica Milne was educated at Oxford University and graduated with a master's degree in modern languages. She spent the war years posted to the Ministry of Economic Warfare including spells in the US, and even at that stage was widely touted as a possible candidate to become Britain's first female ambassador. Milne's acceptance into the Foreign Office was exciting news and reported around the world.[11] Even *The Advertiser* of Adelaide, South Australia, reported on this major development, including a description of her pleasant appearance:

One who has just passed, and in so doing set the Thames alight, is 28-year-old Miss Monica Milne. She is the first woman to be accepted since the Foreign Office opened its sacred ranks to women, and if promotion comes her way, there's nothing to prevent her becoming a full-blooded ambassador. Slim, light-haired and heather complexioned, Miss Milne, with a merry laugh but a serious disposition, who is the first woman to pass successfully all tests, came through the 'house party' test with flying colours. She is an Oxford MA, passed high in the civil service examinations, and is the daughter of a London hospital consulting surgeon, Robert Milne, who was a Surgeon-Admiral during the war. If you ask her about her new career, she says she has been admitted on equality with men and cannot see the reason for all the fuss.[12]

However, soon after Milne returned to Washington DC, as a high-flying Second Secretary and on track for a successful diplomatic career,[13] she became engaged to marry John Britton CBE[14] (later Sheriff of Bristol in 1954), and was obliged to choose between her career and marriage. She left the Service upon her marriage in 1947 and the couple moved to Bristol where she was active in the community serving on various boards and later as a magistrate. In 1985 her husband provided funds for an exhibition hall for the history of medicine at Frenchay Hospital in Bristol in her memory.[15]

The second woman to be admitted into A-Branch was Cicely Mayhew (née Ludham) only a year later.[16] As with many of the early diplomatic pioneers she also had personal experience of life abroad; her father was a metallurgist who made his fortune in Rhodesia and the family's early years were spent in Kenya, Tanzania and South Africa. In Pretoria she attended the Loreto Convent School until 1932, when at aged 10, she was shipped back to England to attend Sheffield High School. There she earned a scholarship to Cheltenham Ladies' College and went on to Lady Margaret Hall, Oxford, to read French and German, graduating in 1944 with a first-class degree in just two years.

Freshly graduated, Mayhew was keen to be involved in the war effort and launched herself into the workforce starting with the Naval Intelligence Department at Bletchley Park (1944–45), translating decoded German navy signals.[17] There she found a large disparity in the treatment and value of women compared to men: '[Women were] being paid significantly lower and being ranked beneath men … [who] could not boast a first from Oxford.' On being asked about her status as one of the first women to apply for and pass the Foreign Office Entrance Exam, Mayhew is reported to have said, 'My attitude was, about time too!'[18]

Mayhew's first overseas posting was to Belgrade accompanied by her shaggy dog, Hamlet, where the reception appears to have been warm. Of her new colleagues, she said, 'They were all very kind, very courteous.'[19]

The next posting was to Geneva in 1949, which soon enjoyed a formal visit from the dashing Under-Secretary of State, Christopher Mayhew. At one of the official dinners that week, Cicely referred to a speech that he had given earlier that day and he responded saying that he had another speech to give, and then suddenly proposed to her. Cicely recalled, 'I was so surprised, I said yes.'

They were married later that year and due to the marriage bar she was also required to resign; her pension was converted to a dowry. Lady Mayhew and her husband had two sons and two daughters, and a long life together, until he died in 1997. When asked about her decision to leave the Foreign Office she said, 'It is silly to pretend I didn't have doubts, then or later […] Did I do the right thing? Should I have stayed? Now of course I have my family, two boys, two girls. How could I possibly wish them away?'[20] She died peacefully on 8 July 2016 aged 92.[21]

Another pioneer diplomat was Margaret Anstee (1926–2016), who joined the Foreign Office in 1948. Anstee was from a relatively humble background but she had flourished from a good school education and went on to achieve a double first in modern and medieval languages at Newnham College, Cambridge. Anstee reportedly demonstrated sound practical application during her university days; when invited to a ball, she got around the stringent post-war rationing by making her own gown from white nylon sourced from a surplus military parachute.[22]

Anstee's career in the Foreign Office was also cut short by her marriage in 1952. However, following her divorce a short time later, she returned to international relations, taking up an appointment with the United Nations (UN). Between 1952 and 1993 Anstee served as a UN representative to countries including Colombia, Uruguay and Argentina, Bolivia, Ethiopia, Morocco and Chile and was the first female staff member to reach the rank of Under-Secretary General, in 1987.

On Anstee's retirement in 1993, Queen Elizabeth II acknowledged her contributions to international relations, bestowing upon her the title Dame Margaret Anstee DCMG. In her autobiography *Never Learn to Type: A Woman at the United Nations*, Dame Margaret wrote:

'Never learn to Type' was a dictum I invented for myself and stuck to throughout my career. … Many of my peers had to take secretarial courses and became high-powered assistants to men often not as bright or as qualified as themselves. I decided very early on that I would never learn to type, in order to avoid a similar fate.[23]

Margaret Anstee in Montevideo, Uruguay, for the United Nations in 1958.
(UN Photo)

In 1948 Patricia Margaret Hutchinson joined the ever-growing female contingent in the administrative grade.[24] Her childhood had also been international; her father, a banker, had been posted to South America and Bilbao, Spain, during the 1930s. The young family had experienced the turbulent period leading up to the Spanish Civil War (1936–39) which precipitated the family's return to England and no doubt formed Hutchinson's interest in foreign affairs.

On graduation from Somerville College, Oxford, in 1947 with a degree in PPE, her first position was with the Board of Trade, but a year later she passed the Foreign Office Entrance Exam. Hutchinson's first posting was as Third Secretary to Bucharest in 1950, with all the intrigues of the Cold War. Hutchinson's career was soon upwardly mobile and she rose through the ranks serving as First Secretary in Bern (1955–58); First Secretary (commercial) in Washington (1958–61), First Secretary and Head of Chancery in Lima, becoming the Chargé D'affaires from 1964 to 1967. She was then promoted and appointed Deputy UK Permanent Representative to the Council of Europe in Strasbourg from 1967 to 1969; Counsellor in Stockholm (1969–72); UK delegate to the OECD (1973–75); and Consul-General, Geneva (1975–80). In 1980 she was appointed Ambassador to Uruguay, although she was not the first woman ambassador by that time.[25]

Uruguay was expected to be a quiet posting but in 1982 neighbouring Argentina decided to invade the Falkland Islands, and so began the Falklands War. While Uruguay remained officially neutral, Hutchinson was a potential target and close protection security guards accompanied her everywhere, even waiting outside her bathroom door. During the war, Uruguay facilitated humanitarian activities, such as the transit of hospital ships carrying wounded troops, and Hutchinson worked hard to maintain good relations with the government there. Hutchinson's final posting was to

Barcelona as the Consul-General up to her retirement in 1986. She received the CMG in 1981 and CBE in 1982 for her services to diplomacy following a stellar career.

Rosamund Huebener (née Benson) successfully took the Foreign Office Entrance Examination in 1949,[26] and was sent on her first foreign assignment as a member of the UK delegation to NATO in Paris, where she met and became friends with Anne Warburton, who was working for NATO at that time.[27] (Warburton would later become the UK's first woman ambassador.) Even though women entering the Foreign Office were tested to the same standards as the men, the equality ended there as they did not receive equal pay until 1955, and they were still required to resign upon marriage under the marriage bar until 1973.[28] Huebener added:

Patricia Hutchinson, UK Ambassador to Uruguay, 1980. (Alamy)

You ask about women's rights in the Foreign Office – I would say there weren't any, in my day at least. Today it seems scandalous that female diplomats had to resign on marriage (until 1973) but then it was accepted as normal. I personally had no problem with nearly always being the only woman in a Department or at a meeting but some of my colleagues later complained about discrimination and mild bullying. […] Women received no pension on resigning (admittedly after only 12 years in my case), but a 'dowry' of a month's basic salary for each year of service. We were paid slightly less than our male colleagues but that didn't bother me.[29]

Huebener reminisced on her early years at the FCO, remarking on a lack of guidance and training for new entrants of either sex: 'You were just flung into a department head-first and told to get on with it […] I had no idea what I was doing and nobody knew what to do with me. It was tremendous fun.'[30]

The lack of initial guidance was not a gender issue, but rather a reflection of how the FCO handled its new recruits. The number of women joining the diplomatic service in the early years was small, constituting only about 2 per cent of A-Branch and about 12 per cent of B-Branch.[31] Some entered through annual recruitment into A-Branch, others transferred from B-Branch and others came across from other government departments. In the autumn of 1946 Monica Milne was the first female appointed to A-Branch and she was then joined by three others over the next year and two more in 1948. Seventeen female officers were directly recruited into A-Branch between 1946 and 1951. Some older women, such as Barbara Salt, also joined A-Branch after service in the SOE in Tangier during the war. Others, such as Daphne (later Baroness) Park, were on secondment from MI6 and were using their diplomatic position as cover for their covert intelligence work.

In the 1950s the small number of female selectees was, in part, due to the fact that it was proportionally harder for a smart young woman to gain entrance to an elite college, especially Oxford or Cambridge, and it was from these establishments that 90 per cent of the recruits were drawn. At least twenty of the women recruited between 1945 and 1965 had been educated at one of Oxford's women's colleges, with Somerville College alone supplying ten of them. The marriage bar also served as a disincentive to women looking for a long-term career.

It was of course somewhat intimidating for women joining the nearly all-male bastion of the Foreign Office, as Dame Rosemary Spencer described when she first started in 1962:

> I have to admit that the FO's introductory sessions for new recruits seemed somewhat intimidating, with 22 men (many having done National Service) and just 2 women in the 1962 entry. But once I joined the West & Central African Department, I found the working atmosphere business-like and congenial, without any feeling of masculine bias. The same went for subsequent postings, both in London and abroad. Perhaps I was fortunate.[32]

Dame Veronica Sutherland, who joined the Foreign Office in 1965, echoed the same sentiment:

> I have often been asked questions about women in the Foreign Office and been told how difficult it must have been for me. I haven't found it so. When I joined, in the 1960s, it was very unusual for women to be appointed to the fast stream. There were very few of us. I wasn't the first by a long way – I could mention quite a number of others – but it was unusual. But you were treated, or I was treated, with absolute courtesy.[33]

While the Foreign Office itself was not for 'turning' in 1948, there were new thoughts about the meaning of equal rights happening around the world. The UN Universal Declaration of Human Rights of 1948 was a significant development on the road to women's rights and it was born of a new robust, international parent organisation to replace the ineffective League of Nations. At the conclusion of the Second World War in a climate of goodwill, a global desire for long lasting peace and a need for reconstruction, the United Nations (UN) was established. The UN still operates on a grand scale and has many constituent organisations under its umbrella. In establishing the UN's charter, the issue of women's rights was addressed, at least in part. Article 55 provides that the UN should promote 'Universal respect for, and observance of, human rights and fundamental freedoms for all without distinction as to race, sex, language or religion.'

One of the organisations formed under the UN's umbrella was the Commission on Human Rights, whose mandate included the preparation of an International Bill of Rights and international declarations or conventions on civil liberties, including the status of women. Other organisations such as the ILO and UN Educational, Scientific, and Cultural Organization also participated, and in 1948 the UN General Assembly adopted the Universal Declaration of Human Rights.[34]

The Commission on Human Rights considered itself responsible for all women's issues, and stated that it intended to raise the status of women, irrespective of nationality, race, language or religion, to equality with men in all fields of human enterprise. It went on to declare that women should be given equal rights with men with respect to labour, wages, holidays and other economic and social rights.

Towards the end of the Second World War, with victory looking increasingly certain, the ILO held a key policy conference at

Temple University in Philadelphia. This conference resulted in a declaration (the 1944 Declaration of Philadelphia) which became the new charter for the ILO and was made into an annex of the original constitution. It clearly stated, 'All human beings, irrespective of race, creed or sex, have the right to pursue both their material well-being and their spiritual development.'[35]

Meanwhile across the Atlantic America appointed its first female ambassador, Eugenie Anderson,[36] who led a remarkable, though these days largely forgotten, life. She was born in Adair, Iowa, in 1909 and studied music at the Julliard School in Germany and New York. Anderson and her husband, John, an artist, travelled through Nazi Germany in 1937 and witnessed 'a totalitarian state in action'. Anderson was shocked and, understanding what was to unfold, became an activist. She joined the League of Women Voters[37] in Minnesota, supporting Hubert Humphrey, a candidate for Congress for the Democratic Farm Laborer Party. After losing the election to a Republican candidate there was a bitter fight within the party resulting in Anderson being appointed a Delegate to the Democratic National Convention, and becoming a high-profile campaigner for Truman's election.

Following Truman's election Anderson expected to return to a quiet life but a call from the President changed everything. At first the Danes were reluctant to have a woman fill the role of ambassador, concerned about a 'call me madam' situation,[38] but these fears were put to rest on meeting with the Danish ambassador in Washington. On 12 October 1949 Eugenie Anderson was officially named as the US Ambassador to Denmark, the legation in Copenhagen having been raised to an embassy on 18 March 1947 when Ambassador Josiah Marvel Jr. presented his credentials to the Danish monarch.[39] As for any concerns about Anderson's new role, she is quoted as saying, 'I have always believed that if you approach your job seriously and if you have an attitude of respect towards

Eugenie Anderson, c. 1960. (Alamy)

the people you work with, you will have no trouble in getting their cooperation.'

Anderson's goal was to reach the Danish people directly, which she felt was an important means to foster US–Danish relations. Immediately, upon her arrival, she began to learn Danish and six months later at the annual 4 July Independence Day party she gave a speech, in Danish, to about 3,000 people. The Danes responded with deafening applause, and afterwards she was frequently asked to speak across the kingdom. When Eisenhower succeeded Truman as President of the United States in 1953, Anderson offered her resignation and returned to private life. Before she left Denmark, King Frederick IX decorated her with the Grand Cross of the Order of Dannenborg,[40] the highest honour ever accorded to a woman in Denmark's history up to that time.

In 1960 J.F. Kennedy became President and Anderson was offered a new diplomatic post as head of the American legation in communist Bulgaria. She found that the Residence was dilapidated and it was necessary to exercise constant vigilance in case their rooms were bugged. She engaged in a battle of wills with the Bulgarian authorities, on one occasion concerning whether she could distribute a pamphlet at a large trade show where the US was exhibiting. In the end, not only did she hand out her pamphlets to attendees, but also pressed one into the Bulgarian Premier's hand when he visited the booth. Later she requested an opportunity to appear on television to address the Bulgarian people, which was initially

Evelyn Adelaide Sharp, Baroness Sharp by Elliott & Fry, 16 February 1950.
(National Portrait Gallery, London)

denied, but she pointed out to the Bulgarian Foreign Minister that he had addressed the American people several times when he was Ambassador to the US. He resisted again, explaining that he had spoken in English. Therefore, on 4 July 1963, Anderson gave her speech, in Bulgarian.

She retired as Ambassador in December 1964 and went on to serve as the US Representative to the UN Trusteeship Council.[41] The following year she served on the UN Committee for Decolonization.[42] She died in 1997, aged 87, and we can recommend reading a more detailed description of her colourful life in the book *Women in the Department of State*.[43]

Back in Britain in 1955, as the country continued its recovery from the war, the UK Civil Service marked a huge milestone with the appointment of Dame Evelyn (later Baroness) Sharp (1903–85) as the first female Permanent Secretary, in the Ministry of Housing and Local Government.[44] Baroness Sharp joined the Civil Service via the Civil Service Entrance Examination in 1926 (the second year that women were allowed to take this exam), and twenty-nine years later held one of the most senior government positions. The tide was turning in favour of women in the Civil Service.

4

MODERN HISTORY AND A BRIEF OVERVIEW OF THE STRUCTURE OF THE BRITISH FOREIGN OFFICE

At the start of the twentieth century the landscape of the British Empire was rapidly changing, and the Foreign Office was subsequently evolving. Around 1900 there were three government departments responsible for the implementation of British foreign policy. The first was the Foreign Office, created in 1787 when the Southern and Northern Departments of Secretary of State were amalgamated, and responsibilities reassigned into either 'Domestic' or 'Foreign' matters under the 'Home' and 'Foreign' Office respectively. Foreign policy for India was controlled through a second department, the India Office, created in 1858 when the British government took over administration of India from the East India Company. The remaining British overseas territories were administered through a third department, the Colonial Office, created in 1854 upon the division of the War and Colonial Offices.

Following the disintegration of the British Empire (and, therefore, a reduced global influence) after the twentieth century world wars, these departments were rationalised and eventually consolidated. In 1925 the Dominions Office had been separated from the Colonial Office but, in 1947, following the independence of India, Pakistan and Bangladesh, the India Office was absorbed into the Dominions Office to form the new Commonwealth Relations Office. This later combined with the Colonial Office in 1966 to form the Commonwealth Office and two years later that too was merged with the Foreign Office to create the FCO. These changes are illustrated below:

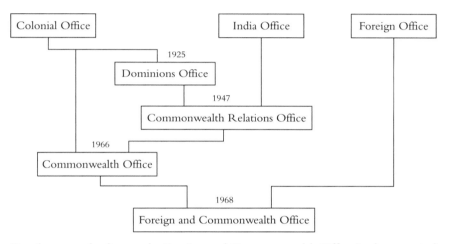

Developments leading to the Foreign and Commonwealth Office in the twentieth century.

The main purpose of the Diplomatic Service is to promote British interests abroad and to provide assistance to British nationals and businesses when overseas.[1] The Head of the FCO is her Majesty's Principal Secretary of State for Foreign and Commonwealth Affairs, more informally referred to as the Foreign Secretary. Economic development and foreign aid was managed by the Department of International Development.[2] This department was rolled in under the FCO from 1970 to 1974, then out and back in again from 1975 to 1997, but with effect from September 2020 is now fully merged and appears under the new twenty-first century name; the Foreign, Commonwealth and Development Office (FCDO).

Diplomatic grades are established by international treaty and define the hierarchy of positions between countries. The current treaty is the Vienna Convention on Diplomatic Relations of 1961, which prescribes the privileges of a diplomatic mission, enabling diplomats to perform their function without fear of coercion or harassment by the host country.[3]

The ranks within an embassy are as follows:

Ambassador (High Commissioner in Commonwealth missions to other Commonwealth countries);*
Minister;
Minister–Counsellor;
Counsellor;
First Secretary;
Second Secretary;
Third Secretary;
Attaché;
Assistant Attaché.

*A Permanent Representative is equivalent to an Ambassador but accredited to an international body such as the UN, not a head of state.

A mission will have a number of First and Second Secretaries. For example, the UK mission to the United Nations in New York has fifteen First Secretaries and sixteen Second Secretaries.[4]

5

CHANGES FOR A MODERN ERA, FROM THE 1960S

In 1962, Prime Minister Harold Macmillan appointed Lord Plowden to lead a new committee[1] tasked to examine Britain's representational service overseas and to review the Foreign Office's effectiveness, in light of world changes since the last reorganisation in 1945. In particular, Britain's economic and military role had decreased and much of the former Empire had been encouraged to become independent.

The Plowden Committee issued its report in 1964 and recommended that the Foreign Office and the Commonwealth Office be combined to form HM Diplomatic Service, and a new employee grading system should be implemented instead of the former A, B, C, D and T branches. It also recommended that there be no discrimation in the appointment of women or in their hiring:

118. When the Foreign Service was opened to women in 1945, a rule was made limiting their recruitment to posts in Branch A to 10% of the total intake in any one year. This 10% limitation is in fact a dead letter. There has never been occasion to apply

it. Its retention is a pointless irritant and we recommend that it be dropped:

[…]

123. We endorse the view that women officers should be employed as widely as possible in the Diplomatic Service. No artificial or unnecessary restrictions should be placed on their duties or postings. There are some appointments for which women are especially well suited and others in which they are less likely to be successful. But we should like to make it clear that we received no evidence which would suggest that women in the Foreign Service have proved 'tender plants'. We came upon a few instances in which, to put it no higher, they had withstood disagreeable climatic, political, or living conditions with fully as much resource and fortitude as their male colleagues.[2]

The Plowden Committee, however, did not class the marriage bar as a form of discrimination and its preservation, albeit with some flexibility in exceptional cases, was recommended:

119. The 'marriage bar' represents a more serious problem. Even for unmarried women diplomats, there are often severe difficulties in arranging suitable overseas appointments. We were assured, and accept it, that these difficulties are not due to restrictive attitude on the part of the Foreign Office but are related to the customs and practices of some foreign countries, the Middle East for example. The difficulties in the way of posting married women overseas would in many cases prove overwhelming. If the husband has a job of his own, this will normally preclude him from accompanying his wife on her postings abroad. If, on the other hand, he is able to move from post to post with his wife, and few will in fact be able to do so, it is hard to see what contribution he can make to the work of the Service. We are

convinced that there are some valid reasons for the existence of the 'marriage bar', although none of them reflect in any way on the fitness of the women themselves.

120. The Foreign Secretary has, however, discretion to make exceptions. The Foreign Service Regulations state that 'as a rule a woman member of the Service will be required to resign upon marriage, but the Secretary of State reserves the right in special circumstances to permit her to continue as a member of the Service, either unconditionally or subject to conditions'. Exceptions under this formula have on occasion been made but we think its emphasis is unduly restrictive. We suggest that a new formula should be introduced for the Diplomatic Services on the following lines:

'Any woman member of the Diplomatic Service who proposes to marry must notify the Personnel Department of her intention. The Secretary of State reserves the right to require her to resign either upon marriage or later or to attach conditions to her continuation as a member of the Service'.

We doubt whether it will often happen that a woman will wish to remain in the Diplomatic Service after marriage. In most cases, it will be her intention to settle down with her husband in this country or wherever he may be living. But a revised regulation on the lines we have suggested should encourage a more liberal attitude wherever practical.

Resistance to removal of the marriage bar was based on an assumption that most women would follow their husbands and not the other way around; and granting women London positions would block opportunities for mobile (i.e. male) officers in furthering their careers. The report also recommended combining the Foreign Service, Commonwealth Service, Commonwealth Relations Office and Trade Commission Service into a unified organisation. Following these recommendations, the Foreign, Commonwealth and Trade Commission Services merged to form the Diplomatic Service on 1 January 1965. Then in 1968, the FCO was created, which is how it remained until 2020. In June 2020, Prime Minister Boris Johnston announced that the FCO and the Department for International Development would merge, for reasons of improved efficiency and efficacy, which was received with mixed reactions. In September 2020 the reform took place and it is now known as the Foreign, Commonwealth and Development Office (FCDO).[3]

The 1960s saw dramatic and positive changes for women led by the post-war generation. Betty Friedman's *Feminine Mystique*[4] propelled feminist thought into the mainstream and made women rethink their role in society and whether there was more to life than the traditional role of wife and mother. For many ordinary women it was a time of awakening and determining changes and discovering choices.

This decade enjoyed huge cultural shifts effecting change in every aspect of life.[5] Enormous leaps in technology delivered televisions into homes, which in turn brought new liberal ideas to the masses. The sexual revolution was aided, in part, by the availability of the pill, enabling women to put their goals and desires on a more equal level to those of men.[6] Society also became more sexually liberal, starting with the high street fashions from shocking miniskirts created by designers like Mary Quant[7] to the overturning of the laws against homosexuality for men over 21[8] and a reduction in the obscenity laws, as was illustrated by the well-known acquittal of Penguin Books in their publication of D.H. Lawrence's *Lady Chatterley's Lover*.[9] Drug use became more mainstream along with a much more prominent counter culture.[10]

There were widespread protests in the West, especially in the US against the Vietnam War, and student protests and widespread strikes in France nearly toppled the government in 1968. In comparison, protests in the UK were much more subdued. Other books have been written that do much more justice to the social changes of this period,[11] but it is worth understanding how this period affected society's views on the role of women and the way that women, themselves, reconsidered expectations of their lives and career paths.

While society was changing rapidly, the Foreign Office was not. Business continued much as it always had, as described by Dame Rosemary Spencer (Former Ambassador to the Netherlands 1996–2001):

> At the beginning of 1962, there was a quota of 10% for women appointed to the administrative grade. Moreover, any woman member of the Service, whatever her status or circumstances, had to resign on marriage. The quota was abolished in the same year, but the marriage bar was not lifted until 1972. Not surprisingly, senior women were pretty rare birds in the 1960s.[12]

On joining the Foreign Office in the 1960s modern women did not want special accommodations due to their sex, and they were determined to show that they were as capable as their male colleagues. For example, Dame Veronica Sutherland, who joined the Foreign Office in 1965, said:

> In retrospect, I am struck by how those of us among my contemporaries who thought of ourselves as feminists felt we had to prove ourselves, without concessions. To have suggested that any special allowance be made was a tacit admission of inferiority.[13]

The endless march for equal opportunities had always experienced flurries of apparent progress between periods of calm, and the 1970s was a decade of notable improvements and some rapid change. Progress came about not just through rewriting laws but the gradual and permanent shift in social attitudes and allowing the population to acclimatise to the 'new norms'.

On the cusp of Brexit as this is being written, it is interesting to consider that when Britain joined the European Economic Community (EEC), or Common Market as it was better known in 1973, it was then bound by the Treaty of Rome in 1957, in which equality of pay for men and women was already a requirement. The treaty formed a union of six European countries: Belgium, France, Italy, Luxembourg, the Netherlands and West Germany:

Treaty of Rome 1957
ARTICLE 119
Each Member State shall during the first stage ensure and subsequently maintain the application of the principle that men and women should receive equal pay for equal work. For the purpose of this Article, 'pay' means the ordinary basic minimum wage or salary and any other consideration, whether in cash or in kind, which the worker receives, directly or indirectly, in respect of his employment from his employer. Equal pay without discrimination based on sex means:
(a) that pay for the same work at piece rates shall be calculated on the basis of the same unit of measurement;
(b) that pay for work at time rates shall be the same for the same job.[14]

Women's scales of pay in the Civil Service achieved legal parity, after a long fight, in 1961. These victories were the result of the persistence of the Council of Women Civil Servants, of which Dame Alix Kilroy was on the Executive Board and, for a time, served as Chairman.[15]

For the rest of the country, the Equal Pay Act of 1970 was passed in response to the growing social pressure for equality between men and women. There were some people who believed that it was reasonable for men to earn more than women because they had to support families, whereas women did not. Even Margaret Thatcher recognised the problem in this argument, as she made clear in 1969:

> One of our young lady speakers said that she thought a woman should not have the same pay as a man who has children to support. I think that this is a fallacious argument. On that basis, a man who has ten children should have more pay than a bachelor. But you cannot deal with pay in industry or in public service or pay for a job in that way.[16]

It also helped to bring British law in line with the Treaty of Rome.[17] This act prohibited any less favourable treatment between the sexes in terms of pay and conditions of employment, and was similar to the US Equal Pay Act of 1963, on which it was modelled. The US Equal Pay Act was an amendment to the Fair Labor Standards Act of 1938.[18]

The UK's 1975 Sex Discrimination Act went further and prohibited discrimination based on gender and marital status.[19] In terms of society, social attitudes towards women changed drastically when Margaret Thatcher became Prime Minister. Legally speaking, women shared equal rights to men, and a few had reached the highest professional levels, but that did not mean that there was equality at every level. Dame Mariot Leslie described the status of women in the FCO when she joined in 1975:

> [In] 1975 [...] all the assumptions through school and university had been that discrimination against women not only happened but was legitimate and normal – so it wasn't normal for somebody like me to enter the FCO. There were women in the FCO, but there was a marriage ban until 1973. There were remarkable and distinguished and very effective women in the upper reaches of the FCO, but very few. And there had been

other, again extremely good, woman diplomats who had to leave because they got married; they had to make a choice that their male colleagues hadn't made. So when I joined in 1977 the FCO had relatively little experience of having woman diplomats, little experience of having senior women diplomats, and virtually no experience of having married women diplomats. And they still had an assumption – wrong – that most of the new legislation about equal opportunities didn't apply to them because they dealt with Abroad, and Abroad was self-evidently different. And they assumed that the security circumstances of a Diplomatic Service where everybody was security-vetted were so self-evidently different that foreign postings didn't need to have the same criteria as those that applied to domestic jobs. That was very deeply entrenched.[20]

The Equal Pay Act of 1970 has since been repealed by the passing of the Equality Act of 2010 which combined several anti-discrimination laws with a single act, and most of the provisions of the Equal Pay Act are now included within the Equality Act.

While the laws in both the US and the UK were leaning towards equal opportunities it was still necessary for some individuals who had experienced discrimination to catalyse necessary changes and to take matters into their own hands.

Alison Palmer began her career in the US State Department in 1959, specialising in African affairs, having passed the stringent examination for the prestigious officer class. Despite a promising start to her career she was denied promotion for over a year, while comparable male colleagues were quickly advanced. Furthermore, once promoted, Palmer was then rejected for three postings in a row on the basis of her sex alone. Several ambassadors had objected to her assignment to their embassies across Africa during the late 1960s, and to add insult to injury, at one posting, she was expected to act as the social secretary to the ambassador's wife.

Palmer was livid and decided to rock the boat by proceeding with an internal grievance procedure through the Department's new Equal Employment Office (EEO), charging sex discrimination. The EEO found in her favour, but the State Department refused to enter the report in her personnel file. Undeterred, in 1971 Palmer filed another sex discrimination action against the State Department, which took three years to process, but was successful.[21] Palmer could see that it would take more than one case to change the State Department so she then used her proceeds to finance a class action suit for more than 500 other women.[22] A huge amount of compensation was paid out, but more significantly, Secretary of State Cyrus Vance directed the State Department to adopt equal opportunity employment across all of its activities.[23]

Margaret Thatcher[24] was an unlikely candidate to become Britain's first female Prime Minister. She rose from humble beginnings in Grantham, the daughter of a local grocer, but it was her headmistress, Miss Gladys Williams at Kesteven and Grantham Girl's School who inspired her to think big: 'It is not our business to turn out teachers or typists, or even housewives, but to try to send out girls capable and desirous of doing some part of the world's work well.'[25]

Thatcher's ambition and resilience was evident at a young age. On declaring that she wanted to reach the top echelon of the Indian Civil Service, the succeeding headmistress warned that this career path was male dominated and would be difficult. Thatcher prophetically responded, 'All the better for it. If I succeed, my success will be the more creditable.'[26]

From the local grammar school, Thatcher went on to read Chemistry at Somerville College, Oxford, and graduated with a second-class honours degree in Chemistry (she was reportedly more proud of becoming the first scientist to be Prime Minister than she was of being the first woman).[27] She was active in politics at Oxford, serving as President of the University's Conservative Association. In 1951 she married industrialist Denis Thatcher, and their twins arrived in 1953. Thatcher strongly believed that women could combine marriage and a career and that such a wife would be a much better companion at home.[28] However, she also respected those women who chose the more traditional roles:

> Many women will still make their main job in life the creation of a home. Others at some time in their life will go out to work and possibly seek a part-time job suitable to their special circumstances. Yet others, some married women and some single women, will carry out the same jobs with equal competence and under the same conditions as men. We must make provision for all of these circumstances, but let us recognise that perhaps the most important job of all is the creation of family and family life. Home is where the individual matters, and, as we move into an economy where size seems to dwarf the individual, the home and the atmosphere there becomes more and more important, not less.[29]

Thatcher, the mother of young twins, was also a full-time research chemist while studying to become a barrister in her spare time, and had a keen interest in the political scene. On being called to the bar in 1954, she became a specialist in tax law; but it was evident that she held the conviction that the time had come for women to have an equal place in society. In 1952, following the death of King George VI, she wrote, 'If as many earnestly pray, the accession of Elizabeth II can help remove the last shreds of prejudice against women aspiring to the highest places, then a new era for women will indeed be at hand.'[30]

Her interest and profile in politics ascended when in 1959 she was elected Conservative MP for Finchley (a constituency she held for her entire career in the House of Commons). Thatcher did not actively push the women's rights agenda, but she was seriously committed to equal opportunities, and was known to counter or deflect gender derogatory questions with a sharp wit. For example, in 1966 during the BBC's news programme, *Question Time*, she was asked whether it was right and proper to judge a woman's intelligence by her legs, she answered: 'I really only ever look at a man's head to see whether he is intelligent, and so often, when the answer is that he's not, one doesn't need to look any farther.'[31]

At the 1969 Conservative Party conference she said at a forum for women's rights: 'I think it was Socrates who said long, long ago that when woman is made equal to man, she becomes his superior, and I would not dissent from anyone as wise as Socrates.'[32]

After Edward Heath lost the confidence of the Conservative Party, she joined the leadership race in 1975, surprisingly found herself elected, and became Prime Minister when the Conservatives won the general election in 1979. Thatcher held the office for three terms until 1990, becoming the longest-serving UK Prime Minister of the twentieth century. The highlights of her time in office included defeating Argentina in the Falklands War and orchestrating successful international negotiations ending the Cold War with like-minded US President Ronald Reagan[33] and Soviet leader Mikhail Gorbachev, and transforming the British economy at home. She had challenges at home with industrial strife and her quarrels with Europe, which are beyond the scope of this book.

After she left the House of Commons in 1992, she was appointed life peer in the House of Lords, receiving the title of Baroness Thatcher of Kesteven. In 1995 she was appointed as Lady Companion of the Order of the Garter, the highest order of chivalry; she died on 8 April 2013.

As a lawyer she strove to revise the tax rules that she believed were unfair to married and divorced women and widows. As Prime

Minister she transformed the psyche of British society in terms of what women could achieve. As the *Independent* newspaper wrote, her legacy was 'shattering deep-seated sexist stereotypes which cleared the path for future generations'.[34] A 2016 survey found that Thatcher was the most influential woman of the past 200 years.[35]

Many women's rights activists, however, felt that Thatcher should have done much more; for example, during her tenure she only promoted only one woman to the Cabinet (Baroness Young). Additionally she did not show much inclination to support other professional women through policy to advance their careers;[36] for example, she froze child benefit and criticised working mothers for creating a 'crèche generation'.[37]

6

THE MARRIAGE BAR

One of the most significant obstacles against a keen and capable woman progressing in her chosen government career was the marriage bar. It was assumed by the establishment that married women would focus on their home and family, and would neither desire nor be able to hold down a career. The marriage bar was not uniquely a requirement of the Civil Service; prior to 1946 there was much sentiment for its removal on the grounds of fairness and waste of valuable human resources as the following article from the *Spectator* shows that same year:

> The White Paper on the Marriage Bar in the Civil Service, published a few days ago, throws into the arena once more a subject that for years has been lurking on the outskirts of it. Should women be retained in their work after marriage? The committee appointed after a deputation of M.P.'s of all parties had approached the Chancellor of the Exchequer (Sir John Anderson) does not answer the question. It merely gives both sides. The position today is that women normally resign on

marriage, but heads of departments in consultation with the Treasury may waive the bar; and during the war, of course, numerous married women were recruited as temporary Civil Servants, some to responsible positions. The chief arguments for resignation on marriage are:

(1) that the employment of married women takes employment from those who need it more, which always was a doubtful argument and has no validity at all in a period of labour shortage.

(2) that married women are less reliable and less 'mobile' than unmarried, to which it may be replied that those offending should be asked to resign on those grounds and not because they are married, and

(3) that girls who work for a few years and then retire provide a necessary 'turnover' in the Civil Service which has much routine work and insufficient opportunities for promotion, to which it may be replied that most women will voluntarily resign on marriage or their first pregnancy, and so the position will not be much affected.

The main arguments for making no hard and fast rules are that they restrict individual liberty, that to dismiss women automatically on marriage is to waste education and training and that the female staff of the Civil Service will lack broad-mindedness if it is entirely composed of spinsters. On the whole opinion seems flowing towards the removal of the marriage bar. The teaching profession, the BBC and the LCC have all removed it recently. The Civil Service might well try a period without it.[1]

The marriage bar was not uniquely a civil service requirement. Prior to the Second World War marriage bars existed across many industries, becoming substantially more common during the 1930s depression when bars were deployed as a gear to free up jobs for unemployed men. The BBC introduced a bar in 1932, when the

Civil Service also formalised it, along with large companies such as Sainsbury's and ICI; Lloyds Bank had a marriage bar until 1949 and Barclays Bank only scrapped it in 1961.[2] Other countries had marriage bars too, for example, the Australian Civil Service exercised a bar until 1966, and the Irish Civil Service, like its British counterpart, kept a marriage bar right up until 1973.[3]

It was, of course, inherently unfair that a fixed rule, such as the marriage bar, could be applied regardless of the circumstances of an individual woman. From 1946 most government departments dispensed with the marriage bar, with the exception of the Foreign Office, for reasons of its foreign commitments and suitability for postings, etc.[4] In 1955 journalist Elizabeth Adams wrote an article describing why so few women become diplomats:

> It is the little matter of the marriage bar. For a female diplomat the path to the altar, even with a Briton, leads automatically straight through to the exit door from the service. I admit that a woman might find it difficult to run a husband in Surbiton in sweet accord with a career in Washington, and would have resigned her career on marriage anyway. But at least that would be her free choice […] At least she would not be at the mercy of an arbitrary condemnation to spinsterhood if she wishes to prosper her chosen career.[5]

The question of marriage and female diplomats was considered an intractable problem for decades. The secondary issue, of what a diplomat might do with her husband when posted abroad, also caused consternation along the marble corridors of Whitehall. The unpaid role of a functioning diplomatic wife at overseas missions was clear and actually regarded as an integral part of the effectiveness of her diplomat husband, but the role of an accompanying husband was beyond the imagination of the Personnel Department. Those women who left the Foreign Office to marry were stripped of their pensions and settled with a dowry, amounting to a month's salary for every year they had served.[6]

The marriage bar also presented a significant cost to the FCO due to the high attrition of trained and capable women leaving on their marriage. For example, seven of the eighteen women appointed to the administrative grade between 1946 and 1954 resigned. These numbers should not have come as a surprise to the Foreign Office since in the 1950s over 50 per cent of women over the age of 16 were married and the median age for marriage for women was 26.4 years old.[7]

The resignation of Joan Burbidge upon her engagement in 1954 was a public setback to the Foreign Office. Burbidge had read modern history at Oxford and joined the BBC after graduating in 1941, but with the Second World War raging, she decided to join the Ministry of Information in Washington DC, where she developed pro-British propaganda to help persuade American citizens to join the war. Interestingly, her supervisor, Donald McClean, later gained notoriety as a KGB spy. After the war Burbidge took the Foreign Office Entrance Examination, becoming the second woman to pass, on 8 March 1948.[8] For several years, she was considered a rising star,[9] becoming the second highest-ranking female diplomat after Barbara Salt. In 1952 Burridge was posted to India as First Secretary to the High Commissioner and it was there that she met and married Ian Macintosh, a Scottish banker, in Old Delhi's St Andrews Church. Burbidge was the sixth woman to resign due to marriage since women were first allowed to enter in 1946. By then about a third of the women who had joined the Foreign Office had resigned because of marriage.[10]

The first woman to be forced to resign, Cecily Ludlam, who was serving as Third Secretary at the Embassy in Belgrade, said, 'I was content to resign. It would take a super-woman to run a Foreign

Office job, a husband and a family, but I do think a woman diplomat should be allowed to decide for herself whether she wants to resign.'[11]

The capital cost of losing proficient, trained staff was becoming a problem for the Foreign Office. In the face of this exodus, Foreign Secretary Ernest Bevin apparently snapped: 'We've turned the Foreign Office into a matrimonial bureau!'[12] The newspapers ran with the story: 'The Foreign Office is perturbed […] Its women diplomats are so attractive that it is losing them too fast. All their training and experience is being lost.'

Grace Gardner, who joined in 1947, also left on her marriage, whereupon a 'rather crusty' senior colleague blurted out: 'The trouble with you women is that you will go and get married.'

She responded, 'You've had eleven of the best years of my life […] What are you grumbling about?'

The marriage bar also stood as a key deterrent to talented women considering a diplomatic career. Juliet Campbell (former Ambassador to Luxembourg) wrote:

Equal pay was being gradually introduced in the FO as far back as 1957 when I joined. The main legal discrimination was the requirement that women should resign on marriage which was not lifted until 1972. In looking at the figures it is worth … [remembering] what a deterrent this was to women, and how long it took for the increased numbers recruited after 1972 to gain the necessary experience and rise through the ranks. […] If the Service has changed its attitudes, so too have the women who belong to it … In retrospect, I am struck by how those of us among my contemporaries who thought of ourselves as feminists felt we had to prove ourselves, without concessions. To have suggested that any special allowance be made was a tacit admission of inferiority.[13]

The approach of Dame Rosemary Spencer (former Ambassador to the Netherlands) on joining the Foreign Office in 1962 was, 'My own take on this was to join up for as long as I remained single, which, as it turned out, I did throughout my career.'[14]

The list below highlights the premature departures of female diplomats due to the marriage bar, which ultimately slowed down the progression of all women to the higher echelons of the service:

Name[15]	Entered Foreign Office A–Branch[16]	Left Foreign Office
Monica May Milne	1946, first woman to enter A–Branch[17]	Married John Britton
Cicely Ludlam	1947, previously with British naval intelligence	Married Christopher Mayhew 1949
Caroline Petrie[18]	1947	
Grace Rolleston[19]	1947	Married Robert Neil Gardner
Margaret Anstee	1948	Married 1952
Patricia Hutchinson[20]	1948	1986, retired
Edith Joan Burbidge[21]	1948	1950, married Ian Macintosh
Jennifer Elizabeth Turner[22]	1948	
Rosamunde Benson	1948	Married Dr Huebener
Katherine du Boulay[23]	Unknown	Married Michael Stewart
Barbara Salt[24]	1949, previously with SOE	1973, retired
Rosalind Chevalier	1950	1968
Meriel Russel	1950	1956
Nadia McCaddon	1950	1954
Ann Murray	1950	1950

Name[15]	Entered Foreign Office A–Branch[16]	Left Foreign Office
Kathleen Graham[25]	1951, transferred from B Grade	1963
Elizabeth Richardson	1951	1968
Gillian Brown[26]	1951, transferred from Research	1983, retired
Moira Armstrong	1951	1958
Mary Georgina Galbraith[27]	1952	1961, married Anthony Moore in 1963
Daphne Park	1954 with MI6	1979, retired
Tessa Solesby	1956	1992
Catherine Pestell	1956	1989
Juliet Campbell[28]	1957	1991, retired
Anne Warburton	1958	1985, retired

The high rate of attrition also counted against those women who were already employed, as the Foreign Office was less willing to invest in training their female staff who wanted to participate in year-long language courses.[29] Dame Veronica Sutherland (Former Ambassador to Republic of Ireland) experienced this resistance herself:

I wanted to go to Asia and India above all and what seemed to be exotic places. And I made this very plain. Indeed, I wanted to be put on a 'hard language'. I was not put on a hard language because there'd been a woman shortly before me, one who'd actually been at Westfield with me, who had joined in Branch B. She'd been put on Thai language training and promptly got married, so they were not prepared to risk another woman at that stage. [This was before the marriage bar was lifted in 1972.] So I wasn't able to do a hard language.[30]

Dame Rosemary Spencer also experienced different treatment, based on her gender, when it came to learning hard languages,[31] and Judy Dennison, who joined the Foreign Office in 1968, was refused her application to learn Japanese:

> The only example of discrimination I can remember occurred during an early interview with the Personnel Dept. They said that women were not usually offered the opportunity to learn a hard language, and I would need to make a very strong case to do so – implying that women were reckoned to be a poor long-term investment.[32]

With less language training, most women tended to go to the US or European postings, though some such as Barbara Salt were posted to interesting places such as Moscow and Tel Aviv. The marriage bar also set the expectations of supervisors in the FCO: 'The women of the Office, leaving us as they do on marriage, can never be so permanent an element in it as the men; but those whom I have known have seemed to be happy here, and only to wish to leave us when they must.'[33]

The marriage bar of course took its toll on the women involved by making them choose between a career and family. Baroness Pauline Neville-Jones, who served in the Foreign Service from 1963 to 1996 rising to the rank of Political Director, on being asked by Alex Barker of the *Financial Times* about what she had sacrificed to the marriage bar, answered:

> Well, I'm not married […] Do I regret it? […] It would be nice to be married. But do I look back and say, this is a fearful regret? No, I don't. The one thing I do think about my life is, for God's sake, don't complain. You choose to do something; you take what goes with the territory.[34]

Once the marriage bar was lifted, there remained a 'cultural' expectation that women would probably resign upon marriage. For example, Dame Mariot Leslie (Former Ambassador to Norway and the Permanent Representative to NATO) told the following story:

I did drop a bombshell on the FCO towards the end of our first year, when we had to do interviews about what our first overseas job was going to be. I'd done very well in the language aptitude test. I was clearly a candidate for one of the hardest languages. I was very keen to do a hard language. I had been asking and asking senior personnel people for a meeting with them because I knew I had just agreed to become married. We intended to continue my diplomatic career. My husband was going to come with me. We intended to make it work, but I wanted to tell the personnel people this in the context of my next posting. They never made themselves available; they kept cancelling appointments. So the first chance I got to tell anybody in the administration this was when I went for my language interview. My name was down against various hard languages; and when I said, 'Well, I need to tell you I'm about to get married', the chap who was doing the interview picked up his pen and scrawled my name off every list.

He said in the most delightful way, 'Of course, I don't mind what you do and this wouldn't be up to me, but I am afraid the Personnel Operations "grid" (the committee of postings officers who met regularly with a "grid" showing vacancies and available staff) and the Postings Boards won't agree to invest tens of thousands of pounds in somebody whose future in the Service is clearly not going to be a very long one'. And he then said, equally charmingly, 'But actually, I am seeing my colleague from the Ministry of Agriculture this afternoon. Would you like me to arrange a transfer?' So this was not a huge vote of confidence.[35]

In 1952, Barbara Salt, the first woman to be appointed Ambassador, said that she would probably resign if she married, even though the Foreign Office could, in principle, make an exception for someone of her ability and rank.[36]

In the early 1970s the question of what to do with husbands became moot once Parliament passed the Sex Discrimination Act of 1975, whereupon the FCO risked legal action if it did not change its own policy. Additional pressure had been felt following a 1971 review of the Home Office. The committee, chaired by Elizabeth Kemp-Jones, had examined ways to increase the number of women in the Civil Service and was severely critical of the discriminatory practices which kept women out of top positions.[37] The Foreign Office decided to drop the marriage bar in July 1972 and the following year the changes in regulations were finally implemented.[38] The marriage bar was similarly lifed in other Western countries. Australia was the first to lift the bar for its female diplomats (and other civil servants) in 1966, the US State Department lifted its marriage bar along with Canada in 1971, and Ireland with the passing of the Civil Service (Employment of Married Women) Act 1973.[39] For a more detailed discussion of the marriage bar, especially in the US, the reader is referred to Claudia Coldin's 1988 report.[40]

7

THE LIFE OF FEMALE DIPLOMATS

When women diplomats were first posted overseas, the missions (of all nations) were often unprepared, in terms of infrastructure and work practices. Society still expected women to carry the greater load for rearing children and mothers continued to face challenges in balancing their careers and family, usually without recourse to complain. Angela Bogdan,[1] who served in the Canadian Foreign Service, had to manage office hours from 8 a.m. to 5 p.m., which often ran later, especially for junior officers. She was also a young mother who was continuing to breastfeed around this schedule, having used up her maternity leave. However, one day she was called into a discussion with her boss that ran after 5 p.m.:

> He must have noticed and asked me if the discussion was boring me, or if I had somewhere else to be […] I guess my maternal instincts took over, I remember replying that he had my full attention from nine to five, but I have an infant at home to feed,

and if I don't leave shortly, Niagara Falls will look like a trickle in comparison to what will happen to me in a few minutes.

She said that her (male) supervisor was initially stunned, but later became apologetic. Neither he nor anyone else in the department had worked with new mothers or understood the unique challenges facing women who returned to work so soon after giving birth. She went on to say:

That particular supervisor became one of my biggest supporters […] Thereafter he always supported me to leave when I needed to care for my infant daughter. I learned that day how important it was to speak truth to power and not apologise for being a working mother.

Bogdan remained in the foreign service and served in several high-profile appointments including High Commissioner to Sri Lanka and Maldives and Chief of Protocol. Other diplomats found that there were advantages to being female single women posted to far-off places. Juliet Cambell (Former Ambassador to Guatemala, 2008) recalled:

Society moved in certain sorts of groups and circles and as a relatively senior woman you were neither fish nor fowl, nor good red herring. There were the wives, there were what were then known as dolly-birds, the pretty secretaries, and there were lots of gorgeous Thai girls all over the place. I somehow felt I didn't belong. That's probably the biggest price, at times: you can gather I've had a pretty good life and I'm not fussing, but I would say I had periods of being acutely lonely.[2]

Julie Chappel OBE also remembered:

By being different and not fitting into the norm, I found that I also had much greater freedom to manoeuvre. I could engage with people who didn't normally want to speak to ambassadors; I could do things that ambassadors wouldn't normally be expected to do; and I could attract attention in doing so, which gave me a voice, as well as an audience.[3]

She discovered that being a female diplomat could facilitate access into places where men would have been excluded.[4] A similar comment has been made by American diplomats in an article in *Politico*:

One person called it the '360-degree view': As an American, the male officials in even the most conservative nations can't realistically ignore you. But, unlike your US male colleagues, you also can more easily meet with the local women.

So whether at parties or funerals, American female diplomats can traverse formal and informal gender divides. That gives them fuller insights, not to mention additional sources and contacts. That's especially important because in many more conservative countries, despite the prevailing stereotypes, many local women are highly educated, active in their communities and control a lot of money.[5]

'It is always better if we can reach broadly into any society to take its measure,' said Margaret Scobey, a former Ambassador whose career included postings in Syria, Egypt, Yemen and Saudi Arabia. 'We cannot do that without having access to women.'

Dame Anne Warburton also spoke about the advantages of being a woman:

Or for example I can remember one of my early lessons in New York when I was still Second Secretary, I think, I felt I was beholden to two or three quite senior people and I had a supper party. I remember having three ambassadors to it and realising that you mustn't do that. You only take on one lion at a time! But the point I'm trying to make is simply that I was able to invite them, whereas if I'd been a man I might not have been able to, it was a subtly different relationship. […] You can cross the hierarchical borders more easily, I think, if you're a different gender.[6]

By the mid-1980s women had successfully been appointed ambassadors and high commissioners but that did not mean that the FCO was free of gender bias; significant gender discrimination still existed. In 1986 Susan Rogerson was blatantly refused a posting because she was female. Backed by the Equal Opportunities Commission, she threatened to sue the FCO. The FCO admitted its error and offered her a post of equal seniority.[7] The case summary reads:

Susan Darling-Rogerson, Assistant Head of the United Nations Department at the Foreign Office claimed that she was discriminated against when she applied for a top overseas posting as Deputy High Commissioner in Zambia because there was already one woman on the staff of 12 at the British High Commission in Lusaka and another would be too many. The Foreign Office admitted that it had 'made a mistake' and agreed to a settlement without taking the case to tribunal. Mrs. Rogerson (whose case was backed by the Equal Opportunities Commission) has been promoted and the Foreign Office has agreed to review its appointments procedure to ensure that it does not contravene the Sex Discrimination Act.[8]

While it would have been preferable for Rogerson not to experience discrimination in the first instance, the case did demonstrate to all employees that the FCO was answerable and furthermore that there was a recourse for victims of gender prejudice.

Both the Home Office and the Foreign Office were formed in 1782 during the government restructuring of the time.[9] As with many older organisations, they have tended towards a conservative outlook and have historically been resistant to change. The graph below provides a comparison of the Foreign and Home Offices for several major changes related to women's rights. In general, the Home Office has tended to be somewhat more progressive than the Foreign Office over the last century:

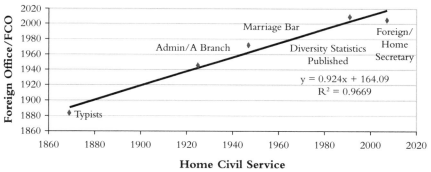

Graph of the timeline comparison of women's rights in the Foreign Office and Home Office.

The 'best fit' line shows that around the beginning of the twentieth century, the Home Office was about twenty years ahead of the Foreign Office, but a century later there is no tangible difference. It should be noted that the choice of comparisons in this graph is of course, somewhat subjective, and that another writer may well have chosen different events, with different dates, but the overall trends would probably have been similar.

Equal opportunities for women within the Foreign Office should be considered in relation to the changes across British society, and likewise they should be compared to concurrent changes abroad. The United States is a natural comparison nation due to its close cultural heritage with the UK and the US's influence across the rest of the world. The graph below compares several milestones for professional women in the Foreign Office to those of their counterparts in the US State Department:

Milestones for Women in the UK's Foreign Office and US's State Department

Graph of the timeline comparison of women's rights in the Foreign Office and US State Department.

Again, the selection of data points is somewhat subjective, but the graph demonstrates that the US and UK are generally well correlated. The 'best-fit' line has a correlation coefficient of 0.78 which shows a strong correlation (1.0 is a perfect correlation, 0.0 is no correlation). Looking at the line, however, it appears that the advancement of women in the Foreign Office tended to be behind their counterparts at the US State Department in the early years. But they have since caught up, perhaps indicating the more conservative approach of the Foreign Office. However, with only five points on the graph, the results are more indications rather than firm conclusions.

One of the early concerns about the suitability of female diplomats was based on how other countries would perceive women in that role and whether they would be taken seriously. The British Ambassador in Bucharest, who was not above painting stereotypes, is reported to have said:

The hard-bitten English woman nurtured in the London School of Economics, with a Marx and Engels outlook; the product of Girton or Somerville, interested chiefly in ancient Greek theatre, but wielding from time to time a forceful hockey stick; the shires girl who breakfasts off an ether cocktail and who will abandon the Chancery entirely for the polo field – none of these would be suitable representatives.[10]

Former American Ambassador Wendy Sherman gave an interesting insight into the 'theatre' of being a woman ambassador during a recent interview with the *Harvard Gazette*:

Madeleine Albright taught me a very important lesson years ago when she was Ambassador to the UN, and that was that when you sit at the table, you are the United States of America. And so it mattered less that I was a woman than that I was the United States of America [...] Having understood what power that brought to the table, I made every use of it.[11]

Dame Veronica Sutherland spoke of similar experience:

I've always found that, if you knew what it was you had to talk about, and if the person you were going to see knew that you had come to talk about this issue on behalf of your Government, being a woman wouldn't make any difference. They didn't have an option but to deal with you. And then after five minutes, as soon as they saw you knew what you were talking about, there wasn't a problem.[12]

Diplomacy is much more about the nation being represented, and the message is much more important than the gender of the diplomat delivering it. However, gender can make a difference, as Baroness Catherine Ashton (European Union's first High Representative for Foreign Affairs and Security Policy, from 2009 to 2014) found:

I am British, I am a woman, and that brings with it, for many people, a view of what you may be like, and actually it's quite a positive view […] I'm always interested in the descriptions of how I do things […] The only thing I want to be is effective. It is probably true that as women we navigate our lives differently because we're navigating relationships, perhaps. But I then stray into my own fear of generalisation […] I guess a lot of the things I've done in my life have been about trying to find solutions or trying to build consensus, so it's partly me, partly the job, partly that I'm a woman.[13]

The life of a junior diplomat has changed considerably over the last half century, as shown in Alyson Bailes's obituary:

She joined the Foreign Office as a junior diplomat in September 1969, having achieved full marks in the entrance exam. It was a very different world from today. All ambassadors were men [the first British female ambassador took up her position in 1976]. Alyson's duties as a junior diplomat included carrying coals for the open hearth fire which heated the office; and writing up policy documents in pen and ink, which would be copied out by typists using carbon paper. […]

A month after joining the FCO, she was interviewed by the *Sunday Times* and was asked whether there would ever be a female British ambassador? Would Alyson be Her Excellency in 20 years' time? She replied that she couldn't begin to imagine herself being that old: 'But I suppose, by the time I am, I might be wanting to be an ambassador.'

Alyson Bailes was British Ambassador to Finland, 2000-02.[14]

Diplomatic wives were considered part of the package, and a good one was definitely an unpaid asset. As a 1964 article about the US diplomatic service commented:

She cannot 'make' his career for him, but she can certainly break it or facilitate it. She is just as active as her husband, and in her own way just as important in the scheme of things.

The success of her husband's assignment, and consequently of the Government's affairs, can depend on how efficiently she keeps a house in a strange and difficult environment, how well and quickly she learns a foreign language, how sensitive she is to, and tolerant of, alien attitudes and customs, how little she complains at having to pack up every few years and go to a new station, how well she can keep diplomatic secrets, how capably she can cope with offspring vexed and disoriented by frequent changes of countries, schools and playmates.

Overseas, it is usually the wife who establishes the congenial social setting that can lead to diplomatic rapport and international agreement. In many instances, it is the wife who, in her dozens of daily contacts with ordinary people, represents the United States more meaningfully than a husband bound to office routine and formal meetings. [15]

It was generally assumed that wives would take on a range of duties such as hosting guests, organising staff, meeting with dignitaries and socialising with other diplomatic wives and with local female dignitaries to gather information that may be useful. In some cases these contacts were used as back-door communications when government wished to convey information 'off the record' or when official contact was prevented. She was also expected to present an image to the world at large, although operating in new surroundings did not always go to plan. Brigid Keenan, an ambassador's wife in the Middle East, remembered one almost disastrous evening:

> The most frightening time was when we arrived in Syria and my husband invited about 60 people for dinner. I decided we would have Thai and Indian curries that I'd never tried before. I didn't know you could only use the tender bits of lemongrass and I chopped the whole thing up so it tasted like thistles. I had to sieve that and make another sauce. Then there was a power cut so we couldn't use the blender. Then a huge rat appeared in the kitchen which the maid beat to death with a broom handle. There was rat blood everywhere. We just wiped it off the saucepan and served up the meal.[16]

In the past some postings were daunting. Life in foreign lands could be lonely, strenuous and sometimes hazardous with extremes of temperature, language barriers and cultural differences. Nowadays spouses and families are briefed about what to expect, but the transition can still be a challenge. Sheila Whitney, who was in Beijing during the Cultural Revolution of the 1930s, saw the anti-imperialist marches directed against foreigners and the Red Guards would sometimes throw paint on the British cars and smash flowerpots. There were also restrictions from the

Chinese government that limited the ability of local people to interact with them.[17] Ill health, a lack of medical facilities, limited possibilities for education, all were challenging for families with children. Judy Denison recounted her experiences educating her children:

> When I refused to send my own sons away from Tokyo at the age of eight, a senior wife reprimanded me for depriving them of a British education. But the same woman added wistfully: 'You lose them, you know. After you've sent them away, you never have the same relationship.' And I know she found it a hardship continuing to attend cocktail parties during the school holidays, when she longed to be tucking her children up in bed in the precious few weeks they were at home. The alternative solution, educating your children locally, also had its difficulties. My own sons' education was severely disrupted, particularly the year we were moved from Mexico City to London to Tokyo in the space of three months.[18]

With the advent of married female diplomats, the Diplomatic Service Wives' Association changed its name in 1995 to the British Diplomatic Spouses' Association. In addition, most spouses either had to give up their careers or at least put them on hold. Brigid Keenan recalled:

> Once, another ambassador's wife came to me in tears. 'You've been married to a diplomat for a long time,' she said. 'Please tell me if it is worth it in the end, or should I leave my husband now and go back to my own career as a doctor?'[19]

Celia Gould, wife of the British Ambassador to Israel, when asked in 2014 about her role, said, 'It's hardly a job. It's not paid, and the

Foreign Service tells you that you're not obligated to do anything, but we're handed a lot of work.'[20]

Brigid Keenan commented similarly:

The Foreign Office and United Nations say that nowadays they don't expect anything from the wives, but it's not true. I was a fashion journalist when I met my husband, but I had to give it up. Most wives get involved in fundraising and we have to entertain. I'm a very bad hostess and get very nervous about it.[21]

American wives were similarly put upon to perform such social duties until 1972 when the State Department issued a directive liberating wives from these expectations, and there have been discussions about whether active diplomatic spouses should be on the payroll:[22]

The wife of a Foreign Service employee who has accompanied her husband to a foreign post is a private individual; she is not a Government employee. The Foreign Service, therefore, has no right to levy any duties upon her. It can only require that she comport herself in a manner which will not reflect discredit on the United States.[23]

Japan went one step further and compensated diplomatic wives for the time they spent entertaining and other embassy-related work.[24] It was generally discouraged for diplomatic wives to use their position to further policies on their own, but there were some exceptions. Dorothea von Benckendorff, the wife of the Prince von Lieven, the Russian Ambassador to London from 1812 to 1834, actively participated in her husband's political deals; and Bertha von Suttner (1843–1914), an Austrian radical, took part in the Universal Peace Congress in Bern in 1892, where she promoted the idea of a union of European states. She and other women tried to exert diplomatic pressure through pacifist actions and she was awarded the Nobel Peace Prize in 1905 for her commitment to peace.[25]

The Foreign Office provides opportunities for people to be involved in matters of national importance and adventure in far off lands, and these incentives provide the main attractions for those who join up. Julie Chappell (former British Ambassador to Luxembourg from 1988 to 1991) commented on the excitement and the difficulties in leading a life with a mobility clause attached: 'Life is never dull – more young people should join the FCO [...] they should not get put off, they should apply for a job.'[26]

Every diplomat's contract includes a mobility clause, meaning they can be sent anywhere at any time. 'There was an assumption that you couldn't expect to spend all your time in green pastures,' said Chappell. 'I remember being told that it was time to go and get my knees brown. You couldn't expect because you had children or, as I later discovered, elderly parents, to think that this was a reason you could stay in easy touch, because you would be told, rather briskly, "we all do at this stage of life".'

She also added how this lifestyle can affect long-term relationships, when asked whether she had ever come close to leaving: 'I did have moments. But, to be honest, I used to ask myself why I didn't get married, and I think maybe belonging to the Foreign Office was part of it,' she said. 'You had this life, you moved on every two or three years or whatever, and you didn't form quite the same forms of relationship.'

The frequent relocation and disrupted spousal careers of course remains an issue, but the Foreign Office works hard to help diplomatic families work out acceptable conditions that meet their requirements. Some of these changes are discussed later.

8

THE FIRST THREE WOMEN TO REACH AMBASSADOR RANK

For all the obstacles we have described in this book, there were some distinguished women who persevered and enjoyed successful careers as senior diplomats and heads of mission. Being the first of their kind, their histories and legacies are significant. They also lived through the dramatic times of the twentieth century and their biographies reveal extraordinairy qualities. We have selected only the first three to reach ambassador status, in order to focus on how these remarkable women broke the mould, exceeded societal, professional and personal expectations, and paved the way for all the female diplomats of today.

Dame Barbara Salt was born at the start of the twentieth century to British parents in California. Her father, Reginald Salt[1] had been offered a position in a bank in California, and the family relocated to Oroville, where Barbara was born, the second of three girls. The family eventually returned to England, and settled first near Oxford and then they later moved to Seaford, a coastal town in east Sussex.[2] Barbara demonstrated an international outlook from an early age by choosing to attend Munich and Cologne universities and learning to speak German fluently.[3]

Salt returned to the UK as a graduate in 1933 to work as a secretary until 1940,[4] at the outbreak of war, when she quickly volunteered and was soon deployed by the fledgling SOE as a fluent German speaker. At that stage Germany had invaded France but Britain was able to offer only limited assistance to the Resistance movements operating behind enemy lines. These activities were primarily run by MI6, which was then part of the War Office. Prime Minister Winston Churchill realised that a much greater effort would be required and founded the SOE in 1940, its charter being to engage in espionage, sabotage and reconnaissance in occupied Europe against the Axis powers, and to aid local resistance movements, or in Churchill's words to 'Set Europe Ablaze'. It assumed several aliases including the 'Inter-Services Research Bureau, War Office Branch 'MOI (SP)'. The SOE's head office was on Baker Street, London, but the overseas stations were staffed by British nationals with sufficient language skills that they could pass as native speakers. There have been many excellent accounts written about the SOE and the incredible stories of its agents, both male and female, that make for fascinating reading.[5]

Following some limited training, Salt was dispatched to Tangier, north-west of Morocco, on 5 October 1942, which was part of the Gibraltar Mission where she was ostensibly the Vice-Consul. Names in the SOE were replaced by an alphanumerical code, and Salt's was GB2502.[6] Her actual role in the Tangier Station was as an operative assistant to Edward Wharton-Tigar (GB2500) and equal to another agent, GB2501, whose identity is not known.

The SOE had its successes and its failures; risk went hand in hand with bravery, cunning, patience and daring. Some of the more remarkable successes were borne out of accidents and clever quick-thinking, rather than from any carefully laid plan.[7]

Salt would later illustrate this with the story of Dick Mallaby. Mallaby was an SOE agent who in August 1943 parachuted alone at night into northern Italy to support the Resistance. He was arrested by the Italian Counter-Intelligence Bureau and imprisoned. Mallaby was soon taken out of prison and, in part because of his language skills, helped negotiate the armistice agreement ending the war for Italy in September 1943. In early 1945 he crossed into Switzerland where he was again arrested and interrogated, this time by the German SS. Again, Mallaby was the right person in the right place and he helped negotiate the surrender of all German forces in Italy in May 1945 in what became known as Operation Sunrise.

The status of Morocco was one of complex political neutrality. In the early twentieth century, there was a dispute between the European powers over control of Morocco, which was settled by an international convention in Paris in 1923, which declared Tangier an international zone under the joint administration of France, Spain and Britain. On 14 June 1940, the day that Paris was occupied by the Germans, Spanish troops took over Tangier, resulting in a diplomatic dispute with Britain. The parties came to an agreement whereby British rights were guaranteed and the Spanish promised not to fortify the area, but the political complexity and little governmental oversight meant that Tangier became a haven for smuggling and spying with agents from all sides.[8]

Salt's first covert role was as part of the secret Political Warfare Executive (PWE), whose task was to produce and disseminate both white and black propaganda to damage enemy morale and sustain the morale of the Resistance in countries occupied by Germany and its allies.[9] White propaganda was material whose source and meaning are clear. Grey propaganda was material of questionable source and accuracy and black propaganda was material with false information put out by one side so that it looks like it came from the other side.

The German Foreign Office and Wehrmacht Intelligence also operated out of their Consulate and were active in disseminating printed matter to promote their cause among locals as well as the foreigners (French middle-class workers, Jewish traders). The SOE created whispering networks in which a 'chief whisperer' recruited ten sub-whisperers, selected due to their contacts with the target groups (politicians, army officers, waiters, hairdressers and barbers). Each sub-whisperer was conscious to the fact that they were working for the SOE, but they had no knowledge of other whisperer identities. They, in turn, recruited ten to twenty more people, who were completely oblivious that they were being deployed to carry and spread contrived rumours for the SOE. The SOE would deliberately send rumours back to occupied France via contacts in nearby Casablanca, and this effort was called Operation Venom. Each week a 'Venom' telegram would be sent from London with suggestions for targets that the local operatives could use. Each rumour had its own reference number and an intended message. For example, a telegram to Mr Gascoigne, 1 September 1942, included some of the following rumours:

P/753 When a British shell hit parts of cement fortifications at Dieppe the mummified body of a German officer rolled out of the split wall. He had been in charge of French workers building the fortifications. [Suggests the fortifications are not very strong]

P/790 Italian officers posted to Yugoslavia are supplied with painless poison pills in the event of capture. [Suggests that the Italian army is weak and making plans in the event of losing.]

P/802 Morocco and Senegalese prisoners of war are being used for poison gas tests at Augsburgh and other gas factories,

265 dead so far. [Suggests that Germans do not treat their Prisoners of War properly.]

P/804 3,000 Algerian Moslems who volunteered for work in France were sent to German-bombed cities to replace German and French workmen who refused to carry on because of raids. [Suggests Moslems are less important to French and German workmen.][10]

Fighting the enemy was a challenge, but another difficulty was working with friends and colleagues under such tense conditions. There was considerable friction between the SOE and the SIS, and between the two British intelligence services and their American counterpart: the newly formed Office of Strategic Services (OSS), the forerunner of today's Central Intelligence Agency (CIA).[11] The British had more experience than the OSS, but the latter had more resources.[12] In addition to using soft propaganda, the SOE in Tangier also conducted various practical exercises as part of Operation Torch, the Anglo-American invasion of German-controlled Morocco and Algeria starting the North African campaign of the Second World War on 8 November 1942 and concluded eight days later. SOE agents gave practical support in assisting the landing parties ashore and providing aerial drops of equipment to Resistance fighters with varying levels of success.

One success story was Operation Falaise. German Military Intelligence (the Abwehr) occupied a cliffside villa at 4 Rue de la Falaise, from where an infrared device was being used to monitor Allied shipping as it passed through the Straits of Gibraltar.[13] On 12 January 1942 the site was destroyed using amphibious SOE and/or SIS forces.[14] Two U-boats were also pinpointed and sunk by the Royal Navy as a result. It is not clear to what extent Salt was involved in these various operations, but the SOE contingent in Tangier was very small, and it is therefore highly likely that she was closely involved.

The Tangier Station fell under the responsibility of the Ambassador to Madrid, who was very concerned that the neutral General Franco would ally Spain with the Germans; and the Ambassador was therefore against any operation that could potentially push Franco that way. Sometimes the business of running covert operations in Tangier did not always run smoothly. Explosives for the successful Operation Falaise had been smuggled into Tangier by Edward Wharton-Tigar[15] in diplomatic bags from Gibraltar. Unfortunately, a few weeks later on 6 February, a second shipment of explosives blew up on the quay, killing fifteen people, including four Gibraltan policemen, and scattering British propaganda written in Arabic all around. Rumours spread, which ignited passions, and rioters attacked the consulate, a British hotel and other British businesses, until order was restored. The SOE's reputation was severely tarnished by this incident.[16]

In another ploy to create chaos for the enemy, Wharton-Tigar distributed Nazi postage stamps, forged by the British, with Hitler's head replaced by Himmler's. The operation was at least partially successful in promoting internal frictions by making Hitler believe that the SS chief was getting above his station.[17] The Tangier SOE station staff also bought low denomination notes for postage stamps, gold sovereigns and diamonds and other precious stones to supply to SOE agents operating behind enemy lines in occupied Europe.[18] Similarly, when Salt was in the UK, she would purchase jewellery in Brighton (cheaper than London) that could be sold in Tangier for Spanish pesetas and other European currencies.[19]

The Germans were simultaneously attempting to undermine British efforts and relations between the Allied forces, and it was via a British bank in Tangier in 1943 that the Bank of England first obtained samples of a high-quality forged British currency. Operation Bernhard was the name of a secret German plan to destabilise the British economy by flooding the country with forged £5, £10, £20 and £50 notes.[20] Salt returned to the UK several times from Tangier, including one time in 1943 for treatment for a dog bite to her right hand that had caused blood poisoning.[21] For her work with the SOE, Salt was made an MBE in the 1946 New Year's Honours.

On returning to London, Salt joined the War Office as a Civil Assistant.[22] From there she transferred to the Foreign Office as a temporary First Secretary in the UN Department. By this time she had earned 'a sterling reputation' from both her superiors and colleagues because of her 'critical and analytical mind, her quickness, her practical common sense, and her mature judgement'.[23] Salt was formally admitted into the Foreign Office A-Branch in 1949, thereby becoming the most senior woman in the service.[24] On joining Salt discovered that there was no formal training or handover, and on reflection, as she approached retirement, she commented: 'That was the way then, and I think it was no bad way.'[25]

Salt's first posting was to the British Embassy in Moscow in 1950 as First Secretary (commercial), but her time there was cut short due to poor health. She was next appointed as the deputy position in the Foreign Office's UN Economic Development Department, at that time headed by Basil Boothby CMG.[26] In this role she was on the front line in preliminary negotiations with the Americans regarding disarmament discussions between the major powers (US, Soviet Union, UK, China, France) in the early 1950s.[27] She was also one of the British representatives in meetings with the US to counter the USSR's 'hate America' campaign.[28]

It was therefore fitting for Salt's next appointment as First Secretary to the British Embassy in Washington DC, and later that year, 1955, she was promoted to Counsellor (6th grade of A-Branch), the first time a woman had held this title.[29] Salt was involved in the key issues coming before the UN including negotiations with the US on the implementation of the UN International Covenant on Civil and Political Rights (ICCPR).[30] Another key issue was the admission of new members to the UN and there are several memoranda on record describing her contribution.[31]

In the 1950s many of the issues on the UN agenda involved sorting out tense territory and border claims, a post-war legacy requiring skilled negotiations. Salt was one of the diplomats charged with the question of Cyprus and the ongoing dispute between Greek and Turkish Cypriots.[32] Another issue was Hungary, which had been under Soviet control since the end of the Second World War and a socialist People's Republic since 1949. In 1956 Hungary, protestors, with encouragement from the West, defied the Soviet Union. The 'Voice of America' radio broadcasts and speeches by President Dwight D. Eisenhower and Secretary of State, John Foster Dulles, had suggested that the US supported the 'liberation' of 'captive peoples' in communist nations. The Soviet Union responded by invading Hungary, and as the Soviet tanks rolled through the streets of Budapest, the Western nations did no more than make public statements of objection.[33] Salt, a key negotiator among the allies,[34] sometimes took the brunt of criticism. British diplomat Jonathan Dean said in an interview in 1997:

In 1956 I happened to be a guest of the German Minister, Albrecht von Kessel, here in Washington, on the day of the Suez invasion. His guests were [journalist] Walter Lippmann and Lady Barbara Salt, Minister at the British Embassy. Lippmann lit into Lady Barbara for carrying out this invasion and confusing international opinion at the very time when this very serious Russian invasion of Hungary was going on. I must say that I and others felt absolutely awful about our inactivity at that time and about the killing that went on.[35]

Salt was also instrumental in discussions with the allies, supporting the requirement for a fleet of Polaris missile submarines and on-land nuclear missile bunkers able to withstand an attack. The missile arsenal was to serve as a deterrent to a Soviet nuclear attack since they could launch a counter–attack after a first strike.[36]

Salt's next posting in 1957 was to Tel Aviv, where she served as both Counsellor and Consul-General.[37] She held this position until 1960 during which time she was made a CBE.[38] Following Tel Aviv, Salt was promoted to Minister, serving as deputy head of the UK delegation to the 1960 UN's disarmament negotiations in Geneva. Again, she was the first woman to reach this rank. A year later, she transferred to New York as the UK Representative on the Economic and Social Council of the UN (ECOSOC). Salt also served on the Economic Commission for South America, UN, in New York 1962.[39]

Barbara Salt at the 10-Nation Disarmament Conference, 15 March 1960, Geneva, Switzerland. (UN Photo)

Salt was by all accounts a very effective diplomat, as illustrated by Sir Nicholas Bayn, who recalled in a 2016 interview with Abbey Wright that:

She [Barbara] was an admirable mentor for me because I could see her diplomatic technique at work with which I was very struck. She made all the use of her femininity, a bit like, although it's an unfair comparison, Margaret Thatcher. Barbara could be extremely charming but she could also be rude to people in ways which would never have been tolerated from a man, but she could get away with it.[40]

Finally, in April 1962 it was announced with great applause that Salt would be appointed as the Ambassador to Israel, succeeding Patrick Hancock, and she would therefore become the first British woman to be appointed an ambassador.[41] Unfortunately, she was not able to take up the position when she developed thromboses in both legs, necessitating amputation and the use of a wheelchair. Since she was unable to take up the position, the Foreign Office cancelled her appointment.[42] The following year, in the Queen's Birthday Honours, Barbara was appointed DBE.[43] It would be more than a decade before the next woman was appointed to an ambassadorial level position, when Eleanor Emery was appointed High Commissioner to Botswana in 1973.

Having come so close to becoming the first woman Ambassador, Salt later said, with her usual reserve and fortitude: 'People keep saying what a tragedy it was that I wasn't able to go to Israel. I don't regard it as such. It's just something you have to live with.'[44]

Despite a significant setback Dame Barbara's working days were far from over. The word 'indomitable' was linked to her name in both press reports and conversations; witnesses commented on her ability to bear pain, disablement, and disappointment.[45] Salt's last decade at the Foreign Office was highly productive; for example, she was involved in negotiations with the government of Israel from June to October 1964 in London over various financial matters.[46] Between 1963 and 1966 she also led UK delegations to Romania and the USSR. And outside of the office she was an active member of the Duke of Edinburgh's Council of Volunteers Overseas.[47] Encylopedia.com states, 'As a negotiator, she had few equals. Besides being a perfectionist, she could be formidable in her obstinacy and had a superb grasp of details.'[48]

In 1949 Sir Marcus Checke wrote his whimsical 'Guidance on Foreign Usage and Ceremony and other Matters for a Member of His Majesty's Foreign Service on His First Appointment to a Post Abroad':[49]

> There are countries where […] it is the virtues which are emphasised in the Old Testament rather than the New Testament which impress the most […] The late Mr. Chamberlain might have done well to remember this when he flew to Munich to negotiate with Hitler; had he been accompanied by a platoon of picked men from the Guards instead of a secretary or two carrying umbrellas, he might have produced a different effect on the Nazi mind.

Some of the whimsy was not especially diplomatic and so this book was kept classified until 1993 to avoid any diplomatic incidents, and diplomats were warned not to share it with their counterparts from other countries. Salt was tasked with updating the guidance, making it both more practical and with less risk of offence should it fall into the wrong hands. She produced her very practical guide in 1965, as an internal Foreign Office document.[50]

Another task where Salt's expertise was sought was to deliberate on whether to publish a broader history of the SOE. Historian Michael Foot was given access to some of the SOE records of its operations in German-occupied France and published his book *SOE in France: An Account of the Work of the British Special Operations Executive in France 1940–1944*. However, the SOE operations outside of France were mostly covert and there was an argument that they should be documented so that the incredible operations that SOE agents undertook, the large number of agents killed and the major impact that these operations had could finally be recognised. The other side of the argument was that there were still some delicate matters that the intelligence services and UK government did not want disclosed, such as revealing the names of possible double agents in Paris. In 1967 Dame Barbara was asked to review the delicate topic and write a report recommending the best option. Salt considered giving access to a limited number of historians to document the events but she recommended against further publication. The Intelligence Services took her advice and in 1969 decided not to allow further access to the confidential/secret records.[51]

Similarly, in 1972 when the BBC wanted to make a programme about the Second World War Operation Postmaster, in which SOE forces boarded and sailed away with Italian and German ships in the harbour of the Spanish island of Fernando Po (Bioko) in January 1942, Barbara Salt, speaking for the Foreign Office, pressured the BBC not to broadcast the story for fear of upsetting the Spanish.[52]

Dame Barbara retired in January 1973, the same year that Eleanor Emery was appointed High Commissioner to Botswana. On being asked whether she had found it difficult being a single woman in the diplomatic service, Salt responded, 'It's just as difficult if you're a single man, you still have to get someone to help you at parties. Besides, I was lucky working in emancipated places, Moscow, Washington, New York and Tel Aviv.'[53] When asked why no other woman had succeeded in being appointed ambassador, Salt responded modestly, 'There hasn't been anyone old enough, but it is just a question of time.'

Dame Barbara died at her home in Montagu Square, London, aged 71, on 28 December 1975,[54] the year before Anne Warburton became the first female Ambassador to take up her appointment. Even though Warburton was the first to be received as an ambassador, whenever the topic was discussed she always paid tribute to Dame Barbara Salt, a pioneer for women generally and particularly for female diplomats. Salt was one of the key figures in the progress of women's rights in the FCO. She believed that success came through hard work rather than special dispensations. When asked about the progress of women in the diplomatic service, she responded, 'Women have got their opportunities, now let them take them!'[55]

Salt lived a remarkable life, with a list of accomplishments that very few others could meet. However, preserving her legacy was not a priority for her and in her will she left her estate to her sister Laura, with the instructions that all her private papers were to be destroyed unread.[56] Salt's most significant legacy was to set an example as to what women could achieve and demonstrated that there were no longer limits to their ambitions. In 1977, Lord Gore-Booth discussing women in the Foreign Service stated in the House of Lords:

I express the hope that we shall see more women in higher places in our Service abroad. I believe that they receive every encouragement and I live in the memory of Dame Barbara Salt who was first appointed to ambassadorial rank. I hope that they will be forthcoming because they add a dimension to our representation which is extremely valuable. I also hope, and I am sure that this will happen, that we shall have the closest and ever-increasingly close relationship between the Diplomatic Service and the Home Civil Service.[57]

★

Eleanor Emery became Britain's first female High Commissioner on her appointment to Botswana, in 1973.[58] She too had started her life abroad as her father, Robert Emery, was serving with the 10th Infantry Battalion, which was part of the renowned Canadian Expeditionary Force. Emery was born on 23 December 1918 in Glasgow, but the following year the young family departed for Canada, where her father was still serving in the army, and arrived in Halifax.[59] The family settled in Seebe, but later moved to Calgary where Robert worked in the Federal Customs and Excise Office as an inspector of weights and measures.[60] Emery attended the Western Canada High School in Calgary, leaving her with a Canadian accent that she kept through her life.[61]

Emery returned to Scotland to attend Glasgow University to read history, and spent the next four years living with her mother's married sister.[62] Her time in Glasgow was not all work; she especially enjoyed many long walks with friends in the beautiful Scottish countryside. Her father continued to work in Calgary until his retirement in 1944 when the family returned, as they had always intended, to Scotland at the end of the Second World War.[63]

In 1941 Emery applied for a position in the Dominions Office and was accepted.[64] 'It was at a time when everyone seemed to be joining either the armed services or the government. I think we all felt we had to do something.'[65] She became the Assistant Private Secretary to the Dominions Secretary, who at that time was Clement Attlee. Attlee was shy and withdrawn, and Emery liked him very much.[66] He was succeeded by Viscount Cranbourne, the future 5th Marquess of Salisbury, whom Emery is reported to have described as charming and lovable.[67] Emery's role initially was to convey messages, between her superiors and various officials.[68–74] Emery's first overseas appointment in 1945 was back to Canada, to the High Commission in Ottawa as Second Secretary. 'At the time I was what they called the "worm" in chancery,' she said, 'which meant I did a little of everything, but not a great deal of anything.'[75]

In 1947 she returned to Whitehall[76] to take up the position of Private Secretary to the Right Honourable Patrick Gordon-Walker, who was briefly Secretary of State for Commonwealth relations.[77] At this time Emery was one of the younger generation with fresh ideas who were shaping the new Commonwealth Relations Office;[78] she was pleased to accompany Gordon-Walker on various overseas trips to Australia, New Zealand and Canada in 1950.[79]

After London, Emery spent three years serving in the High Commission in Delhi, India. She returned to London in 1955, and she was then asked to work on a new continent as the Higher Executive Officer in the Commonwealth Relations Office on the Basutoland, Bechuanaland and Swaziland Sub-Department General Policy and Administration Desk.[80]

One of major issues of the day was the story of Seretse Khama, King of the Bamangwato people in Bechuanaland, who had studied at Balliol College, Oxford, and married a white English woman, Ruth Williams. The union greatly upset Bechuanaland's neighbour, apartheid-ruled South Africa. Britain's Labour government was still heavily in debt from the Second World War, and therefore was dependent on cheap gold and uranium supplies from South Africa. The uranium was needed for development of Britain's nuclear weapons, since the US ended nuclear weapons cooperation after the Second World War. Despite British pressure, Khama absolutely refused to divorce his wife and so the British exiled both of them in 1951. Winston Churchill, then the Leader of the Opposition, called the whole affair 'a very disreputable transaction'.[81] The Labour government steadfastly refused to admit that it was exiling Khama to appease South Africa,[82] but Prime Minister Clement Attlee later confessed that both the Labour and Conservative governments had indeed behaved dishonourably towards Seretse with an agenda of appeasement towards South Africa.[83]

When Emery became involved with the Khama matter she took a much more humane and sympathetic approach, advising Lord Home (Secretary of State for Commonwealth Relations) to meet with tribal representatives in London to find a settlement. For Emery, it was apparent that 'a new leaf should be turned over' and she made a point of respectfully addressing Khama's wife as Mrs Khama in all correspondence, in stark contrast to how she had been referred to previously. She insisted that press statements about Khama's return to Bechuanaland should refer to his wife and children, and maintained that the proper reference was to 'Mrs Khama', rather than 'Ruth' or 'that woman'.[84] Additionally, officials' wives should be given guidance as how to behave towards Mrs Khama. Emery minuted that this would be an important factor in keeping him 'happy and co-operative'. Bechuanaland became the Republic of Botswana on 30 September 1966 and Seretse Khama returned as Botswana's first President, ruling until 1980, the longest and most stable period of all southern African nations.

In 1958 Emery was posted to the High Commission in Pretoria, South Africa.[85] Three years later South Africa left the Commonwealth due to the international dispute about its apartheid regime, becoming a republic, whereupon the High Commission was renamed as an Embassy. In 1994, when South Africa re-entered the Commonwealth, the Embassy reverted to being a High Commission once again.[86] During Emery's time in Pretoria, one of the major issues was the trial of Nelson Mandela and other leaders of the African National Congress (ANC) on charges of high treason against the State.[87]

Emery's next appointment was as Head of the South Asia Department. Decolonisation had been going on since the end of the Second World War and it continued rapidly during her tenure.

Even small islands such as the Gilbert Islands were looking for self-government in some form. In November 1969 Emery visited the Gilbert Islands to reiterate the UK policy of independence for those colonies that desired it, and had the capability to support themselves. For those islands that could not support their independence, the UK was willing to draft special arrangements. Emery met with the council at Tarawa (Tarawa is an atoll and now the capital of the Republic of Kiribati, in the central Pacific Ocean) and discussed the colony's economic prospects, educational development, migration outlets and other factors leading towards some kind of self-rule.

Emery was also involved in negotiations with the New Hebrides, which was controlled by both the British and French governments. Emery recognised that the National Party 'was one of the first signs of an emerging New Hebrides Nationalism' and believed that material action was required to satisfy the islanders. Neither the British nor French governments, however, considered the New Hebrides a priority and both were reluctant to take any action. Instead, they favoured the existing tri-partite system, whereas Emery argued that:

A cumbersome tri-partite system of government, an antiquated and inequitable judicial system, denies the local people any national status and makes no provision for democratic institutions. [...] We cannot, incidentally, divest ourselves of these responsibilities nor could we without offence to France and incurring international criticism wriggle out of them by negotiation.[88]

The independence movement grew and there was some violence in what became known as the Coconut War. The final outcome was the founding of the Republic of Vanuatu in 1980, with Father Walter Lini as its first Prime Minister.[89]

Another colony seeking independence was Fiji, which had been a British Crown Colony since 1874. Fiji had progressed towards independence through the 1960s, encouraged by international and British pressure. From 1968 to 1969, Emery was a key player in the discussions as to what form of government should be established there.[90]

Similarly, there had been discussions about self-rule for the Seychelles for several years. In 1969 France Albert René met with Emery during an official visit to London to discuss self-rule for the Seychelles. In Kevin Shillington's biography of René,[91] he claims that Emery was clearly charmed by him, and following a luncheon at her club, she described him as 'an intelligent, moderate and rather agreeable personality'.[92]

The Seychelles became independent in 1976, with René as Prime Minister, but he unexpectedly led a coup d'état against the first President, James Mancham, on 5 June 1977, installing himself as President and ruled as a strongman under a socialist one-party system until in 1993, when he was forced to introduce a multi-party system. There were accusations of human rights abuses, but even after multi-party elections were held, he was relected several times. He eventually stepped down in 2004 in favour of his Vice-President, James Michel.[93]

Emery returned to Ottawa at a time of minor constitutional tensions in the 1960s[94] involving the status of Quebec.[95] She was appointed as Political Counsellor to the High Commission in 1964, the first woman to hold that position.[96] Emery's area of interest in Ottawa is best described in her own words:

I enclose a memorandum about Canadian views on the Commonwealth. In sum, you will see that our view is that Canada has a positive and constructive attitude to the Commonwealth; the concept of the new, multi-racial, Commonwealth plays a significant part in Canada's external policies; and continuing association with and interest in the Commonwealth on the part of Britain and Canada are important and generally beneficial factors in British–Canadian relations.[97]

According to Sir Wynn Hugh-Jones (Head of Chancery, British High Commission, Ottawa 1968–70), Emery was 'embedded there, loved Canada and wanted to stay'.[98]

Emery's next posting was a return to Whitehall in 1968 which also brought her back to the Pacific as Head of the Pacific and Indian Ocean Department. One of the most controversial incidents that she was involved in concerned the Chagos Archipelago. In the 1960s, it became apparent to the American government that their military bases in foreign lands were vulnerable to being shut down from local unrest or changes in the political mood of their host countries. They therefore decided to locate and occupy an unpopulated island, in a strategic location. Unfortunately, the US did not own any such islands, but there were a number of suitable locations in the possession of friendly European countries. However, the pool of prospective candidates was rapidly diminishing as many small islands became independent with decolonisation. Diego Garcia, part of the British Indian Ocean Territory (BIOT), was strategically situated in the Indian Ocean halfway between Tanzania and Indonesia and looked like a prime candidate. The territory comprises seven atolls of the Chagos Archipelago with over 1,000 individual islands – many very small – amounting to a total land area of 60 square kilometres (23 square miles). Diego Garcia, 27 square kilometres (10 square miles) is the largest and most southerly island, and ideally situated in the Indian Ocean.[99]

The British and American governments came to a confidential arrangement on 30 December 1966,[100] whereby the American military could build its base and the British would get the Polaris nuclear submarine and missiles at reduced cost to update its nuclear deterrent.[101] There was, however, a small indigenous population, the Chagosians, who were quietly but forcibly relocated. Britain initially claimed publically that the islands were uninhabited and in 1971 the BIOT Commissioner, acting under instructions from ministers in London, enacted an Immigration Ordinance thereby making it illegal for a person to enter or remain in the BIOT without a permit, and allowed those remaining to be removed. Unfortunately, the islands were not as unpopulated as the British and Americans initially claimed and under the agreement the British forcibly deported the entire population of between 1,400 to 1,700 indigenous people.[102] The issues surrounding Diego Garcia and the Chagosians fell within Emery's mandate at the South Asian Department.

The Chagos Archipelago was originally part of Mauritius, which became a British colonial possession in 1810 and remained so until 1968, when it became independent. In 1965, before independence, the British government took the Chagos Archipelago out of Mauritius, and it remains a British territory to the present day.[103]

In 1970, British MP Tam Dalyell gave notice that he intended to ask questions in Parliament about the depopulation of the Chagos Archipelago. Emery, as Department Head, drafted a 'memorandum of guidance' for internal circulation which resurfaced in 2001 and Tam Dalyell cited it in the House of Commons. It says in part:

> Apart from our overall strategic and defence interests we are also concerned at present not to have to elaborate on the administrative implications for the present population on Diego Garcia of estab-lishment of any base there. We would not wish it to become general knowledge that some of the inhabitants have lived on Diego Garcia for at least two generations and could, therefore, be regarded as

'belongers'. We shall therefore advise Ministers in handling sup-plementary questions about whether Diego Garcia is inhabited to say that there is only a small number of contract labourers from the Seychelles and Mauritius engaged to work on the copra plantations on the Island. That is being economical with the truth.

Should a Member ask about what would happen to these contract labourers in the event of a base being set up on the Island, we hope that, for the present, this can be brushed aside as a hypothetical question at least until any decision to go ahead with the Diego Garcia facility becomes public. One of my objections is that the questions were indeed brushed aside. Since then the papers have become available from the court case.[104]

Mauritius has long sought the return of the Chagos, and in June 2017 the UN General Assembly voted to refer the territo-rial dispute between Mauritius and the UK to the International Court of Justice.[105] The Court started hearings in September 2018 and issued an advisory legal opinon in favour of Mauritius,[106] and the UN General Assembly adopted a resolution demanding that the UK unconditionally withdraw its colonial administration from the area within six months.[107] So far, the UK has rejected this non-binding resolution.[108] Most of the unfortunate depor-tees ended up in Mauritius and the Seychelles, with only a small financial compensation fifteen years later, and many now live in poverty. There have been a number of legal attempts to enable the population to return to the Chagos Archipelago, but in 2016 the UK's Supreme Court upheld a 2008 House of Lords ruling that the exiles could not return.[109] ITV produced a short docu-mentary on the plight of the people displaced from the islands, showing that the British government had been frugal with the truth.[110]

Tam Dalyell later wrote a letter:

Before I say anything else, it is legitimate to ask [...] for at least an explanation from Eleanor Emery and others as to why they did that [deported the inhabitants]. If a case can be made for their actions, it is up to the Minister and the Foreign Office to tell us why they did what they did. I suspect that it was about the Anglo-American relationship.[111]

However, it would be unfair to blame Emery or any of the other FCO personnel for their actions. They were career civil servants whose role was to implement the policies of the elected representatives of the electorate, even if that policy was an uncomfortable task. When Dalyell rang to inform Emery that he was raising the matter again, after the thirty-year restrictions on publication had expired, Emery was true to her instincts and her duty, tearfully expressing her sadness for those historical events and that she was not in a position to comment.[112]

In April 1973 it was announced that Emery would be appointed High Commissioner to Botswana, the first woman to hold this position.[113] She is reported to have said that it was an entirely unexpected honour,[114] and also modestly commented: 'Of course, I'm thrilled and immensely pleased. But I don't think all this fuss about being the first woman is justified. After all there are five or six other women in the service with equal rank and responsibility.'[115]

She filled that role with style and distinction, establishing easy and effective working relations with the Botswanan government and, through her enthusiasm and energy, earned much admiration and affection among expatriates and Botswanans alike.[116]

In the House of Lords, Baroness Tweedsmuir of Belhelvie declared, 'First of all, I shall gladly convey the congratulations, which I hope I may say will come from the whole House, to Miss Eleanor Emery who will be our first British lady High Commissioner. She certainly has achieved this honour on merit.'[117]

In 1973 Lord Shepherd also conveyed his congratulations to Eleanor Emery:

> Before coming to the debate itself I feel I ought to ask the noble Baroness to convey, as I hope she will, our sincere congratulations to Miss Eleanor Emery, a very good friend of many of us, who is the first woman High Commissioner to be appointed. There was a previous diplomatic appointment, but unfortunately, on account of illness, it could not be taken up; so this is the first occasion upon which a woman has become a High Commissioner. I can say to my noble friend Lady Summerskill that in my view this has nothing to do with 'Women's Lib.', or a recognition of the valiant campaign that she fights on behalf of her sex. I believe this is an appointment arising solely as a consequence of merit, and of great sensitivity and great service to many dependent territories and to one new Commonwealth country, Fiji.[118]

That same year Kenneth Baker (now Baron Baker of Dorking, CH PC) said, in response to a question about female diplomats, in the House of Commons:

> My honourable friend will no doubt have seen the announcement on Saturday that Miss Eleanor Emery has been appointed High Commissioner of Botswana. I can assure my honourable friend that over 300 women have posts in the Civil Service with salaries over £4,000 a year.[119]

The announcement on 3 April of Emery's appointment as High Commissioner to Botswana made headlines in newspapers around the world.[120] Reporters asked her questions about being the first woman High Commissioner and whether the Foreign

Office was an intimidating place, heavy with protocol and difficult for a woman. She responded, 'It's not at all intimidating, seen from the inside. In the end, it all comes back to people, basically what we are trying to do is reconcile conflicting interests and promote mutual ones.'[121]

In an interview for the Canadian press Emery was quoted as saying that she had never found being a woman, in the male-dominated world of international politics, an obstacle to her advancement. 'Women are treated strictly on their merits in the British Foreign Service. One woman had been named an ambassador in 1961 but she was unable to take up her duties because of illness. Others had risen to positions of equal importance with the Foreign Office.'[122]

Even if she had experienced discrimination, it is unlikely that she would have discussed it with reporters at that time. When asked why there had not been a female High Commissioner before, Emery said in an interview with Terry Coleman, 'You would expect there to have been others. Dame Barbara Salt had been appointed Ambassador to Israel ten years ago, but had been unable to take up the post because of illness.'[123]

She went on to say:

There were about half a dozen women in the Foreign Service with her rank, and they were heads of departments […] in the nature of things, women were less mobile than men. Some women had husbands whose careers did not enable them to go with their wives to the end of the earth. Furthermore, women did not begin to enter the service much before the last war and would thus only now be achieving the necessary seniority.[124]

She also gave her three golden rules for success in the Foreign Service:

Trust in God
Honour the Queen, and
Keep your Martinis dry.[125]

When asked about Britain's relationship with the Commonwealth, Emery commented that its recent entry into the European Common Market meant that relations with Commonwealth Countries would change over the next few years. However, she went on to say:

> But that doesn't mean Commonwealth relations become less important. They don't. I'm absolutely certain the Commonwealth has a vital role to play in future as a means of promoting international understanding and facilitating communications among member countries.[126]

On arriving as High Commissioner in Botswana, Emery found that Gaborone, the Botswanan capital, was developing rapidly from the proverbial 'one-horse dorp' which she had visited years before. The economy was switching from cattle to mineral resources, though it was the diamond operations rather than the earlier nickel-copper mine which proved the greater earner. Emery performed her tasks as High Commissioner with aplomb, making slow, deliberate speeches and overcoming the initial disapproval of the President, Sir Seretse Khama. She set high standards in the office and the Residence, and colleagues and staff found her sometimes demanding but always appreciative. She saw to it that the High Commission supported local charities and, like Lady Khama, Emery also took a particular interest in the Livingstone Mission Hospital at Moleopole, run by a Scots missionary doctor.[127]

Emery diplomatically declined to discuss what role she might play in ongoing negotiations between Britain and Rhodesia's government.[128] The Rhodesian government had declared independence in 1965 to preserve white rule, as other African countries were being encouraged to decolonise and establish democratic governments. However, as High Commissioner to a neighbouring country, Emery was very involved in the discussions.[129] In August 1978 the British organised an all-parties conference at Lancaster House in London. Under the resulting settlement, the British supervised the election, guerrilla fighters were rounded up as part of the ceasefire, and the US lifted sanctions. Robert Mugabe won the majority of seats in Parliament and became Prime Minister; Prince Charles officially handed power over on 17 April 1980 to an independent Zimbabwe. Robert Mugabe was re-elected Prime Minister until 1987 when he became Executive Head of State.[130]

Emery's achievements were honoured by her being awarded the CMG in 1975. She retired in 1977 and first settled in Dulwich and worked for Toynbee Hall in Tower Hamlets before moving to Cambridge.[131] She lived near Cambridge until 2005 when she moved to Worthing in West Sussex.[132]

Emery's creative drive to help Botswana continued into retirement and she was part of a group who assisted Aloysius Kgarebe, an old friend from her time as High Commissioner (who had been the reciprocal High Commissioner in London), to set up a society 'to encourage and strengthen ties between Britain and Botswana and to foster friendship and a better understanding between the peoples of the two countries'.[133] She was elected Vice-Chairman of the UK Botswana Society at its inaugural meeting in April 1981, becoming a highly effective Chairman in May 1984. In later life Emery stayed informed about world events and made her voice known in newspapers and other outlets as she felt appropriate when incorrect information was presented about Botswana and other subjects dear to her heart.[134] She was also Governor of the Commonwealth Institute from 1980 to 1985.

Emery died on 23 June 2007, at the age of 88.[135] In her will she bequeathed funds to the University of Glasgow, to establish the Eleanor Emery Botswana Fund, whose purpose is to support postgraduate Botswanan students.[136]

Anne Marion Warburton[137] was the younger daughter of Captain Piers Eliot Warburton MC, (who had served in the Royal Artillery and been awarded a Military Cross and bar in the First World War), and Mary Louise Thompson, an American from Anniston, Alabama. When the Second World War broke out Eliot returned to uniform and Mary Louise took their four children to stay with relatives in the United States. Warburton attended the Virginia Intermont College before entering Barnard College in 1944; a women's college affiliated

Eleanor Emery, *c*. 1973. (Crown Copyright, Open Government Licence)

with the University of Columbia, from which she graduated *Magna cum Laude* in 1946 with a degree in government and economics. On the family's return to London, Warburton went up to Somerville College, Oxford, to read PPE.[138] Warburton was interested in foreign affairs and accepted a position with the Economic Co-operation Administration, also known as the Marshall Plan, whose purpose was to rebuild Europe after the war. Two years later she took a position as an economist with the NATO Secretariat in Paris from 1952 to 1954 and then joined the merchant bank Lazard Frères.[139]

Warburton had thought that she was too old to take the Foreign Office Entrance Examination, but a temporary relaxation in the rules provided a late opportunity and in 1957[140] she joined the other successful aspirants appearing before the Civil Service Selection Board (CSSB, colloquially pronounced 'sisby'). Candidates were put through the ringer and tested for a range of skills and talents, including chairing mock committees, developing policies for fictitious territories and coming up with potential solutions for diplomatic real-world problems. *The Advertiser* newspaper from Adelaide, Australia, gave the following description of the process:

The taxpayers have recently acquired a lovely old manor house, Stoke Dabernon, to conduct 'country house' tests for civil service candidates under 30 […] The mansion in extensive grounds has terraced lawns run down to the river, and pleasant views over park-like country. The staff live in the main house and their 'guests' in converted cement Army huts in the grounds. Each hut contains 13 bedrooms and two bathrooms. Both examiners and examinees share the lounges, dining room and bar, where beer and whisky are plentiful. These 'house parties' are mixed, with women on the same footing as men. When the guests arrive at 6 pm, a pleasant hostess pins a label with a number on each one's front and back; by these numbers they are known until departure.

Psychological Tests. They are placed in groups with psychologists and observers attached to each group, eating and relaxing with them and watching them during tests. They are subjected to a quiz, practical tests and debates. A budding ambassador, for instance, must nail two bits of wood together or pile bricks on each other. Future foreign secretaries got so angry dismantling and re-assembling a fire service water tank that its bolts are now unserviceable.[141]

The last step was the Final Selection Board, during which the candidates were interrogated individually by a panel of six for one to two hours on their background, interests and motives for wanting to join the Foreign Service. Female candidates were also asked whether they planned to get married and if so, what they would do. Male candidates were not asked this question.

Warburton was appointed an officer in A-Branch in 1957[142] and given a position in the Economic Relations Department. Her first posting was to the UK Mission to the UN, in New York, followed by a posting to the British Embassy in Bonn. She played a major role in the State Visit of Queen Elizabeth to West Germany in May 1965, which was widely viewed as a reconciliation between the UK and Germany after the Second World War, and was eagerly welcomed by the German people. Large crowds turned out to see the Queen and the visit was considered a great success by both governments.[143] The Queen bestowed the honour of CVO upon Warburton in recognition of her efforts,[144] and the West German government awarded her the Verdienstkreuz (Merit Cross), First Class, for her service to West Germany.

Warburton returned to London in 1965 to take up a position in the Personnel Department. The Plowden Report (discussed earlier) had just been accepted and Warburton spent much of her time implementing its recommendations. She believed that people should be promoted based on merit, but she also recognised that there was resistance to women in some quarters and she had no desire to send a woman into a situation in which she would fail, because that would not be of help to anyone.

Later that year Warburton was promoted to the newly created Diplomatic Service Administration Office, and in 1967 she was appointed Assistant Head of the UN political department. Her next posting was as Counsellor to the UK's Geneva Mission to the UN. Following Geneva, Warburton returned to London to serve as Head of the Guidance and Information Policy Department (GIPD).

Warburton's appointment as Ambassador to Denmark in 1976 by the then Foreign Secretary, James Callaghan, received widespread attention, and some silly remarks.[145] When she travelled to Copenhagen to present her credentials to Queen Margrethe, a journalist asked her how she was coping with 'a two-pronged life [...] doing the job of both husband and wife'. She quickly responded, 'Socially speaking, a husband would be useful, but I suspect that a bachelor ambassador would miss a wife more.'[146]

Had it not been for the marriage bar, Warburton is unlikely to have been the first female Ambassador. For the FCO, it was important to show that with Warburton's appointment, they had, at last, put the issue of gender inequality behind them.[147] Once the appointment had been announced the FCO gave it much publicity. Sir Michael Palliser, Permanent Under-Secretary for the FCO, later recalled, 'The Foreign Office were very keen for us to show that we were letting women into the top jobs, and of course Anne did a very good job.'[148]

The choice of Denmark was not random. For the FCO, it was important that the appointment be a success and given that the Danes had a progressive cultural outlook and history of women's rights they would be receptive to a female representative. Sir Michael explained that Copenhagen was 'certainly chosen with the feeling that in Denmark a woman ambassador would be totally acceptable in the way that in Saudi Arabia she would not be'.[149]

Lord (Paddy) Ashdown, who worked with Warburton in Geneva and became a lifelong friend, described her as 'greatly loved and held in extraordinary awe and respect and none of us were surprised that she was the first woman Ambassador to Copenhagen [...] where she did a very good job'.[150]

Lord David Owen (Foreign Secretary from 1977 to 1979) also worked with Warburton and paid his respects to her professional contributions:

In my day, which started in fact as Minister for Europe in the FCO, before I became Foreign Secretary, it was a matter of great pride that at long last we had a female British Ambassador. And for me an important Embassy. Denmark was interested in Africa and had a Foreign Minister who was committed and involved. And in the framework of what was then called Political Cooperation, I found the Danish voice a very helpful one and there is no doubt that Anne Warburton played a big part in this drawing on her experience of the UN in the UK's Geneva Mission.[151]

In the Queen's Silver Jubilee Birthday Honours in 1977, Warburton was made a CMG.[152] She travelled extensively in Denmark and loved the country and the people, eventually publishing a guide book called *Signposts to Denmark* in 1992.[153] She felt a great affiliation with Denmark and described the Danes as a nation:

They feel especially close to us, and not only because of Britain's role in the liberation of Denmark, celebrated in this 50th anniversary year. They are right in thinking that they have many things, including their sense of humour, in common with us. Yes, I can heartily recommend being British Ambassador to Denmark![154]

The highpoint of her posting to Denmark was the State Visit in 1979, which Warburton spent considerable time organising. The visit was a great success, and afterwards the Queen appointed her DCVO.[155]

The Falklands War also occurred during Warburton's time in Copenhagen, and she worked hard to keep the UK's Danish allies on side as the conflict deepened.[156] She was so successful in promoting Anglo-Danish relations that in 1986 she became a Life Member of the Anglo-Danish Society.[157]

Warburton's next assignment after Denmark was to Geneva as the UK's Permanent Representative to the UN, holding the rank of Ambassador.[158]

In 1986 Warburton retired from diplomatic service a little earlier than required in order to take up the position of President of Lucy Cavendish College at Cambridge University. Lucy Cavendish was

Dame Anne Warburton DCVO on her appointment as the Permanent Representative at UKMIS Geneva, 1983. (Crown Copyright, Open Government Licence)

then just a collegiate society founded as a place for 'mature' women; i.e. those who typically had taken a break from professional or academic life for reasons of family etc., and who wished to restart. Warburton explained the mission of Lucy Cavendish:

> So many women have been brought up to think simply that they are somebody's daughter, wife, mother, neighbour. At Lucy Cavendish they can become a person in their own right. Perhaps the greatest personal reward for me is to see undergraduates, some of whom are so unsure of themselves when they first come up, being able to say when they leave: 'Now I can do something.' [Dame Anne Warburton's obituary, *Guardian*, 15 June 2015]

Under Warburton's leadership Lucy Cavendish upgraded its status to a college, which enabled it to access the university to build its capital funds, improve its infrastructure and improve financial aid to students.[159] The number of research fellows increased as did the number of undergraduates. The *Guardian* wrote:

> What had begun in 1965 as a small foundation with only 10 students became a full college at the University of Cambridge in 1997, in part because of Warburton's efforts. She was committed to its focus on attracting older women from diverse backgrounds. Student numbers at Lucy Cavendish almost doubled [from 77], to 133 [from 1988 to 1993], during her tenure, and she planned the development of several new buildings, including the spacious dining hall which has been named after her. Her steely-eyed portrait surveys today's 380 students as they enjoy the status of full members of Cambridge University.[160]

Meanwhile, in the former Yugoslavia during the early 1990s, the civil war had unfolded and accounts of mass murder and atrocities against citizens were making headlines in the Western newspapers. In particular, there had been rumours and press reports about large-scale systematic abuse of Bosnian women, and Warburton was tasked by the then Prime Minister, John Major, to lead a fact-finding mission to Bosnia-Herzegovina to determine whether the horrific accounts were credible and to lay down recommendations for Britain's policy on the crisis.

In 1992, then aged 65, Warbuton led two European Council authorised missions to Bosnia-Herzegovina to hear first-hand accounts of how women were being subjected to rape, abuse and other atrocities because of their gender and ethnicity. Giving an estimate of the number of women raped was difficult for the Mission. However, they believed that it was better to give a reasonable estimate with large uncertainty than to provide no estimate at all:

> However, on the basis of its investigations, the Mission accepts that it is possible to speak in terms of many thousands. Estimates vary widely, ranging from 10,000 to as many as 60,000. The most reasoned estimates suggested to the Mission place the number of victims at around 20,000. [Section 14, Warburton Mission Report][161]

The European Council issued a press statement endorsing the Warburton Report and promising to act on its recommendations,[162] and the report received widespread coverage in the press.[163] As Paddy Ashdown said:

> Her report had a huge impact and it was the first report that identified the sexual violations of women as an instrument of war as used by the Serbs. It [Rape] has been used before, certainly, the Serbs were not the only ones by any means, but they were the worst. And she [Warburton] did a brilliant report, very well

founded, very well received and it had a profound influence on the way that we began treating women in warfare.[164]

In addition to the European Council, the UN, Amnesty International and Human Rights Watch sent their own missions to Bosnia to determine the facts.[165] The Warburton Report, in combination with the reports from these other missions, had an enormous impact. There was widespread condemnation of the Serb forces by many countries,[166] as well as in the UN.[167] One of the most significant outcomes of the reports was the establishment of the International Criminal Tribunal for Yugoslavia (ICTY)[168] by the UN Security Council in February 1993. The only previous tribunal under Chapter VII of the United Nation's charter[169] had been the Nuremburg tribunals after the end of the Second World War.[170] The ICTY and a similar tribunal for Rwanda (ICTR), led to the formation of the Permanent International Criminal Court, which investigates and tries individuals charged with genocide, war crimes and crimes against humanity.[171]

Warburton also served on the Nolan Committee charged with developing ethical guidelines for politicians and others in public service. She additionally served on the Equal Opportunities Commission dealing with sex discrimination in the workplace. Dame Anne Warburton DCVO CMG died on 4 June 2015, aged 87. Her funeral service was held in Thornham Magna, Suffolk, where she had lived in her retirement. Both her funeral and memorial service were attended by a huge number of people from all walks of life.

Women such as Dame Anne Warburton, Eleanor Emery and Dame Barbara Salt had a lasting impact on the Foreign Office and those who served in it, especially younger women following in their footsteps. For example, Dame Rosemary Spencer (former British Ambassador to the Netherlands 1996 to 2001) commented that:

> There were one or two [earlier women diplomats] who inspired me on the way up. One was Barbara Salt, though I never met her. She was clearly a formidable personality. The other was Anne Warburton, one of our first women ambassadors, and another very strong personality. I got to know her slightly in the FCO before she became Ambassador in Copenhagen.[172]

9

NEW AMBASSADORS AND DEVELOPING EQUALITY

Equality for women has dramatically improved in the last 100 years both across society in general and within the ranks of the Foreign Office. In 1918, a select number of women received the right to vote and nearly a century later, in July 2016, Theresa May became Prime Minister without causing much excitement about her gender, since Margaret Thatcher had already dispelled the novelty. At the turn of the twentieth century, female staff in the Foreign Office existed only in the lower and service grades, but now they number among the most senior levels of political and diplomatic appointees.

In the last two decades women who have joined the Foreign Office were, for the most part, treated as equals by their male counterparts. There were a few cases when this was not the case, as illustrated by Sally Jane Axworthy, who was appointed the Britain's second woman Ambassador to the Holy See in 2016. She commented about her early years after she joined the FCO in 1986 and how the organisation has since adopted women-friendly practices:

When I joined the FCO 30 years ago there were few senior women, and none with children. I experienced being assumed to be the PA; being subject to inappropriate propositions; and being told not to think about promotion! Now we have many senior women. For me, the FCO's excellent flexible working provisions – and supportive line managers – were what enabled me to stay. I look forward to us completing the transformation: we still need a female PUS, and female ambassadors to Washington and Paris!

The way that we present ourselves carries a message. People make snap judgments when they see us, even before the first word is spoken and so it is important that women diplomats look the part, although sometimes their appearance is given more attention than their message.[1]

John Kerry, while US Secretary of State, emphasised the importance of fashion as a means of diplomacy:

The clothes we create, the food we eat, the sports we play and the traditions that we honor are all part of a nation's identity and therefore an integral part of how countries relate to one another [...] We know that America's standing in the world isn't determined solely by political and security policies [...] On many occasions, cultural diplomacy can achieve what traditional diplomacy cannot because it speaks a universal language.[2]

Dame Karen Pierce, the current British Ambassador to Washington, takes the view that her clothes can be used to convey confidence; part of the costume and theatre of a high-ranking position:

Generally, I think if you're an ambassador you do need to look the part, and if you're in somewhere like Kabul, being able to dress in a way that makes you feel confident when you take the body armour off is very important. I would wear stilettos in Kabul and even, depending on the distance, walk places in them. My protection team once said, 'We didn't know it was possible to walk this slowly, ma'am.'[3]

In discussing women's style she went on to say:

There's a part of me that loves to talk about style. I do wonder if it's not an older woman/younger woman thing, because I can think of plenty of younger colleagues who actually would be a bit cross with that approach.

The key is getting the balance right, because if you come across only as superficial and interested in how you look, no one's going to take what you say about any diplomatic issue seriously; you're not doing justice to the cause of promoting women to senior positions.

When Pierce was asked by *PassBlue* why the press focuses so much on women's clothing, she answered:

There's a demand. One thing I learned about journalism when I was in the Foreign Ministry Press Office: people like to have something, a specific characteristic to latch on to, something personal that hooks the reader. I think, when the person is a woman, most of the time it's going to be your shoes, your hair, your handbag, and that's not particularly fair. I don't imagine anyone sets out to put the focus on the accessories, it's just the way things are at the moment, and it will probably take a long time to change.[4]

Dame Karen Pierce DCMG at the Foreign and Commonwealth Office speaking at the Week of Women panel discussion and networking event, 17 November 2016. (Foreign and Commonwealth Office)

Kirsty Hayes who joined the Foreign Office in 1999 and rose to become Ambassador to Portugal (2014–18) said that in her early career she was told or overheard the following:

> At the end of the day there is no place for women in the diplomatic service because all they want to do is go off and have babies.
>
> I'm sure Kirsty will find being the wife of a busy head of mission a rewarding role in its own right.
>
> The trouble with this policy, Kirsty, is it is not very manly.[5]

Based on a life-long career in the Service, her advice to women joining the Foreign Office is:

Aim high and seek to be the change you want to see – and don't forget to 'pay it forwards' by supporting more junior colleagues [...] The FCO can make the best policies in the world but our ability to promote genuine equality will only ever be as strong as our weakest manager.[6]

Later women who were the first female ambassadors to their respective countries also encountered uncertainty about how they should be treated based on their gender until the novelty of a female ambassador had worn off. Dame Denise Holt ,who was the UK's first female Ambassador to Mexico (2002–05) recounted one of her experiences after being appointed ambassador there:

There was an institution known rather unattractively as the Snuffers' Club, which had been begun by a British ambassador probably 50 or 60 years earlier, where he had identified a group of mates and they would get together at the luncheon club every month, and at the highest point of this they would take snuff. Now because the British Ambassador was the convening point, and because the group was really seriously interesting, it had a former President, high court judges and quite a lot of [people] you welcome the opportunity to meet. So there was quite a debate before I joined, because it has always been a men only club, but how could they not include the British ambassador. The matter was settled by ex-President de la Madrid [President of Mexico 1982 to 1988], who said he was not prepared to continue coming if the group did not respect the right of Her Majesty to nominate such ambassadors as she wished. And if I was there as ambassador then clearly I must be invited. And that was that. They had a problem and once they sorted it, they were absolutely polite. I joined in fully and there were no problems.[7]

Since the first three ambassadorial level women were appointed, there was an initially slow but steady increase in the number of female heads of missions appointed. Each woman broke new ground on being appointed ambassador to a new country and by 2016, over ninety countries have had female British ambassadors. Sometimes it took a while for a host country to get used to the idea of a female British ambassador; for example, Jane Marriott, who was formerly the Ambassador to Yemen, said:

When I was younger, I'd walk into a room and people would glance behind me because they'd be looking for a man in a suit and wondering where the 'real' Ambassador was [...] But either things are getting better or I have a few more lines on my face now.[8]

Catherine Arnold, Britain's Ambassador to Mongolia (2015–18), commented, 'I can't go to an event without someone rushing up to shake my hand and marvel at the fact that I'm "young and a woman and an ambassador". I'm proud of what this says about the UK.'[9]

More recently, Sally Axworthy MBE, Ambassador to the Holy See since September 2019, said that 'as an ambassador, as a diplomat, you tend to be treated as a representative of your country, irrespective of being male or female'.[10] This comment suggests that much of the novelty of female diplomats has worn off, which may not be surprising since Axworthy was the UK's second female Ambassador to the Vatican. Much has changed since 1970 when the Vatican rejected a proposed Minister from West Germany because she was female.[11]

While most comments were encouraging, not all were, as Julie (Jules) Chappell OBE recounted in her speech 'The future of activism in a pussy-grabbing world',[12] which was adapted from her recent Ted Talk.[13] While many were supportive of her arrival, there were some in diplomatic circles who regarded her appointment with scepticism, opining that she was not a 'proper' ambassador and, worse, that she owed her position to nepotism: either her father's friendship with David Miliband or, even more insultingly, to sexual favours.

Other women reported that being female was an advantage. Several female American diplomats told *Politico* that it was key to know when to use your femininity and when to draw the line.[14] The funny thing about men, the women interviewed said, is that they like talking to women. This can prove very useful.

'We're not as threatening as men,' says Barbara Bodine, whose many postings have included being Ambassador to Yemen. 'There isn't quite the proving themselves, there isn't that chest-butting kind of thing going on. And so in that sense you can often get a whole lot more information.'

When she was Deputy Chief of Mission in Kuwait in the late 1980s, Bodine once went to meet an important Kuwaiti official. They talked for two hours, she says, some of it substantive and some of it about the television shows he liked as a child. When she emerged, her colleagues looked at her in awe, saying they'd never gotten as much information about that official before.

The first such female pioneers through to 2000 are listed below:[15]

Country	Name	Appointment
Botswana	Eleanor Emery	1973–77
Denmark	Dame Anne Warburton	1976–83
Uruguay	Patricia Hutchinson	1980–83
Norway	Dame Gillian Brown	1981–83
UN (Geneva)	Dame Anne Warburton	1983–85
Panama	Margaret Bryan	1986–89
Ivory Coast	Dame Veronica Sutherland	1987–99
Chad	Charlotte Rycroft	1989–90
Mozambique	Dame Maeve Fort	1989–92
Ivory Coast, Niger, Burkina and Liberia	Margaret Rothwell	1990–97

Country	Name	Appointment
Costa Rica	Louise Croll	1992–95
Holy See	Maureen Macglashan	1995–98
Rwanda	Kaye Oliver	1995–98
Uzbekistan and Tajikistan	Dame Barbara Hay	1995–99
Ireland	Dame Veronica Sutherland	1995–99
South Africa	Dame Maeve Fort	1996–2000
Netherlands	Dame Rosemary Spencer	1996–2001
Chile	Dame Glynne Evans	1997–2000
Luxembourg	Juliet Campbell	1988–91
Angola	Caroline Elmes	1998–2002
Mongolia	Kay Coombes	1999–2001
Sri Lanka	Linda Duffield	1999–2002
Lesotho	Kaye Oliver	1999–2002
Finland	Alyson Bailes	2000–02
Estonia	Sara Squire	2000–03

Following the appointment of the first female High Commissioner and first Ambassador, the number of women in senior positions and heads of mission remained small, only one or two for another twenty-five years, until a notable increase in the late 1990s. For the next couple of decades there continued to be only one or two women in head of mission roles, and the number of women in senior positions remained small. Dame Denise Holt commented on the number of women when she joined the Foreign Office:

> When I joined the Foreign Office, a woman was almost never seen, so by the time I got to the 1990s there were always a couple of women in the room and I thought that was pretty good and then I would go to a meeting in the Home Office where the majority of people were women. So I realised that we did still have a way to go.[16]

Society has changed in women's favour, as evidenced, for example, by the seminal House of Lords ruling in 1991 that a husband who forced himself on his wife committed rape.[17] This decision overturned at least 400 years of precedence since Sir Matthew Hale (1609–76) wrote on the subject.[18] Another example is the UN Convention on the Elimination of All Forms of Discrimination against Women, which the UK ratified in 1986.[19]

The new era of social intolerance to discrimination caught up with FCO in the 1990s with a couple of high-profile examples that made the newspaper headlines. The first was Susan Rogerson and the second was Baroness Neville Jones. Rogerson's case was discussed earlier and Baroness Neville Jones is discussed later; both of which undoubtedly caused embarrassment to the FCO. Other factors probably played a role too, but by the late 1990s the FCO made much more effort to encourage larger numbers of female diplomats to reach the higher levels.

Since then, the number of female Heads of Mission has grown steadily, as may be seen in the graph below. In 2018 there were sixty-five female heads of mission around the world, and by 2018 nearly half of UK embassies across Europe were headed by female diplomats:[20]

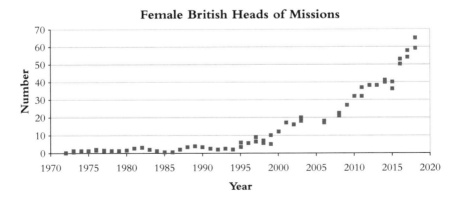

Graph of female heads of mission over time.

Marriage as a female diplomat has been a significant obstacle, not

Marriage as a female diplomat has been a significant obstacle, not just due to the historical employment restrictions, but because women typically face more family-based challenges than do men and the demands of diplomatic service require mobility and a willingness to be posted anywhere in the world. The pre-1946 discussion of feasibility of female diplomats had focused on the difficulties of what a trailing spouse would do. It is easy to criticise the naysayers, but they did have a valid argument, especially in the early twentieth century when the majority of families expected the husband to earn the money and the wife to look after children and manage the home.

If the Foreign Office was to encourage female diplomats then it had to reduce the burden on women. The first barrier was institutional: the marriage bar which forced female diplomats to resign upon marriage was removed in 1973. However, there were still significant barriers for female diplomats balancing career and family demands.

The first married female Ambassador was Dame Veronica Sutherland, who arrived in Abidjan in 1987 with a husband, Alex, who was also working as a Director of the African Development Bank. The following year Juliet Campbell, Ambassador to Luxembourg, was also accompanied by her husband.[21] Many husbands did not want to trail around the world after their wives, and by 1988 there were still only 284 married women in all grades of the diplomatic service,[22] out of the roughly 4,000 UK-based civil servants who work for the FCO.[23]

Ambassador Vivien Life was appointed to Denmark in 2012, while her husband Tim Dowse, also a senior FCO official, continued to work in the UK with their two college-age daughters.[24] When asked about the toughest lessons she had learned, she answered:

As a working mother, especially one who travels and works with 24 hour a day issues, you will not escape feeling guilty either about not being there for some key moment for your children or not being where the action is for your job. But you have to live with that and aim to have confidence in the decisions you have taken.[25]

Dame Anne Pringle, the first British female Ambassador to Moscow and the Czech Republic, spent most of the first twenty years of her marriage apart from her husband:

I don't think anyone would pretend it's easy. I'd say my husband and I are past masters at shuttle diplomacy [...] It is quite a long haul. But it's worked for us. We have barely missed a beat and certainly barely ever missed a weekend [...] Most people find it slightly bizarre that we are still very, very together. But you have just got to find what works for you. The joy of nowadays is that you are not in a straitjacket. Spouses thirty years ago were in quite a straitjacket in terms of not having many choices for what to do. Now things are a bit more flexible and that helps both sides.[26]

The push for change increased in the 1980s and more so in the 1990s as the politics of diversity became more mainstream. Dame Rosemary Spencer (Ambassador to the Netherlands from 1996 to 2001) described the changes that she saw:

In 1995 the FCO's Departmental Action Plan for Women set in motion a more radical look at the impediments to women in the Service. It was accepted that change was necessary. The review looked at maternity packages, flexible working hours, part-time work, job sharing, and help with childcare. During the 1990s the proportion of senior women increased: in 1995, there were three female heads of mission, rising gradually to twelve in 2000. By 2017 things had improved to the extent that 30 per cent of senior grade posts at home and abroad were filled by women.[27]

Where both spouses were diplomats, the Foreign Office had more room to be creative. For example, when two spouses are at ambassadorial rank, the Foreign Office has sometimes arranged appointments in adjacent countries. For example, Dame Judith MacGregor was appointed to Slovakia as Ambassador while her husband, Sir John MacGregor, was Ambassador to Austria. The distance from Bratislava, Slovakia, to Vienna, Austria, is about 50 miles (80 km) or about an hour's drive. The previous posting arrangements for Ambassadors Dame Judith and Sir John MacGregor are set out below:

Year	Dame Judith MacGregor	John MacGregor CVO
1998–2000		Ambassador to Poland
2004–07	Ambassador to Slovakia	Ambassador to Austria (2003–07)
2009–13	Ambassador to Mexico	Retired
2013–17	High Commissioner to South Africa	

One of the programmes that the Foreign Office has to assist married couples, where both partners are diplomats, is special unpaid leave. If one spouse is posted abroad and there is not a suitable position for the second spouse, then the latter can take unpaid leave until an opening comes along without harming his or her career. Dame Denise Holt discussed when her husband David was sent abroad:

David was then posted to Trinidad and Tobago as Deputy High Commissioner and there wouldn't have been a job for me there. But that was fine, I was very happy, our son was now five, and I was very happy to take a little more time out to be with him, which I did. We did two and half years in Trinidad and Tobago and at that point my husband retired and the floor was all mine. It worked out pretty well.[28]

The Foreign Office has in some cases used some very unconventional methods to accommodate married couples. For example, when Tom Carter and his wife Carolyn Davidson were appointed to Zambia, they were equal High Commissioners, the first married couple to job-share a Head of Mission posting for Britain.[29] Similarly, in 2011 Kathy and Jonathan Leach, a married couple with young children, were appointed joint Ambassadors to the Republic of Armenia.[30] Kathy Leach wrote in the Civil Service blog:

My husband and I have been job-sharing the role of Ambassador in Armenia for the past two years. We decided to use the format pioneered by the first couple to job-share the head of post role – four months on/off – and have found this has worked very well, for us, for the Embassy team and for our wider external contacts. It is a long enough period to see a lot of decisions/ business through and to (re)establish yourself as the person in the hot seat; but it is not so long that you lose touch with the key issues or the key people.

We thought about it a lot before going into it and established a few ground rules. First: the importance of continuity of decision-making – you need to discuss in advance and both be happy with the big decisions, but to trust (and not later undermine) the lower-level decisions which the 'on' Ambassador has to make quickly every day. Second: to avoid appearing in public together at official events. People quickly learn that the person who turns up is the person in charge [...] We have encountered some scepticism (particularly from fellow Ambassadors, who perhaps prefer to feel irreplaceable, not interchangeable!). But we have found that once contacts have met us both, and realised that we are both credible, informed, and committed, then the issue drops away.[31]

As mentioned previously, Parliament has passed several anti-discrimination laws that have helped to further the advancement of women in the Foreign Office. The Equality Act of 2010 marks the most recent major legislative step towards gender equality in the United Kingdom.[32] This Act incorporated the mission of several prior Acts, including the Sex Discrimination Act of 1975, the Race Relations Act of 1976, and the Disability Discrimination Act of 1995. The Act applies to both public and private organisations and has had a significant impact on the FCO. Public bodies such as the Foreign Office are now required to publish relevant statistics showing compliance with the equality requirements, and to set equality objectives. To this end, each year Foreign Office publishes its Diversity and Equality Report. A recent one is 'Foreign and Commonwealth Office (FCO) Diversity and Equality Report 2016–17 in response to the Equality Act 2010', which discusses the employee composition by gender, race and other protected groups. For example, the 2016–17 gender breakdowns by employment and average pay gap are summarised below:[33]

Position	Grade	Proportion female	Average pay gap
Senior Civil Service (SCS)	Senior management structure (SMS)	30.0%	
SMS 3 & 4			−6.5%
SMS 2			−2.2%
SMS 1			+0.4%
Grade 6	D7	42.1%	−1.6%

Position	Grade	Proportion female	Average pay gap
Grade 7	D6	39.2%	–1.2%
Senior Executive Officer	C5	37.3%	–2.0%
Higher Executive Officer	C4	42.5%	–0.5%
Executive Officer	B3	55.5%	–0.3%
Administrative Officer	A2	61.4%	0.5%
Administrative Assistant	A1	57.8%	0

The FCO has been successful in terms of hiring new recruits. In November 2009, according to Tayln Rahman, 2,013 female candidates and 2,057 male candidates applied for employment. Only 3 per cent of the candidates were successful, of whom 58 per cent were women.[34]

Francis Adamson, Secretary to the Department for Foreign Affairs and Trade (DFAT), while reflecting the progress of women in the Foreign Office said the following:

When I joined the FCO in 1989, there were still very few women in senior roles, and just two female Ambassadors posted overseas. This meant a dearth of role models, of women like me, and a working culture which felt stuck at an earlier stage of our history. It was unfamiliar, strange and pretty intimidating.

We've made huge progress since then: nearly 30% of our senior managers are now women; our Board of Management is 55% female; and we have around 50 women (including me) who are Heads of Post – Ambassadors, High Commissioners, Consuls-General […] In broader terms too, the FCO has become a more diverse organisation with a less hierarchical and elitist culture: we are more representative of modern Britain. And we're taking care to celebrate the lives and contributions of our early female pioneers, who laid the path for the rest of us to follow. Last year, we named one of our 'fine rooms' in the main FCO building on Whitehall after Dame Anne Warburton, Britain's first female Ambassador (to Denmark, in 1976). Yes, it took nearly 40 years, but we got there in the end.[35]

The Foreign Office continued to make improvements towards equality in the early 2000s, and tried hard to accommodate the family commitments of diplomats. As Dame Rosemary Spencer recalled the changes in the years prior to her retirement:

By the time I retired in 2001 after a fulfilling career, the FCO had come a long way in accommodating women with families and enabling them to make the most of their talents for the benefit of the country. In Berlin, I had a married woman Deputy, whose young family were no obstacle to her fulfilling all aspects of her job with success. In The Hague, our woman Head of the Political Section arrived with young children; her husband was on sabbatical leave and looked after the family. When another child was on the way, we were fortunate to find another woman member of the FCO, on leave to look after her family while her husband worked for Shell in The Hague. She was ready to return to work, and a job-share was successfully arranged.[36]

The FCDO has made significant strides in gender equality compared to its early days, and women diplomats are no longer a novelty. In 2014 an FCO official said in an article in *The Guardian*:

[The FCO takes] equality extremely seriously and it's important that we recruit the best people into the most senior roles regardless of their gender or background [...] We know there is more to do to increase the number of women reaching the very senior roles but we are making progress. The number of female heads of mission is at an all time high of 40, up from 22 in 2008 and 40% of the FCO management board are women.[37]

The FCO has been actively trying to improve the status of women and now has a special envoy for gender equality. Special Envoy for Gender Equality. Joanne Roper CMG, who held this position until July 2020, describes the role:

> The Foreign and Commonwealth Office's Special Envoy for Gender Equality leads the FCO's work to deliver the Foreign Secretary's vision of a foreign policy that consciously and consistently delivers for women and girls and that showcases the UK's leading international reputation in this area.
>
> The Special Envoy is responsible for promoting this agenda across the FCO, by encouraging bold and ambitious policy making and programme support and developing and leading a network of FCO gender champions to support colleagues in doing so. Externally, they work with other government departments, Parliamentarians, civil society, academics and other governments to help deliver a more robust and coherent approach to promoting gender equality at country and international level.[38]

The Foreign Office has taken other steps to be more family friendly, including:

- Encourages flexible and remote working.
- Allows career breaks and unpaid leave for up to 10 years.
- Has a nursery in the FCO where staff can leave their children while they work.
- Checks every job advertisement to make sure it does not put women off.

- Is committed to having a woman on the shortlist for all senior jobs.
- Is committed to mentoring and coaching to develop women's talents.
- Insists on diverse interview panels (i.e. not just men conducting the interviews).[39]

Unpaid leave is a great benefit for couples where one spouse can be appointed abroad and the other trail. It also allows, and the Foreign Office encourages, people to go into private industry, and later return to government service but now with a much broader experience. Julie (Jules) Chappell (the youngest ever Ambassador) recently took a leave of absence to work as Head of International Relations at Hawthorn Communications, a boutique agency based in London, in which she has been promoted to Partner:

> I'm on unpaid leave from government [...] The Foreign Office does this brilliant thing whereby they encourage people to get private sector experience. As ambassador a big part of my job was lobbying British expertise in certain areas or where there was a sense of a British company not being given fair treatment. This type of work is so much easier – I think – if you've had experience of working in a business and understand how different organisations do different things.[40]

Ambassadors face many unique challenges. Chappell went on to say:

> What I really underestimated about being an ambassador was the step up to being a visible leader [...] I'd always advised leaders and suddenly I was the leader and had to get used to not pleasing everyone. And I'm a natural extrovert, so when I talk about ideas

with my team I like to brainstorm – this is my way of bringing people along and also genuinely getting stuff done. I suddenly realised that as ambassador they take your brainstorming ideas as read, which wasn't the case at all. So I had to adapt very quickly to that level of scrutiny, which I hadn't experienced previously. I had completely underestimated the pressure that it brought on me and my boyfriend at the time.[41]

There are other challenges to being ambassador, which apply to both men and women. Jane Marriott OBE, whilst Ambassador to Yemen, required a security detail wherever she went and commented that one of the big challenges of the job is maintaining a personal life. 'I was seeing a lovely chap for five years but he didn't want to go overseas [...] When I was in Yemen, I had three cars full of men with guns following me everywhere I went, which definitely curtailed the social life.'[42]

By the 1980s senior female diplomats no longer received any special treatment regarding hazards, meaning that they were reviewed for suitability for overseas postings against the same criteria as their male colleagues. One of the first such female heads of mission was Patricia Hutchinson, who entered the diplomatic service in July 1948,[43] and was appointed British Ambassador to Uruguay in 1980. While a relatively peaceful posting was anticipated, Uruguay was not considered a docile posting since one of her predecessors, Sir Geoffrey Jackson, had been kidnapped and held for eight months by guerillas in 1971.[44] However, in 1982 the Falklands War broke out, anti-British sentiment rose among some parties and, as mentioned previously, Hutchinson had to operate with constant close protection.[45]

She is not the only ambassador to require extra security. Similarly Jane Marriott, Ambassador to Yemen, lived within a heavily guarded compound and regular lockdowns, sometimes for weeks at a time.[46]

In discussing the appointments of male and female diplomats overseas, there are two questions that are central to the issue of gender differences:'Are women posted to safer locations than men?', and 'Are men posted to more prestigious postings than women?'

A comparison of the hazards of the location for male and female ambassadors was made as follows. The Institute for Economics and Peace has ranked the countries of the world according to how dangerous they are, in their Global Peace Index Report,[47] and this hazard ranking was used as a measure of how dangerous the posting was. On this hazard scale the most peaceful country was Iceland with a ranking of 1.11 and the most hazardous was Syria, with its active civil war and a ranking of 3.81.

A list of the current ambassadors and high commissioners[48] was matched by country to the peace index. Not all countries were included on the hazard scale (e.g. some of the very small ones) and not all countries have UK missions; for example, the Mission to Syria was withdrawn because of the war there. For those countries with a hazard ranking and an active UK mission, comparisons of the hazard ranking for male and female heads of mission were calculated to see if there was a significant difference between male and female heads of mission. The results are summarised below:

Description	Male	Female
Number	102	45
Average	1.995	1.814
Median	2.013	1.938
Standard deviation	0.719	0.735
Max	3.567	3.524

The following conclusions can be drawn:

- In terms of hazardous postings, the numbers for both sexes are similar. The average for the men is only slightly higher than for the women by 0.18, and the difference in median is only 0.08. These numbers are much smaller than the standard deviation for the men (0.719). Compared to the men, the per cent deviation for the women is (0.08/0.719 = 11 per cent).
- The standard deviation for the women at 0.735 is very similar to the men's, indicating that the women are not posted to a narrower group of countries by hazard than their male counterparts. For example, if men were posted everywhere, but women were only posted to 'safe countries' the standard deviation for the men would be much larger than the women.

If we look at the current two most dangerous postings, Afghanistan (3.567, Ambassador Sir Nicholas Kay)[49] and South Sudan (Ambassador Alison Blackburne),[50] in combination with the above statistics, the conclusion is that women do not appear to have been placed in more sheltered positions than men.

Notes:

1.   These numbers indicate that men outnumber women almost 2.3 to 1, but that is presumably because of the historically larger male intake into the diplomat service. By 2017, the FCO had fifty-four female heads of mission around the world out of about 200 missions.[51]

2.   Not all heads of mission were included in this survey, since countries that were not on the hazard index were excluded. It is likely that some of the countries excluded were too small to be included in the Global Peace Index hazard ranking.

It is unclear what impact their absence has on the numbers and conclusions.

3.   In calculating the per cent deviation and coefficient of variation, the median was used rather than the more common mean, in order to avoid distortion caused by a few outliers. If the mean is used, then the numbers are (0.18/0.719) 25 per cent for the per cent deviation and (0.719/1.995) 36 per cent.

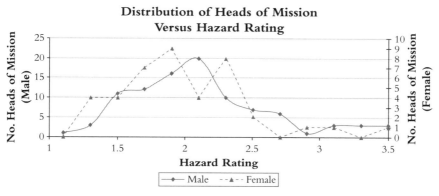

Distribution of heads of mission as a function of hazard rating.

The data was also plotted for male and female heads of mission in hazard rating increments of 0.2, shown in the graph. The above statistics assume a normal distribution (bell curve), but the number of points is not large and from the graph, it may be seen that though the graphs are generally bell-curve shaped, there are significant differences from normality. More importantly, for this discussion, the graph indicates that there is no obvious difference in placement of heads of mission by gender. If, for example, women had been sent to safer locations, then their female curve would be skewed to the left of the male curve. However, the two curves more or less overlap each other, with some point to point fluctuation that may be expected for a modest sample size, such as the present data set. The data is therefore consistent with no significant bias at present in favour of one gender with respect to the hazard index for the assigned locations.

Let us look at the most important postings: United States, Russia, China, France, Germany, Saudi Arabia and the United Nations. Dame Barbara Woodward served as British Ambassador to China (from 2015 until 2020), and Dame Karen Pierce is the current British Ambassador to the United States,[52] both of them being the first woman to hold their respective positions. The other positions are held by men; however, the ratio of men to women at the top is 5:2, which is greater than the overall ratio of male to female heads of mission. The statistics indicate that the FCO has made significant progress towards gender equality in recent years; however, the sample size for prestigious appointments is so small that the statistics are of only limited value as indicators. Pierce has been an inspiration for younger women in the Foreign Office. Julie (Jules) Chappell, former Ambassador to Guatemala, and also Non-Resident Ambassador to El Salvador and Honduras in 2008, said:

> Karen Pierce, the UK Representative to the UN, is an incredible person. People often think women need a certain style of leadership to succeed in the FCO, but Karen is a very natural person to talk to; she has done it her own way and I really respect that. We need lots of different types of people.[53]

A 2016 article which reviewed the American Foreign Service Association's Female US Ambassador Tracker data[54] found that:

> The countries that have hosted the highest number of [American] women ambassadors tend to be, first, those less central to U.S. foreign policy (such as Liechtenstein or Micronesia) and, second, those most Americans have probably never even heard of (including Kiribati, the Kyrgyz Republic, or Palau). The countries

that are most central to American foreign policy, such as China, Germany, Saudi Arabia, and Russia, have had exclusively male ambassadors, whereas the country that has hosted the most female ambassadors overall is Luxembourg, a small European country with a population of just 500,000.[55]

If this article is still accurate, then the American State Department has some more work to do to improve parity of opportunity between sexes. A similar disparity was found for most of the other major countries in a 2016 study.[56]

This book has focused on the development of women's rights in the Foreign Office, but women were not the only under-represented group. The story of exclusion for other groups is generally similar, though usually not with the legal structure banning or allowing entry as for women. In the last decade or so, the Foreign Office has worked hard to ensure that minorities of all kinds are included in its ranks and thus ensure that the best person is selected for the position regardless of attributes such as the colour of their skin, gender or sexual orientation. The section below very briefly outlines some of the people involved.

The 1948 Nationality Act granted UK citizenship and residence for all Commonwealth and Dominion subjects, which resulted in large numbers of people from Jamaica, India and other parts of the Empire/Commonwealth moving to the UK. The Foreign Office did not officially have racial criteria for selecting diplomats; however, the policy was put forward by Sir Percival Waterfield, the first Civil Service Commissioner, who in 1951 said:

Commissioners should not let themselves be influenced in any way by colour prejudice, but that: a person of manifestly un-English appearance or speech might be held unsuitable for a situation in which he would not act as a representative of the United Kingdom to foreigners.[57]

By the mid-1960s, the Foreign Office's policy for selecting diplomats was a little more nuanced, as stated below:

a) he or she was 'at all times since birth' a British or Irish citizen; unless his or her parents were at all times British or Irish citizens;
b) the 'Secretary of State is satisfied that the candidate is so closely connected with the United Kingdom, taking into account such considerations as ancestry, upbringing and residence';
c) he or she undertook to become a British citizen if not already one.[58]

Section b) provided great latitude for officials to ensure that only people of the right background were admitted and effectively raised the bar for those of immigrant ancestry. There were of course people both in and out of the Foreign Office who were concerned about such discrimination, and who sought for a merit only basis for advancement, regardless of skin colour. For example, Home Secretary Roy Jenkins envisioned a more racially tolerant society, which was one of the goals of the Race Relations Acts of 1965 and 1968. The former made it an offence to refuse service in public facilities based on race and the latter outlawed racial discrimination in housing and employment. The Race Relations Act of 1976 further broadened the protections and additional amendments were added in 2000 and 2003.

The number of racial minorities in the Foreign Office was very low, especially in the administrative grade. There were a few exceptions, for example, Noel Jones, who was of Indian ancestry, having joined the Foreign Office in 1962, became the first Head of Mission when we he fulfilled his post as Ambassador to Kazakhstan in 1993.[59] In contrast, in the United States the first black American diplomat was Ebenezer Don Carlos Bassett, who was appointed General Consul to Haiti in 1869,[60] and the first black Ambassador,

Edward Richard Dudley, was appointed to Liberia in 1949.[61] The first female black US Ambassador was Patricia Roberts Harris, to Luxembourg, in 1965.[62]

In May 1999 Foreign Secretary Robin Cook hired an Ethnic Minorities Liaison Officer, whose role was to help create an environment within, and present an outward image of, the Foreign and Commonwealth Office which was more attractive to minority ethnic communities and supportive of minority ethnic staff.[63] The next significant advance came with the 2010 Equality Act, which was discussed earlier, which combined and strengthened previous anti-discrimination legislation and required annual public reporting by government departments on minorities in the workforce. Each year the FCO publishes its FCO Diversity and Equality Report. The 2018 report[64] indicates that 13.7 per cent of its UK workforce is BAME[65] with 5.6 per cent at the highest senior management structure (SMS) level and higher proportions at lower grades. Despite all the history of racial strife in the US, the State Department appears to have been more progressive racially than the UK's Foreign Office in which the first black female diplomat to be appointed High Commissioner was NneNne Iwuji-Eme, who was appointed to Mozambique in July 2018. She had joined the Foreign Office sixteen years before and had worked her way up through the ranks.[66]

Male homosexuality had been illegal in England since the 1533 Buggery Act, which made buggery of any kind a felony punishable by death. Female homosexuality was not even considered at that time and though lesbians often faced discrimination and ridicule, they did not face the same legal challenges as gay men. The Act remained on the books until 1828 when it was replaced by the Offences Against the Person Act of 1828, which included a wide range of violent and criminal acts. However, the penalty for buggery remained unchanged and the last two men executed by hanging for buggery were James Pratt and John Smith in 1835.[67]

The next major change was the 1957 Wolfenden Committee Report,[68] which recommended decreasing the crime of buggery to a misdemeanour, and making it legal between consenting men over the age of 21, if performed in their privacy of their own homes. These changes became law in the Sexual Offences Act of 1967, and the age of consent was reduced to 18 in 1994, and to 16 in 2000, the same as for heterosexuals. In 2003 sexual activity between two men was made no longer a crime.[69]

These dramatic changes in the law reflected changes in society. Maureen Colquhoun, MP for Shoreham, was the first MP to declare that she was a lesbian in 1975, but her local constituency party deselected her, citing her 'obsession with trivialities such as women's rights'.[70] In November 1984 Chris Smith, MP for Islington South and Finsbury, came out and announced that he was gay, and went on to become the first openly gay cabinet minister when Tony Blair made him National Heritage Secretary in 1997.[71] By 2015, 32 of the United Kingdom's 650 MPs described themselves gay, lesbian or bisexual, which, at 4.9 per cent, is close to a fair representation of the general population[72] and demonstrates a remarkable change in British society in less than a generation.

The Foreign Office's attitude towards homosexuality and gender identity has largely followed the prevailing social trends. Prior to 1967 male homosexuality was illegal and so was not accepted in the Foreign Office; there were undoubtedly many homosexuals at all levels of the institution, but they had to remain discreet. After 1967, the Foreign Office was concerned with security and believed that homosexuals were susceptible to extortion and so they could not get a security clearance. This belief came in part from the infamous spy ring known as the Cambridge Five which had provided information to the Soviet Union from the 1930s to 1950s. Of the spies, Guy Burgess and Anthony Blunt were gay and Donald MacLean was bisexual. John Vassal was another homosexual who was caught in a Soviet honey trap and extorted to provide information from 1952 to 1964.[73] Since the Foreign Office believed that homosexuality presented a security risk, it was therefore believed to be incompatible with serving in the diplomatic service. A special internal investigator was appointed, who, armed with list of characteristics and tendencies that gay men would be likely to exhibit, set out to spot and expel homosexual employees from all ranks.[74] In the 1980s official documents and memos addressed the risks of having gay employees:

> [They would be] open to compromise if they indulge in unlawful activities, or mix with unsavoury elements in louche bars ... [and should not be allowed in the service as] homosexuals tended to promiscuity which involved mixing with 'undesirable elements' with consequent security implications.[75]

Society was changing quickly. In July 1991 Prime Minister John Major announced that 'changing social attitudes' meant that homosexuality should no longer be a barrier to employment in the diplomatic service. Subsequently the Foreign Office announced that homosexuality would no longer be a bar to full security clearance, and thus working for the diplomatic service.[76] However, the FCO went on to encourage employees to 'come out' because 'the extent to which an officer is open about his or her sexuality, lifestyle and relationships' was relevant to susceptibility to blackmail. Two years later they asked all overseas posts to compile a list of local laws that banned homosexuality, and went on to say that sexual orientation would therefore continue to be a factor in getting a security clearance. Homosexual officers were supposed to discuss the local laws with the Security Department before any overseas posting.[77]

It was clear that policy makers at the time were struggling to decide what to do. For an excellent discussion of the issues, the reader is directed to 'Homosexuality at the Foreign Office 1967–1991' by James Southern.[78]

As homosexuality moved more into the mainstream, the last vestiges of official discrimination fell away. In 2000, the ban on gay men in the armed forces was lifted.[79] In the FCO, openly gay diplomats rose through the ranks and in 2004 James Clark became the first openly gay man to be appointed Ambassador (to Luxembourg).[80]

Civil unions were allowed in 2004 and same-sex marriage became legal in the UK in 2014,[81] whereupon British diplomat Brian Davidson married his American husband, Scott Chang, at the British Ambassador's Residence in Beijing, China. They now live with their baby son, Eliot, born to a surrogate mother in California. Having met ten years before in China, where they were both posted, their marriage created a firestorm on social media, especially since same-sex marriage is not allowed in China.[82] Davidson said the Foreign Office had been 'nothing but extremely supportive as it is of all its LGBT employees and their partners'.[83] In less than a generation, gay men have gone from being treated as criminals to being granted equal rights and full acceptance across most echelons of society and the Establishment.

Since embassies are legally considered an extension of that country, its laws apply rather than local laws. Now that same-sex marriages are legal in Britain, the UK announced in June 2014 that same-sex couples could marry at British consulates in twenty-five countries, even in countries where such arrangements are illegal. The first such marriage was between a British and Dominican man at the British Embassy in Santo Domingo, Dominican Republic where same-sex marriage is illegal.[84]

Judith Gough, British Ambassador to Ukraine, told Buzzfeed:

You get used to the double take […] But I get that for a couple of reasons. One is because often when I'm introduced to people they think I am the Ambassador's wife. So I get the double take. I've had said to me, 'Oh, but you're young and female, you can't be the Ambassador.' And then if you introduce a female partner, yes, you get another double take. But on the whole in those situations people are polite.[85]

She has received a few harsh comments from other diplomats, telling her that she should be at home looking after her children and not being an ambassador. However, one of her replies is, 'I represent the UK and we are a diverse country based on a certain set of values. I therefore reflect that country.' With regard to the Foreign Office, she said, 'I can genuinely say that within the Foreign Office I have never experienced discrimination or harassment on the grounds of sexuality.'

Since the passing of the Equality Act of 2010, the Foreign Office issues its Diversity and Equality Report each year which tracks the statistics of gender, race, sexual orientation, disability, religion, age and maternity. The report promotes women's rights, lesbian, gay, bisexual and transgender (LGBT) rights, and the rights of people with disabilities, and seeks to prevent discrimination based on religion or belief and race.[86]

One of the challenges facing the Foreign Office (and all organisations) in promoting diversity is to ensure that individuals of protected groups are not hired to meet quotas, but because they are the best person for that role. By promoting diversity, the candidate pool from which to select individuals is larger, and the organisation should be getting better candidates. The Foreign Office promotes diversity but avoids using quotas for this reason. As Dame Barbara Woodward said: 'I hope that we don't go to quotas because I think then you risk undermining the concept of merit. If I got this job because we had quotas, I would be haunted slightly by the doubt that it was unfair in some way.'[87]

She also commented on Former First Secretary to Beijing and Ambassador to Cairo, Miles Lampson, 1st Baron Killearn, who in 1933 said that the possibility of a future with a female ambassador to China would be 'unsuitable and highly inadvisable'. 'Well, if I hadn't already been Ambassador, I would have been inspired right out there to go out and do the job and prove him wrong!'[88]

And that's what so many great women have done: proved people wrong and challenged stereotypes.

In brief summary, the history of women's rise to senior leadership in the FCO has been both slow and difficult, and for many years the Foreign Office either opposed women diplomats or dragged its feet as much as possible. However, the most significant reason for the Foreign Office being so far behind the rest of the British government was the conservative nature of the office itself. Even when the first female diplomats were hired in 1946, their number remained very small, and attrition due to the marriage bar was very high.

As society changed toward greater equality for women, the Foreign Office slowly came along, appointing its first female Ambassador, Dame Barbara Salt, to Israel in 1962. Due to a medical condition she was unable to take up the position but the office continued to make progress by eliminating the marriage bar in 1973, and appointing the first female High Commissioner, Eleanor Emery, to Botswana the same year and first female Ambassador, Dame Anne Warburton, to Denmark in 1976.

It took another twenty years before the number of female heads of mission rose to more than a handful, but their number started increasing steadily from the late 1990s. The rise was gradual because the pool of female candidates at senior level from which the heads of mission are drawn was small, but increasing. Most of the appointments were to smaller and less prestigious countries, in part because the more prestigious appointments were given to their more senior male colleagues, but discrimination was also an issue for some women.

The next major milestone was the 2010 Equality Act which required government departments, including the Foreign Office, to keep statistics on gender, race and other minority groups, and to publish those statistics annually. The Foreign Office took up the challenge and worked hard to create an even playing field for women. In our society, women usually face more of the burden of children in the household than do men, and this burden is especially difficult for female diplomats who are expected to be mobile and ready to serve in whatever country they are sent to.

The Foreign Office realised that when senior women left it was both a great loss of talent and investment, and they needed to have as wide a talent pool as possible to select the best candidates, and so could not afford to lose women or minorities because of old-fashioned ideas. The Foreign Office developed plans such as extended leave without loss of seniority, on-site childcare and other programmes to help women. Programmes to support female employees, where a married couple held similar levels, job-sharing and geographically close postings might be used.

Today, while there is still progress to be made and there is not full parity in the most senior ranks, the Foreign Office has worked very hard to create a level playing field for women and minorities and strives to improve. In a relatively short space of time, the Foreign Office has changed from being the obstinate old guard that only changed its ways under great pressure, to being a very progressive organisation with respect to equality, for which it should be sincerely commended. The Foreign Office is now a leader in employment equality, and often well ahead of commercial entities. Dame Denise Holt compared the situation for women in the Foreign Office compared to the commercial world:

> In the last ten years I have mostly worked in business, in banks and other businesses and I think the Foreign Office is streets ahead of most of them in its ability to encourage part time working, job sharing, time out if you need it, without damage to the career.[89]

10

SENIOR MANAGEMENT AND MINISTERS OF THE FCO

The Foreign, Commonwealth and Development Office (FCDO) employs over 14,000 people in 229 diplomatic missions around the world. As with any organisation it requires a large management system to ensure its many functions and security are performed well. The senior leadership comprises both members of the government and civil servants. The hierarchy at the top levels of the civil service management is the SMS, in which there are three main grades: (i) Permanent Under-Secretary (ii) Directors General (iii) Directors, Heads of Departments, Ambassadors and High Commissioners.

In addition to the SMS, there are two boards that overview the operations of the FCDO and many subject-specific committees. The FCDO Supervisory Board, which is chaired by the Foreign Secretary, forms the collective strategic leadership of the FCDO, bringing together ministers, officials, and senior non-executives from outside government. The second board is the FCDO Management Board, chaired by the Permanent Under-Secretary (PUS) which provides corporate leadership to the organisation by delivering the policies and services decided by the ministers. The current structure of the Civil Service SMS, including the FCDO, is shown below:[1]

Position	Senior Civil Service pay band	Unified grading structure (1971)	Old titles of positions
Cabinet Secretary	4	1A	Cabinet Secretary
Permanent Under-Secretary		1	Permanent Under-Secretary
Director General	3	2	Deputy (Under-) Secretary
Director	2	3	Assistant Under-Secretary
Director or Deputy Director	1	4 or 5	Assistant or Under-Secretary, Superintendent

The PUS is the most senior civil servant in the FCDO and Head of the Diplomatic Service. The current FCDO PUS is Sir Philip Barton KCMG OBE, who has been in the role since August 2020. To date, no women have been appointed as PUS.

Heads of Department report to Directors, who report to Directors-General, who report up to the PUS. Dame Marion Leslie described the FCO in 2008 when she became Director General of Defence and Security:

By that stage there were only three Directors-General dealing with foreign policy work. There was also one dealing with administration, personnel and so on, and a Finance Director-General. Of the three dealing with policy there was me doing the defence and security side of things; the D-G Political as we called it, dealing mostly with the UN, with the conflict in Afghanistan, with the big European political issues; and then there was the D-G Economic, the person for the rest of the world and 'global issues', dealing with trade, economics, third world, development, plus a whole range of regional issues.

The three of us divided the world [geographically] between us, in a sort of post-Napoleonic war way of dividing up the Christmas pudding. I had all of the Americas, the Caribbean, the Overseas Territories. I was, absurd though it seems, the line manager of our Ambassador in Washington. I held the budget of all our Embassies in the Americas. I chaired the Cross Government Committee on the Falkland Islands, kept a watching brief to see that it remained safe. I dealt with the Caribbean independent states, but also the Overseas Territories – so we were always having to make sure the MOD didn't withdraw its frigates in the hurricane season. So I was dealing with all of that, plus the personnel and budgets and ambassadors which went with Embassy management and discipline. Those [latter] subjects, though, were mostly delegated to my good Directors.[2]

The first woman to reach the level of Director-General was Pauline Neville-Jones, now Baroness Neville-Jones. She joined the Foreign Office in 1963 and served in British missions in Rhodesia, Singapore, Washington DC and Bonn. In 1977 and 1982 she was appointed Deputy and then Chef de Cabinet to Commissioner Christopher Tugendhat of the European Commission. She was appointed CMG in 1987.[3]

In 1991 Neville-Jones became Head of the Defence and Overseas Secretariat in the Cabinet Office and Deputy Secretary to the Cabinet and in 1993 and 1994 she was appointed Chairman of the Joint Intelligence Committee. She became Deputy Under-Secretary of State and Political Director in 1994, becoming the second-highest civil servant in the FCO after the PUS. The following year, in recognition of her service to the country and her great professional accomplishments, she was appointed DCMG.[4]

Neville-Jones was interested in taking an ambassadorship position and believed that someone of her position should have been offered a Grade 1 ambassadorial post, i.e. Paris, Bonn, Washington or Moscow, and Grade 1 on the promotion scale. The Paris ambassadorship was open, but it was given to a man six years her junior and instead she was offered Bonn, leaving her at Grade 2.

Neville Jones was outraged, believing that she was a victim of overt gender discrimination and so she resigned, accusing the FCO of sexism in a very public manner.[5] The *Independent* reported:

> The angry fumes can be seen rising from her Chelsea house, where she has been sulking in her tent since December, quite understandably. For her head has just crashed against the glass ceiling and the sound of the collision is reverberating around the vaulted corridors and marbled stairwells of the Foreign Office.

Official portrait of Baroness Neville-Jones by Chris McAndrew, March 2018. (Creative Commons)

She is speaking to no one. The news of her imminent departure from the second-highest post in the Foreign Office emerged from hostile leaking at the very top. Her friends are gleeful that it has rebounded sharply upon the head of Sir John Coles, the Permanent Under-Secretary, who, they say, has done her down. He does not like the public accusation of sexism at the top of the Foreign Office, and the Prime Minister is not pleased.[6]

Her high-profile departure made the newspaper headlines providing fuel to the women's rights issues and the FCO's poor record on employment for women. After leaving the FCO in 1996, Neville-Jones went to serve on the BBC Board of Governors, before being elevated to the House of Lords. She has since served as the Minister of State for Security and Counter-Terrorism, and is a Member of the Privy Council.[7]

In October 2018 there were thirty-one directors covering the major areas of responsibility with the FCO, of whom only eleven (35 per cent) were female.[8] The number of women in senior management positions has increased steadily over time, as shown in the graph below. Directors and ambassadors are at a similar level and often people move between these roles:

The number of women at director level and above at the FCO over time.

The number of women rising to senior leadership roles has increased steadily over the last twenty years and the trend of the graph suggests that the percentage of women in these roles will continue to increase with time.

It is the role of civil servants to take instructions from, and to answer to, representatives of the elected government. The appointment of the Foreign Secretary and Ministers are made by the Prime Minister and Ministers are drawn from Members of the majority party/parties in the House of Commons or the House of Lords and therefore change with each government.

There are three levels of government minister in the British system. The highest level is a Secretary of State (e.g. the Foreign Secretary), the intermediate level is a Minister of State, and the most junior level is the Parliamentary Under-Secretary of State (also called a Parliamentary Secretary). The Foreign Secretary is a Member of the Cabinet, whereas the other levels are usually not. In the entire British government, there are twenty-two Cabinet Members (Secretaries of State from all Departments and some other Ministers) in addition to the Prime Minister. There are a larger number of more Junior Non-Cabinet Ministers. The current Foreign Secretary, at the time of writing, is the Right Honourable Dominic Raab, First Secretary of State and Secretary of State for Foreign, Commonwealth and Development Affairs since July 2019 following a reshuffle in Prime Minister Boris Johnston's Cabinet.[9]

Eirene Lloyd White served as Parliamentary Secretary of State for the Colonies from 1964 to 1966, and so has a claim as the first female Parliamentary Secretary in the FCO, since the Colonial Office was one of the predecessor organisations to today's FCDO.[10] White was born in Belfast in 1909, into a political family:

her father was Dr Tom Jones, Deputy Cabinet Secretary to four Prime Ministers (Lloyd George, Bonar Law, Ramsay MacDonald and Stanley Baldwin). Following her graduation from Somerville College, Oxford, where she read PPE, White studied housing conditions and the provision of public libraries in the US, during which time she met the singer and civil rights activist Paul Robeson. One evening they were barred from entering a restaurant together due to the racial segregation laws, and this experience cemented a vocal, lifelong opposition to racial discrimination.

During the Second World War White served in the Ministry of Labour to train women for the war, but afterwards she took a different career path and became the first accredited female

Eirene White, Labour Minister of State at the Foreign Office, pictured in her office at the Ministry, 1 April 1966. (Alamy)

political correspondent with the *Manchester Evening News*. She unsuccessfully ran for Parliament as Labour MP for Flintshire, but at the next election five years later she was successful in winning the seat of East Flint, which she held for twenty years. She married fellow journalist John Cameron White in 1948.

Following White's appointment as Parliamentary Secretary she became the Minister of State at the Welsh Office. White then served as the Foreign Affairs Minister from 1966 to 1967 at the Colonial Office, becoming the first women to hold this senior position.[11] In 1966, the Commonwealth Relations Office merged with the Colonial Office to form the Commonwealth Office, and merged again with the Foreign Office to form the FCO in 1969. She also served on Labour's National Executive Committee and was chairman of the Labour party 1968–69. She worked hard to promote women's rights including equal pay, nursery provision, divorce reform and further education, and successfully strove to end the punitive earnings rules for widows, which reduced or eliminated their meagre pensions.

On retirement from the Commons in 1970 White was elevated to the House of Lords as Baroness White of Rhymney, and soon after became Chair of the Select Committee on the European Communities and served as Deputy Speaker from 1979 to 1989.[12]

In the Foreign Office, the first female Minister of State was Priscilla Jean Fortescue Buchan, Baroness Tweedsmuir of Belhelvie (1915–78).[13] Born in 1915 in Kensington, the younger daughter of Brigadier Alan F. Thomson DSO and Edythe Unwin,[14] she married her first husband, Major Sir Arthur Lindsay Grant, 11th Baronet, of the Grenadier Guards in 1934 and they had two daughters.[15] While Sir Arthur was on active duty during the Second World War, Priscilla, now Lady Grant, worked in welfare helping the women in the munitions factories. Sadly, Sir Arthur was killed in action in 1944.

A year later, with the war over and finding herself a young widow, the Dowager Lady Grant ran for Parliament and was elected as the Conservative MP for the seat of Aberdeen South in 1946, which she held for twenty years. Aged just 31, she was the youngest woman in the House of Commons at that time. As a new MP, she met John Buchan, the 2nd Baron Tweedsmuir, who helped her find her feet and whom she married in 1948, producing a daughter a year later.

In the House of Commons, Buchan sponsored a Private Members' Bill that became the Protection of Birds Act of 1954. Lord Tweedsmuir introduced the bill into the House of Lords, the second time ever that a husband and wife had steered a bill through both houses. This bill became a model for later environmental bills.[16]

On one occasion, when asked about being a female MP, she said, 'It wasn't always easy even with his [Lord Tweedsmuir's] help. I think a woman has to work a little harder than a man to get anywhere.'[17]

Buchan was appointed to her first ministerial position, Joint Parliamentary Under-Secretary of State for Scotland, in 1962, but lost her seat in the General Election of 1966. She then joined the Cunard company as a Director, the first woman to be appointed to the shipping line's board. She was very active in that role; for example, she advised Cunard on the 'practical outlook of the passenger areas' for the newly designed *QE2* liner.[18]

On 1 July 1970 Buchan was created a life peer in her own right as Baroness Tweedsmuir of Belhelvie, of Potterton in the County of Aberdeen and returned to politics sitting in the House of Lords for the first time on the same day.[19] She was quickly appointed Minister of State at the Scottish Office by Prime Minister Edward Heath in 1970. Heath then appointed her to the FCO from 1972 to 1974, as Minister of State in the Foreign Office, the first woman to hold this position.[20]

She responded to many of the events of the day, such as introducing a bill for the independence of the Bahamas, and she visited many countries including West Africa and Zambia, and was a member of the British delegation to the United Nations General Assembly.[21] One of her roles was to lead the negotiating team during the so-called Cod Wars, a heated dispute over the rights of British fishermen to access the Icelandic fishing grounds. The sea around Iceland had been rich fishing grounds on which the British fishing fleet had long depended. When Iceland made a series of unilateral declarations to increase its exclusive fishing area, there were tense trade disputes, backed up by warships on both sides. Buchan worked to keep calm, balancing British rights while not appearing to take advantage of a much smaller country, or appearing weak. This was the first time a 'war' had been run by a woman in Britain. Mary Kenny of the *Evening Standard* wrote, 'The Government can be completely confident of Lady Tweedsmuir. She is a sort of gentler version of Barbara Castle: very charming and able. Dead Post and tough.'[22] The *Daily Mail* wrote, 'Lady Tweedsmuire, our tough and very feminine negotiator over the Icelandic Cod War is […] quite the mistress of her own kitchen.'[23]

Eventually the Icelandic government ended diplomatic relations with the UK on 19 February 1976. There were several iterations of the conflict and Iceland prevailed each time it extended its exclusive fishing area. Britain eventually conceded to a 200-nautical-mile (370-km) Icelandic exclusive fishery zone following threats that Iceland would withdraw from NATO, but the closure of the Icelandic waters effectively ended British long-distance fishing.

During this time Buchan was sworn on to the Privy Council in 1974 and in the House of Lords she also served as Principal Deputy Chairman of Committees, 1974–77, and simultaneously as Chairman of the Select Committee on European Communities.[24]

In 1974 she became the first female Deputy Speaker in the House of Lords. She died of cancer in 1978, aged 63, which her family attributed to her chemical exposure in the wartime munitions factories.

Lord Home of the Hirsel paid tribute to Buchan following her death:

> Then she came to the Foreign Office as Minister of State and, whenever we were faced with a real difficulty in any part of the world, I used to ask, 'Where is Lady Tweedsmuir?'. Whether it was in Europe, Africa, or at the United Nations, she was about the best ambassador that this country could have sent and she always returned having held the respect of those with whom she went to deal.[25]

The second female Minister of State at the FCO was Joan Lestor, later Baroness Lestor of Eccles, who served as the Under-Secretary of State for Foreign and Commonwealth Affairs for just over a year.[26]

Barbara Castle, later Baroness Castle of Blackburn, should also get a brief mention since she served as Minster for Overseas Development from 1964 to 1965.[27] The Ministry for Overseas Development has had an on/off relationship with the Foreign Office, sometimes standing as a Ministry in its own right and at othertimes being incorporated as part of the Foreign Office. Barbara Castle was born Barbara Betts in Chesterfield and went on to study at Oxford. During the Second World War she served as the housing correspondent for the *Daily Mirror*, where she met and married fellow journalist Ted Castle. Barbara Castle was elected MP for Blackburn in 1945 and nineteen years later was appointed head of the Overseas Development Ministry (ODM) by Prime Minister Harold Wilson, becoming the only female member of the cabinet and fourth woman ever. Castle always maintained her femininity, saying once, 'I have never consciously exploited the fact that

I am a woman. I wouldn't dare try that even if I knew how to. I have too much respect for my male colleagues to think they would be particularly impressed.' (*Labour Orators from Bevan to Miliband*, Manchester University Press, 2015.)

Castle raised the profile of the ODM and introduced interest-free loans for the poorest countries. In 1965 she was appointed Minister of Transportation, the first woman in that position. One of her first tasks was getting a women's restroom installed, since there had not been the need for one previously.

In 1968 she was appointed Secretary of State for Health and Social Security and Secretary of State for Employment and Productivity. In June that year, female upholsterers at a Ford plant went on strike. Castle invited them and Ford's management for tea in her office. The dispute was settled when the women received a pay rise from 85 per cent to 92 per cent depending on the Ford plant, to achieve parity with their male counterparts. Her major accomplishment was pushing for equal pay for women that resulted in the 1970 Equal Pay Act.

Labour lost the election in 1970 but regained power in 1974, and Castle became Secretary of State for Social Services. She introduced a child benefit payable to all mothers with children at home, and a minimum pension to protect the elderly who did not have a pension from their employer. Women retired five years before men, and had previously received lower payments, Castle made women's contributions and payments the same as men, even though the earlier retirement favoured women. She later explained, 'I knew this was discrimination in their favour, but I argued that men had been discriminating against women for centuries and it would not do them any harm to wait until we could afford to bring down the retirement age to sixty for them as well.' (*Stories of Women in the 1960s: Fighting for Freedom*, Capstone, 2015.)

In 1976 she was removed from this position by incoming Prime Minister James Callaghan, on the basis that she was too old (she was two years older than him). She was asked if she would have liked to have been Prime Minister. She said, 'People sometimes ask me if I would have liked to become Prime Minister. The answer is yes [… but] in my day the Labour Party was not ready for a woman leader.'

In 1979, Margaret Thatcher became Leader of the Conservative Party and Prime Minister. Castle went on to serve in the European Parliament and later in the House of Lords. One of Castle's main achievements, early on in her career, was to raise the expectation of what a woman could do in politics.

Judith Hart, later Baroness Hart of South Lanark, was born Constance Mary Ridehalgh in 1924, but adopted the name Judith at age 12 when she went to Clitheroe Royal Grammar School, and later the London School of Economics and the University of London. At age 26, she married Anthony Bernard Hart. She was MP for Lanark from 1959 until 1983 and for Clydesdale until 1987.

She was appointed by Harold Wilson as the Minister of State at the Commonwealth Office from 1967 to 1968, the first woman to hold that position, whereupon she was almost immediately thrown into the Rhodesia problem. Kenneth Kaunda, the Zambian President, believed that Britain supported Ian Smith's government, and even called for Britain to be expelled from the Commonwealth. Hart visited Kaunda on her arrival, to try to get negotiations going again.[28] In 1969 she was appointed Minister for Overseas Development, serving until 1970, and again in 1974–75 and 1977–79.[29] She was made a Dame in 1979 and a life peer, entering the House of Lords in 1988.[30]

The determination of the first female ministers with the FCO and related offices is complicated. The timeline of female ministers and the various ministries and offices is shown overleaf.[31]

Year	Colonial Office	Commonwealth Relations Office and Commonwelth Office	Ministry of Overseas Development	FO and FCO
1964	Eirene White, Under-Secretary, Colonial Office 1964–66		Barbara Castle, Minister for Overseas Development 1964–65 [New Ministry]	
1966	Eirene White, Minister of State for Foreign Affairs 1966–67 [Merged with CRO]	Judith Hart, Minister of State, 1966–67		
1969	[Merged with FO]		Judith Hart, Minister for Overseas Development 1969–70 [Merged with FCO]	
1972				Rt. Hon. Lady Tweedsmuir, Minister of State, 1972–74
1974			Judith Hart, Minister for Overseas Development 1974–75 [New Ministry]	Joan Lestor, Under-Secretary, 1974–75

Official Portrait of Margaret Beckett by Chris McAndrew. (parliament.uk, distributed under Creative Commons 'Attribution 3.0 Unported' licence)

Dame Margaret Beckett, Britain's first female Foreign Secretary, started life as Margaret Mary Jackson in 1943 in Lancashire.[32] Her father, Cyril, was a carpenter and her mother, Winifred, was a teacher. Unfortunately Cyril became disabled due to an injury when Becket was only 3 and then he died when she was just 12 years old, leaving her mother to become the sole breadwinner for the family.[33] These experiences and her parents' views about the role of women had a major impact on Beckett's outlook on life. She later said:

> In our household, it was taken for granted that a woman might have to work and support her family and you weren't just there

to just sort of run the house and look after the kids kind of thing. My father was also immensely supportive, he absolutely made it clear, this is what women should do, women should have independence, women should have their own career, women should do what they want to in life. That was innate.[34]

Beckett was educated at the Notre Dame High School for Girls in Norwich,[35] then she obtained a degree in metallurgy from the University of Manchester Institute of Science and Technology. She started to take her first steps into politics while at college, in part at least because an old boyfriend was Chair of the Labour Club.[36] Though raised a Catholic, Beckett has consistently made a point of never discussing her personal beliefs in public.[37]

She started work for Associated Electrical Industries as a student apprentice and three years later she joined the Transport and General Workers' Union. As the Experiment Officer she oversaw the Scanning Electron Microscopy (SEM) laboratory in the Metallurgy Department of the University of Manchester,[38] but four years later she found that politics was more interesting and so she joined the Labour Party as a researcher in industrial policy. She recently reflected from this period that:

> I well recall being fulsomely praised for some work I had done, but stunned by the punchline, 'you ought to marry some nice young Labour MP. You'd be such a help to his career' – and the astonishment when I politely indicated that I might like the career for myself.[39]

Four years later, in the October 1974 general election, Beckett was elected as the MP for Lincoln, part of the narrow swing towards Harold Wilson's Labour Party with a majority of only three seats. The following year she became a Government Whip and in 1976 she was appointed the Under-Secretary of the Department of Education and Science.

Beckett married Lionel (Leo) Beckett, an ex-fitter, who was Chairman of her local constituency, in 1979. He continues to serve as her Election Agent and support, travelling with her and working in her office. She relies greatly on Leo, and has commented, 'Most of my female colleagues, and some male ones, say they wished they had a Leo.'[40]

She lost her seat at the general election in 1979 but returned to the House of Commons as the MP for Derby South in 1983, joining Neil Kinnock's Shadow Cabinet for several years. When Kinnock resigned, following the loss at the 1992 election, John Smith was elected Leader and Beckett was elected Deputy Leader, the first woman to hold that position. She was appointed to the Privy Council the following year. In May 1994, Smith died unexpectedly of a heart attack and Beckett became Acting Leader of the Labour Party, another first for a woman.

Though she stood in the contest for the leadership of the party, she lost to Tony Blair, who went on to lead the party to a strong win in the 1997 general election. Beckett was then appointed President of the Board of Trade, a position which later became Secretary of State for Trade and Industry,[41] another first for a woman, and a position Beckett held until July 1998. During this time she was involved in the UK's opposition to the proposed merger between British Airways and American Airlines, and the merger of brewers Bass and Carlsberg.[42]

One anecdote from the time was that there was some panic after she had been negotiating with the US about companies trying to get into the British gas market, after the *Guardian* obtained documents from these meetings under the Freedom of Information Act. The *Guardian* reported, 'It was not the official words that worried her, but the fact that some of the documents could have contained her doodles of the US characters she was meeting, plus her acerbic comments about them.'[43] Luckily for her the US kept them to themselves, avoiding a major diplomatic incident. According to her husband her doodling is quite extensive, including at cabinet meetings.

In 1998 she became Leader of the House of Commons and in 2001 Blair appointed her Secretary of State for the Environment, Food and Rural Affairs, where among other things she was the UK's negotiator for the Kyoto Protocol for reducing global warming. She described the protocol as follows, 'This is the first multinational environmental agreement with teeth. It's a historic step forward and it will make an enormous difference in reducing greenhouse emissions.'[44]

In 2006, Beckett was asked to become Foreign Secretary, the first woman to hold that position and only the second woman after Margaret Thatcher to hold one of the four great Offices of State (Prime Minister, Home Secretary, Foreign Secretary and Chancellor of the Exchequer). Beckett has always had a reputation for using colourful language, but she admitted that she was surprised to be offered the position. Her first response to the Prime Minister was 'F★★k, I'm stunned'.[45] She later accepted, 'I did, for an instant, resort to less than diplomatic words out of sheer surprise [...] it was not a move I was expecting.'[46]

She recounted in an interview with Nicola Hughes that soon after she was offered the position of Foreign Secretary, a woman from the Foreign Office confided in her that, 'You do realise that there are people in the Foreign Office who don't think a woman should be Foreign Secretary?'[47] Needless to say, given that nearly two decades had elapsed since Margaret Thatcher was elected the first female Prime Minister, she was a little taken aback:

When I was told that some of them in the Foreign Office didn't think there ought to be a woman in the job, I thought to myself, I know exactly what sort of person they think should be Foreign

Secretary. It should be somebody who went to the right school, who went to the right university, who is regarded as an intellectual and has wide knowledge of the world. And that's what they've got.[48]

The major foreign policy issues that she faced were the ongoing Iraq war, Iran's active nuclear programme and the conflict between Israel and Hezbollah in Lebanon. Another issue was the decision by the Blair government to upgrade the Trident nuclear missile system, and while her politics have shifted over time from the left wing to more centre, it was probably a difficult decision for a former member of the CND to support. When asked if she would ever use nuclear weapons, she responded, 'You never answer that question […] Nor would I ever rule out [using it].'[49]

It is possible that her support for modernisation of the Trident system was a reflection of her loyalty and adherence to the policy that all ministers must publicly support cabinet decisions (collective ministerial responsibility)[50] resigning being the only honourable alternative. After Tony Blair left office, Beckett gave a policy speech in Washington DC that advocated for nuclear disarmament, presumably with the blessing of Blair's successor Gordon Brown.[51] The *Wall Street Journal* reported that she said:

What we need is both a vision – a scenario for a world free of nuclear weapons – and action – progressive steps to reduce warhead numbers and to limit the role of nuclear weapons in security policy. These two strands are separate, but they are mutually reinforcing. Both are necessary, but at the moment too weak.[52]

Beckett was also asked whether foreign policy would have different priorities if conducted exclusively by women. She responded, 'Sadly, we will probably never know but my guess is a woman's way of doing business would be different even if the priorities remained unchanged.'[53] She was asked whether she had an unfairly negative press, just because she was a female Foreign Secretary. Beckett responded, 'It is hard to judge but few of my male predecessors have had any interest taken in their wardrobe.'[54]

Prior to 2006, departing or especially retiring ambassadors would often write confidential valedictory dispatches about the country and institution they were leaving, often drafting exquisitely penned descriptions, warts and all. After one such dispatch was leaked to the *Sunday Times*, resulting in great embarrassment to the FCO, Beckett stopped the practice. Even without the leak, the presumption of publication of government documents except where there was a need for them to be kept secret, helped nail shut the coffin on valedictory dispatches.[55]

Blair resigned as Prime Minister on 27 June 2007, and the following day Gordon Brown replaced Beckett with David Miliband as Foreign Secretary. Brown brought Beckett back into government with an appointment as Minister for Housing and Planning, which she held until 2009. The general election the following year saw Labour lose its majority in the House of Commons, though Beckett kept her seat. Since then the Conservative Party has governed and Beckett has been part of the opposition. With only a brief interruption, she has been an elected MP for forty years, the longest-serving woman in the House of Commons.[56] Once when asked if being a woman was a handicap in her leadership bids, she responded, 'Well, let's say it didn't help. Particularly being a woman called Margaret, that really didn't help!'[57]

Beckett also commented about the issues that female MPs were expected to embrace:

In a sense. I mean, it was a conscious decision [not to play the 'women's card'] in the sense that it always seemed to me that the whole point about feminism was that people should be able to do the things that they wanted to do, that they felt were right for them, that they were interested in, not the things that other people thought they [should do].

I mean, especially early on when I was elected, you were always getting letters from people saying, 'You know, as a woman, I care passionately about this and therefore I think you should make this your top priority because as a woman, you should care about this'.

Now of course, we all care about all kinds of things, the health service and social care and all those things but I was actually very interested in Treasury stuff, trade and industry, that kind, manufacturing.

Those are the things that I was passionately interested in and my view was the whole point about this is that if that's what I'm interested in, that's what I should be able to do.

I shouldn't have to specialise in women's issues because I'm a woman. And I didn't.

Former Labour MP Gillian Merron commented on the same topic:

Margaret appears to effortlessly lead by example, continually demonstrating that women don't have to be confined to particular roles. When she was first elected in the 1970s, there was an assumption that women did 'women's things' like health and education. Margaret has shown in deed and word, and by being supportive, that women don't have to do what is expected of them. For her, this is what feminism is about – that we can each do what it is that we seek to do.[58]

Beckett was once asked in a radio interview whether she would describe herself as a feminist. Typically and modestly, she replied, 'I hope others would describe me as one.'

In the 2013 Queen's New Year's Honours, Beckett was made a DBE for political and public service.[59] Reflecting on the role of women in Parliament, Beckett recently said, 'Many of the ground-breaking economic and social changes that we risk taking for granted would not have occurred without the input of more women in Parliament, and we still have a long way to go before we achieve real diversity.'[60]

On the subject of party leadership and gender, Beckett has consistently declared that the best candidate should be elected, regardless of sex.[61] However, at other times she has suggested that some affirmative action to increase the number of women MPs might be appropriate.[62] Nowadays Beckett continues to inspire younger women to stand, and Angela Rayner, then Shadow Secretary of State for Women and Equalities, said at the Labour Women's Conference in 2016:

One inspiration is our very own Dame Margaret Beckett MP, who was born in Ashton and cut her Labour teeth in the local CLP. God knows what it was like in those days, Margaret.

But since then, Margaret has become our first ever female Deputy Leader and the longest serving female MP in the House of Commons.

It is to women like Margaret that we owe a huge debt. For blazing the trail, for showing the way, for inspiring all of us women who follow, to reach ever higher.

That's why I am proud to announce that Margaret's hometown of Ashton will be celebrating all of her achievements with the launch of our Dame Margaret Beckett Prize for Public Speaking for teenage girls.

Encouraging our young women, giving them confidence, spurring on our young women to become involved in politics and the life of our communities.

Inspiring us on – something Margaret has spent her whole life doing.[63]

The *Guardian* had the following to say about Beckett:

Mrs Beckett is neither flashy nor attention-seeking. She makes no effort to cultivate the press, to erect a faction around herself, or to make greater claims for her achievements than they merit. She simply does the job well. No government would survive without such ministers.[64]

At the time of writing, Beckett is the longest serving female MP of all time.[65] In 2017 the University of Derby conferred an honorary doctorate on her in recognition of her commitment and achievements in public service, both regionally and in the national political arena.[66]

The female ministers who served in the Foreign Office up to 2010 are summarised below:[67]

Name	Year	Position	Government
Eirene White	1964–66	PIUS (CO)	Labour
	1966–67	MOS (FO)	
Baroness Tweedsmuir of Belhelvie	1972–74	MOS	Conservative
Joan Lestor	1974–75	USOS	Labour
Baroness Young	1983–87	MOS	Conservative
Lynda Chalker	1986–97	MOS	Conservative
Joyce Quin	1998–99	MOS	Labour
Baroness Symons of Vernham Dean	1997–99	PIUS	Labour
	2001–03	MOS	
	2003–05	MOS	
Baroness Scotland of Asthal	1999–2001	PIUS	Labour
Baroness Amos	2001–03	PIUS	Labour

Name	Year	Position	Government
Margaret Beckett	2006–07	SOS	Labour
Meg Munn	2007–08	PIUS	Labour
Baroness Glenys Kinnock	2009–10	MOS	Labour

Notes:
SOS = Secretary of State for Foreign and Commonwealth Affairs; USOS = Under-Secretary of State; MOS = Minister of State; PIUS = Parliamentary Under-Secretary; CO = Colonial Office; FO = Foreign Office.

Except where stated otherwise, position is in the FCO.

11

BEYOND
THE FOREIGN OFFICE

This book has focused on Britain's Foreign Office, but there have been dramatic improvements in equality across the globe. These developments might well be seen as one of the defining positive attributes of the twentieth and twenty-first centuries. Almost every country has made progress towards allowing female diplomats, even Saudi Arabia, which despite strict guardianship laws for women appointed a female Ambassador, Princess Reema bint Bandar bin Sultan al-Saud, to the US for the first time in February 2019.[1] The country and date for the first female ambassador for a select number of countries are summarised below:[2]

Country	Name	Date	Host country
Argentina	Angela C. Romera Vara	~1962	Panama
Australia	Dame Anabelle Rankin	1971–75	New Zealand
Austria	Johanna Mondschein	1959	Norway
Belgium	Edmonde Dever	1973–78	Sweden

Country	Name	Date	Host country
Brazil	Ivete Vargas	1951	Special ambassador on mission to Lebanon
Canada	Margaret Blanche Meagher	1958–61	Israel
China	Deng Xuesong	1979–81	Netherlands
Denmark	Bodil Begtrup	1955	Ambassador to Iceland
Egypt	Aisha Rateb	1979–81	Denmark
Finland	Tynne Leivo-Larson	1958–66	Norway
France	Marcelle Capara	1972–74	Panama
Iceland	Sigridur Aids Snaeuvarr	1991–96	Sweden and Finland
India	Vijaya Pandit	1948–49	USSR
Ireland	Josephine McNeill	1950–55	Netherlands
Israel	Golda Meir	1948–49	USSR
Mexico	Palma Guillen	1941	Columbia
New Zeeland	Cynthia Mackensie	1949	France
United Kingdom	Dame Barbara Salt	1962	Israel (unable to take position)
	Eleanor Emery	1973–76	Botswana
USSR	Aleksandra Kollontai	1923–24	Norway
USA	Ruth Bryan Rhodes	1933–36	Denmark
Venezuela	Ida Gramcko	1948	USSR

Towns and Niklasson published[3] a study in 2016 of 7,000 ambassador postings around the world and found that only 15 per cent of the world's ambassadors were women; of these, women were less likely to be posted to the most prestigious postings. They attribute these differences both to institutional norms and the fact that the combination of life as a foreign service officer and a marriage (especially with children) continues to be particularly problematic for women. They also found that the distribution of female ambassadors also varies around the world with the highest in the Nordic countries, followed by the other Western industrialised countries, and the lowest in the Middle East:

North America	25%
South America	18%
Nordic Countries	35%
Europe inc. Russia	14%
Middle East	6%
Africa	17%
Asia	10%
Oceania	25%

For comparison in 2017–18, 33.2 per cent of the Senior Management Structure (SMS) of the FCO and 54 out of 134 heads of mission were women (40 per cent).[4] Recent fast-stream recruits were 59 per cent women[5] and so the fraction of women rising up through the diplomatic ranks is higher than at the top levels, and so greater equality is expected in future years.

While the number of female diplomats has increased, men retain the majority in most countries, except for Finland where more than half of the professionals in the Ministry for Foreign Affairs (MFA) are women. About half of the leadership positions in the MFA as well as ambassadorial posts of Finland are held by women.[6]

One of the most famous female diplomats, Madeleine Albright, who served as US Secretary of State during President Clinton's administration described female diplomats as follows:

Women are particularly good at diplomacy. It does require the human touch [...] women are much better at having peripheral vision and also multitasking and having the capability of telling it like it is. Many of the best diplomats are women, although there are men who can do it.[7]

It is fair to say that Albright served to create a much wider path for future female diplomats and she in turn was followed by two more very capable women: Condoleezza Rice and Hillary Clinton. The presence of high-profile women does set the expectation for the younger generation, as Albright illustrates with another story: 'A few years ago, not long after Hillary Clinton succeeded Condoleezza Rice as Secretary of State, one of my granddaughters asked: "So what's the big deal about Grandma Maddy being Secretary of State? I thought only girls are Secretary of State".'[8]

One of the lessons from history is that personal and societal expectations go a long way to determine what should and can be done by its members. In the UK, one of the major groups opposed to women's suffrage was the Women's National Anti-Suffrage League, whose members believed that it was not a woman's role to be involved in national elections or politics. Their expectations were that women's role in society should be focused on running the home, raising children and supporting the husband. A generation later, not having women's suffrage in the UK would be unthinkable. Society's expectations as far as suffrage have been re-written. Ray (Rachel) Strachey wrote in her book:

Surveying the whole female populations, however, and comparing it with that over which Queen Victoria began to reign, it is easy to see that there has been progress in every direction. Something, no doubt, has been destroyed, something innocent and restful and pure; but ignorance, ill-health, and the dangerous spirit of dependence have been banished with it, and in their place there is education and self reliance. No woman of today would go back if she could to the conditions which her grandmother endured. No girl would submit to the clothing and the restraints of 1837; no wife would be content to merge her whole legal and financial existence in that of her husband; no matron would agree to put on her cap and retire from life at thirty-five. And even if women would do these things, men would not approve! For as the Women's Movement has gone along its course, men too, have been influenced thereby. They have found better comfort and joy in companions who have shared their world, and neither sex would now, even if it could, turn back the hands of the clock.[9]

Today women have achieved legal parity with men in almost every field, but there is still discrimination in the workplace. Women are significantly under-represented in positions of leadership, as is illustrated by the following statistics:

- As of January 2019, of the 195 countries in the world, 59 (30 per cent) of them have had a female leader in recent history (since the end of the Second World War).[10]
- As of June 2019, eleven women are serving as elected heads of state and twelve are serving as head of government.[11]
- Of the eight largest economies, France, Germany, Italy, the United Kingdom, Japan, the United States, Canada, and Russia, only three – the United Kingdom (Margaret Thatcher, 1979; Theresa May, 2016), France (Édith Cresson, 1991) and Germany (Angela Merkel, 2005) – have ever had women leaders (38 per cent).

Similar patterns may be seen in legislative leadership roles:

- In 2015 there were 191 women MPs out of 650 in the House of Commons (29 per cent), despite 51 per cent of the voting population being female.[12]

- In 2018, 106 women held seats in the United States Congress, comprising 19.8 per cent of the 535 members; twenty-three women (23 per cent) served in the United States Senate, and eighty-three women (19.1 per cent) served in the United States House of Representatives.[13]
- Globally, only 24.3 per cent of all national Parliamentarians were women as of February 2019, a slow increase from 11.3 per cent in 1995.[14]

In large companies, a similar proportion of board members are women:

- In 2017 in the UK 23 per cent of board positions were occupied by women and only 3 per cent of the chief executives of Europe's 600 largest companies were women.[15]
- In 2017 in the US, women held about 20 per cent of all board seats for companies in the S&P 500 stock index and among all publicly traded companies.[16]

It is not a matter of education or skills. In the UK there are more women enrolled in higher education than men (55 per cent in 2011), similar to their US counterparts (54 per cent in 2014)[17] but the sexes each have their preferred courses. Women dominate veterinary science and subjects allied to medicine and education, whereas men outnumber women in science and engineering and technology courses.[18]

Men and women seem to select their favourite subjects even before university. In the US, more girls take Advanced Placement (university-level courses taught in high school) than boys, but boys outnumber girls 4:1 in computer science exams,[19] and in 2015 women only received 18 per cent of degrees in computer science,[20] 19.3 per cent in engineering, 39 per cent in physical sciences and

43.1 per cent in mathematics, although they receive more than half the bachelor degrees awarded in the biological sciences.[21] Medicine is not obviously a male- or female-specific subject and medical schools were more balanced with roughly equal numbers of women (49.8 per cent) and men (50.2 per cent) entering in 2016 in the US and 56.4 per cent women in the UK (2016).[22]

There is nothing innately different in the ability of men and women to do, for example, computer coding or to teach, but self-selection largely boils down to expectations, including one's own self-expections and self-determination. Sheryl Sandberg wrote an excellent book describing these subconscious expectations and biases and their impact on women's equality today.[23] She cited a 2012 McKinsey study that surveyed more than 4,000 employees in major companies. The survey found that 36 per cent of men aspired to reach the C-suite (executive management level), whereas only 18 per cent of their female counterparts did.[24] Similarly, both men and women also found that women who failed to fit the stereotypes of being caregivers, sensitive and communal were more likely to be rated as selfish and 'not the type of person you would want to hire'. Personal and society expectations can make a big difference in how far women are able to progress in their careers, and there are sometimes personal costs in progressing far in the workplace.

Being the 'first' person to achieve a goal is always challenging to status quo, not only for that person out front, but for all the other interested parties as well. The role of the first achiever is to change perceptions by taking ownership of that role, to realise their own exceptional expectations of themselves, and to leave behind success and confidence in their wake. This is why the first person is so admired, celebrated and usually remembered.

It is naturally the same in diplomatic circles where personalities, policies and politics are all factors in the determination of individuals. The first female high commissioner or ambassador made headlines around the world because she exceeded societal expectations. Later, society accepted the notion of female heads of mission, the novelty expired and the next female ambassador appointed was only a minor story. It is a great challenge to be the first person to raise the bar, as each of the exceptional women described in this book have done for their gender. They individually excelled in their own careers and by doing so, successfully cleared the pathway for their successors. As Joseph Campbell said, 'If the path before you is clear, you're probably on someone else's.'[25]

While many of the women in this book may not have set out to be the 'first', they were probably aware of the longer-term consequences should they fail, than if a male colleague were to fail. As the first female US Supreme Court Justice, Sandra Day O'Connor, said, 'It's wonderful to be the first to do something, but I didn't want to be the last. And, if I did not do the job well, there might be no second woman on the court.'[26]

It is a testament to their strength and perseverance that these women achieved all that they did.

NOTES

Introduction

1   *The Wisdom of The East, The Instruction of Ptah-Hotep and The Instruction of Ke'gemni: The Oldest Books In The World, Translated From The Egyptian with An Introduction And Appendix, by Battiscombe G. Gunn* (London: John Murray, 1906).

Chapter 1

1   Warren Cass, *Influence: How to Raise Your Profile, Manage Your Reputation and Get Noticed* (John Wiley & Sons, 20).

2   Charles W. Freeman and Sally Marks, 'Diplomacy', *Encyclopedia Britannica*, www.britannica.com/topic/diplomacy.

3   www.britishpathe.com/gallery/winston-churchill-quotes/3.

4   Charles Patrick FitzGerald, 'Wuhou Empress Of Tang Dynasty', *Encyclopedia Britannica*, www.britannica.com/biography/Wuhou.

5   Leonie Frieda, *Catherine de Medici* (Weidenfeld & Nicholson, 2004). Joseph Cummins, *The World's Bloodiest History* (Fair Winds Press, 2009), p. 47.

6   Robert Pick, 'Maria Theresa, Holy Roman Empress', *Encyclopedia Britannica*, www.britannica.com/biography/Maria-Theresa.

7   Joyce Hackel, 'Former Secretary of State Madeleine Albright and Ambassador Wendy Sherman speaking at Wellesley College', *PRI's The World*, January 25, 2018, www.pri.org/stories/2018-01-25/madeleine-albright-many-best-diplomats-are-women.

8   Natalie Mears, 'Love-making and diplomacy: Elizabeth I and the Anjou marriage negotiations, *c*.1578–1582', *History*, vol. 86 (October 2001), pp. 442–6.

9   Susan Doran, *Queen Elizabeth I* (NYU Press, 2003), p. 72.

10 Kathleen Spaltro, *Royals of England: A Guide for Readers, Travelers, and Genealogists* (Noeline Bridge, iUniverse, 2005), p. 180.

11 Deborah Cadbury, *Queen Victoria's Matchmaking: The Royal Marriages that Shaped Europe* (New York: Hachette, 2017).

Chapter 2

1   C. Beem and Carole Levin, 'Why Elizabeth never left England', in *The Foreign Relations of Elizabeth I*, ed. C. Beem (Palgrave Macmillan, 2011).

2   2 Chronicles 35, 20–21.

3   Luke 14, 31–32.

4   Freeman and Marks, 'Diplomacy'.

5   'Women leading peace: A close examination of women's political participation in peace processes in Northern Ireland, Guatemala, Kenya, and the Philippines', the Georgetown Institute for Women, Peace and Security, 2015, giwps.georgetown.edu/wp-content/uploads/2017/08/Women-Leading-Peace.pdf.

6   Freeman and Marks, 'Diplomacy'.

7   Ibid.

8   Christine de Pizan, *The Treasure of the City of Ladies: Or the Book of the Three Virtues* (Penguin, 2003).

9   Katie Hickman, *Daughters of Britannia: The Lives and Times of Diplomatic Wives* (Harper Collins, 1999), p. xxiii.

10 Gary M. Bell, 'Introduction', in *A Handlist of British Diplomatic Representatives 1509–1688* (Cambridge University Press, 1995).

11 *Journals of the House of Commons*, vol. 71 (HM Stationery Office, 1816), Appendix, p. 770.

12 Freeman and Marks, 'Diplomacy'.

13 Herodotus, *The Histories*, ed. A. D. Godley, 7.133.1, www.perseus.tufts.edu/hopper/text?doc=Perseus%3Atext%3A1999.01.0126%3Abook%3D7%3Achapter%3D133%3Asection%3D1.

14 Ibid. 7.132.2.

15 Jonathan Wright, *The Ambassadors: From Ancient Greece to Renaissance Europe, the Men Who Introduced the World to Itself* (Harcourt, 2006), p. 3.

16 'The lawe of nations: How diplomatic immunity protected an Elizabethan Assasin', warwick.ac.uk/newsandevents/knowledgecentre/arts/history/shakespearediplomacy/.

17 'Diplomatic Immunity', 3 July 2018, diplomatmagazine.com/diplomatic-immunity/. Full text of the act of 1708: 7 Anne c.12: An act for preserving the privileges of ambassadors, and other publick ministers of foreign princes and states, the Statutes Project, statutes.org.uk/site/the-statutes/eighteenth-century/1708-7-anne-c-12-diplomatic-privileges-act/.

18 Emmerich De Vattel, 'Of the Rights, Privileges, and Immunities of Ambassadors and Other Public Ministers', in *The Law of Nations or the Principles of Natural Law* (1758), Book 4, Chapter 7, the Lonang Institute, lonang.com/library/reference/vattel-law-of-nations/vatt-407/.

19 Convention Regarding Consular Agents, signed at Habana, 20 February, 1928, history.state.gov/historicaldocuments/frus1928v01/d366.

20 The text of the treaty is United Nations, Treaty Series, vol. 500, p. 95. treaties.un.org/doc/Publication/UNTS/Volume%20500/v500.pdf.

21 'The Iranian Hostage Crisis', Office of the Historian, Department of State, history.state.gov/departmenthistory/short-history/iraniancrises, accessed 20 October 2020.

22 Michael de Ferdinandy, 'Charles V Holy Roman Emperor', *Enclopedia Britannica,* www.britannica.com/biography/Charles-V-Holy-Roman-emperor.

23 'Eighty Years' War', *Encyclopedia Britannica,* www.britannica.com/event/Eighty-Years-War.

24 *De navorscher-Nederlands archief voor genealogie en heraldiek, heemkunde en geschiedenis,* vol. 19; 1869, books.google.com/books?id=FtwSAAAAYAAJ&dq=Bartholda+van+Swieten&source=gbs_navlinks_s.

25 'Swieten, Bartholda van (1566–1647)', Huygens ING, resources.huygens.knaw.nl/vrouwenlexicon/lemmata/data/Swieten.

26 Robert O. Crummey, Holm Sundhaussen and Ricarda Vulpius, *Russische und Ukrainische Geschichte Vom 16.-18. Jahrhundert* (Otto Harrassowitz Verlag, 2001), pp. 240–1.

27 Glenda Sluga and Carolyn James, *Women, Diplomacy and International Politics since 1500* (Routledge, 2015), p. 115.

28 Sue Cameron, 'Why British women need a diplomatic coup', *Telegraph,* 9 Aug 2014, www.telegraph.co.uk/comment/columnists/sue-cameron/11022551/Why-British-women-need-a-diplomatic-coup.html.

29 In a meeting between John Adams (the US's first ambassador to the UK), Thomas Jefferson (US minister to France) and Sidi Haji Abdrahaman (Tripoli's ambassador to the United Kingdom) in 1786, the latter explained that according the Qur'an 'all nations which had not acknowledged the Profet were sinners whom it was the right and duty of the faithful to plunder and enslave'. Brian Kilmeade and Don Yaeger, *Thomas Jefferson and the Pripoli Pirates: The Forgotten War that Changed American History* (New York: Penguin Random House, 2015).

30 'Articles of peace & commerce between […] Charles II […] and the […] Lords the Bashaw, Dey, Aga, Divan, and governours of the […] kingdom of Tripoli concluded by Sir John Narbrough […] the first day of May, 1676', quod.lib.umich.edu/e/eebo2/A32172.0001.001/1:2?rgn= div1;view=fulltext.

31 *Hertslet's Commercial Treaties: A Collection of Treaties and Conventions, Between Great Britain and Foreign Powers, and of the Laws, Decrees, Orders in Council, &c., Concerning the Same, So Far as They Relate to Commerce and Navigation, Slavery, Extradition, Nationality, Copyright, Postal Matters, &c., and to the Privileges and Interests of the Subjects of the High Contracting Parties*, vol. 1 (HM Stationery Office, 1827), p. 143.

32 *Scots Magazine*, Volume 26, Sands, Brymer, Murray and Cochran, 17, p. 166.

33 'Tripoli: Attestation of Cosme Conty, Comte Palatin, that following the death of Robert White, Imperial Consul to Tripoli, his wife Jean acted as chargee des affaires at the British Consulate with the approval of the Bashaw', 22 June 1765, TNA T 1/441/156–157.

34 'Lord Shelburne, enclosing accounts and application of Mrs Jean White, widow of Robert White, consul of Tripoli, for usual allowance and expenses for her management of the consulate's affairs from the death of her husband to the arrival of his successor Mr Fraser, a period of above a year', 1767, TNA T 1/458/165–170.

35 'Tripoli: Letter to the King from the Bashaw of Tripoli on the appointment of Robert White as British Ambassador', TNA, T 1/438/223–224.

36 Frederick C. Leiner, *The End of Barbary Terror, America's 1815 War Against the Pirates of North America* (Oxford University Press, 2006).

37 *Illustrated London News*, 1859, cited in Steven Roberts, *Distant Writing, A History of the Telegraph Companies in Britain between 1838 and 1868*, archive.is/IC4G#selection-3851.5-3851.37.

38 Report to the Playfair Commission Report of 1874–75 (reproduced in the 1929 Royal Commission, p. 105), cited in 'A History of Women in the UK Civil Service', www.civilservant.org.uk/library/2015_history_ of_women_in_the_civil_service.pdf.

39   Helen McCarthy, *Women of the World: The Rise of the Female Diplomat* (London: Bloomsbury, 2014).

40   Reproduced in the 1929 Royal Commission, p. 105, cited in www.civilservant.org.uk/library/2015_history_of_women_in_the_civil_service.pdf.

41   'Women and the Foreign Office', FCO Historians, 30 April 2018, issuu.com/fcohistorians/docs/women_in_diplomacy_history_note__5b.

42   www.ekathimerini.com/40188/article/ekathimerini/news/women-and-diplomacy-a-british-diplomat-looks-back. John Dickie, *The New Mandarins: How British Foreign Policy Works* (2004), p. 23. Under Clause VII of the Order in Council of 4 June 1870. The Honourable Stephen Powys, *Foreign Office: Clerk on the Establishment or Attache in the Diplomatic Service*. Sophia Isabella Fulcher and Ethel Gunton, *Woman Typists*, www.thegazette.co.uk/London/issue/26519/page/3261/data.pdf.

43   'Under Clause 7 Of The Order In Council Of 4th June 1870', *The Edinburgh Gazette*, 8 June 1894, www.thegazette.co.uk/Edinburgh/issue/10577/page/660/data.pdf. *London Gazette*, 5 June 1894, www.thegazette.co.uk/London/issue/26519/page/3261/data.pdf.

44   'Women and the Foreign Office', 30 April 2018, issuu.com/fcohistorians/docs/women_in_diplomacy_history_note__5b.

45   *Evening Post*, 25 May 1914, paperspast.natlib.govt.nz/newspapers/EP19140525.2.6.

46   'A History of Women in the UK Civil Service', www.civilservant.org.uk/library/2015_history_of_women_in_the_civil_service.pdf, citing Appendix to Part 1 of minutes of Evidence to the Royal Commission on the Civil Service, 1929.

47   Ibid.

48   Mildred A. Joiner and Clarence M. Welner, 'Employment of Women in War Production', report prepared in the reports and analysis division, Bureau of Employment Security, www.ssa.gov/policy/docs/ssb/v5n7/v5n7p4.pdf.

49   www.civilservant.org.uk/women-bertha_phillpotts.html.

50   McCarthy, *Women of the World*.

51   Her book is still available on Amazon. *The Desert and the Sown: Travels in Palestine and Syria*, by Gertrude Bell (Dover Publications; Illustrated Edition, September 2008)

52   *Review of the Civil Administration of Mesopotamia*, archive.org/details/reviewofciviladm00iraqrich/page/n2.

53   www.legislation.gov.uk/ukpga/Geo5/9-10/71/section/1/enacted.

54   Ray Stracey, *The Cause: A Short History of the Women's Movement in Great Britain* (Kennikat Press, 1969), pp. 229 and 376.

55   Ibid., p. 380.

56 R. K. Kelsall, *Higher Civil Servants in Britain: From 1870 to the Present Day* (Routledge, 2013), p. 173, citing the Leathes Committee Report.

57 Alan Travis, 'First female PC wins Theresa May's acclaim and apology', *Guardian*, 1 December 2015, www.theguardian.com/uk-news/2015/dec/02/first-female-pc-wins-theresa-mays-acclaim-and-apology.

58 The ILO is an unusual organisation in that it encourages participation by both government labour and employer representatives. Each member nation has four delegates, two governmental and one each from employer and labour organisations.

59 www.ilo.org/dyn/normlex/en/f?p=1000:62:0::No:62:P62_LISt_eNtrIe_ID:2453907:No.

60 Grant R. Pogosyan, ambassador of Armenia, 'Appreciating the long history of friendly relationship with Japan', *Japan Times*, 22 September 2014, classified.japantimes.com/nationalday/pdfs/20140922-Armenia_national_day.pdf.

61 Erika Rackley and Rosemary Auchmuty, *Women's Legal Landmarks: Celebrating the History of Women and Law in the UK and Ireland* (Bloomsbury, 2018).

62 Helen Davenport Gibbons and Diana Abgar, *The Armenian Massacres of 1909* (Sophene, 2019).

63 Diana Agabeg Apgar, *On the Cross of Europe's Imperialism: Armenia Crucified* (Yokohama, 1918), archive.org/details/oncrosso-feuropes00apca/page/n3.

64 The Rosika Schwimmer Papers 1890–1983 Mss Col 6398, New York Public Library Humanities and Social Sciences Library Manuscripts and Archives Division, archives.nypl.org/uploads/collection/pdf_finding_aid/schwimmerr.pdf.

65 'Rosika Schwimmer', *Encyclopaedia Brittanica*, jwa.org/encyclopedia/article/schwimmer-rosika. www.britannica.com/biography/Rosika-Schwimmer.

66 Simon Karlinsky, 'The Menshivik, Bolshevik, Stalinist Feminist', *New York Times*, 4 January 1981, www.nytimes.com/1981/01/04/books/the-menshivik-bolshevik-stalinist-feminist.html.

67 McCarthy, *Women of the World*.

68 Madeleine Herrren, 'Gender and international relations through the lens of the League of Nations (1919–1945)', in Sluga and James, *Women, Diplomacy and International Politics since 1500*.

69 Congressional Record Senate, 4 December 1922, www.govinfo.gov/content/pkg/GPO-CRECB-1922-pt1-v63/pdf/GPO-CRECB-1922-pt1-v63-12.pdf.

70 Marilyn S. Greenwald, *A Woman of the Times: Journalism, Feminism, and the Career of Charlotte Curtis* (Ohio University Press). Review: 'A Life in Public Service', www.nytimes.com/books/first/g/greenwald-times.html.

71 www.historic-uk.com/HistoryUK/HistoryofBritain/margaret-bondfield/.

72 'Margaret Bondfield', *Encyclopaedia Brittanica*, www.britannica.com/biography/Margaret-Bondfield.

73 www.guide2womenleaders.com/United_Kingdom.htm.

74 'Frances Perkins, United States Secretary of Labor', *Encyclopedia Britannica*, www.britannica.com/biography/Frances-Perkins.

75 www.localhistories.org/womensrightstime.html.

76 Richard Severo, 'Gertrude Ederle, the first woman to swim across the English Channel, dies at 98', *New York Times*, 1 December 2003, www.nytimes.com/2003/12/01/sports/gertrude-ederle-the-first-woman-to-swim-across-the-english-channel-dies-at-98.html.

77 www.civilservant.org.uk/women-history.html.

78 *Royal Commission on the Civil Service 1929–1931*, Report (HM Stationery Office, 1931).

79 Ibid.

80 Helen Jones, *Women in British Public Life, 1914–1950: Gender, Power and Social Policy* (Harlow, Pearson Education, 2000), p. 157.

81 Fiona MacCarthy, 'Dame Alix Meynell: A towering pioneer for women in the civil service and an unconventional figure in British society', *Guardian*, 1 September 1999, www.theguardian.com/news/1999/sep/02/guardianobituaries.

82 'Women of French diplomacy: France in the United States, Embassy of France in Washington, D.C.', 4 May 2018, franceintheus.org/spip.php?article8625. Linda L. Clark, *The Rise of Professional Women in France: Gender and Public Administration since 1830* (Cambridge University Press, 2000), p. 173.

83 'A guide to the United States' history of recognition, diplomatic, and consular relations, by country, since 1776: Denmark', history.state.gov/countries/denmark.

84 Anne Miller Morin and Kristie Miller, 'The Dame among the Danes: America's first female envoy remembered as beloved, eloquent and controversia', *Foreign Service Journal*, 1997, p. 40. www.usdiplomacy.org/downloads/pdf/representative/Morin1997.pdf.

85 British Nationality Act, 1948, www.legislation.gov.uk/ukpga/1948/56%20/pdfs/ukpga_19480056_en.pdf: 'A woman who, having before the commencement of this Act married any person, ceased on that marriage or during the continuance thereof to be a British subject shall be deemed for the purposes of this Act to have been

a British subject immediately before the commencement of this Act'. See Jones, *Women in British Public Life*.

86   Daniel B. Rice, 'The Riddle of Ruth Bryan Owen', *Yale Journal of Law & the Humanities*, vol. 29, October 2017.

87   Philp Nash, 'A Woman's place is in the embassy: America's first female chiefs of mission, 1933–1964', in Sluga and James, *Women, Diplomacy and International Politics since 1500*.

88   adst.org/oral-history/fascinating-figures/frances-willis-the-first-career-female-ambassador/. history.state.gov/departmenthistory/people/willis-frances-elizabeth.

89   Nicholas J. Willis, *Frances E. Willis: Up the Foreign Service Ladder – To the Summit – Despite the Limitations of Her Sex* (Privately printed, 2013).

90   A. Scott, *Ernest Gowers: Plain Words and Forgotten Deeds* (Springer, 2009), p. 148. The final report of the Committee on the Admission of Women to the Diplomatic and Consular Services (Schuster Committee) to the cabinet, 7 November 1934 is pages.wustl.edu/files/pages/imce/caddel/uk_1934_committee_on_the_admission_of_women_to_the_diplomatic_and_consular_services.pdf.

91   Inter-Departmental Committee on the Admission of Women to the Diplomatic and Consular Services, Chairman Sir Claud Schuster (HM Stationery Office, 1936).

92   Memorandum by Sir Robert Vansittart, 30 January 1934, FO 366/929, TNA.

93   Jones, *Women in British Public Life*.

94   Miscellaneous No. 5 (1936) Documents relating to the Admission of Women to the Diplomatic and Consular Services, 1930, 1934 – April 1936. Presented by the Secretary of State for Foreign Affairs to Parliament by Command of His Majesty (HM Stationery Office, 1936).

95   History notes 20 'Women and the Foreign Office, 1782–2018', FCO Historians, 2018.

96   Proposals for the Reform of the Foreign Service (White paper of January 1943, Cmd. 6420), in Lord Strang, *The Foreign Office* (London: The New Whitehall Series, 1955), Appendix III.

97   '1941: Women Ask to Be Diplomats', *New York Herald Tribune*, 17 September 1941, iht-retrospective.blogs.nytimes.com/2016/09/16/1941-women-ask-to-be-diplomats/?_r=0.

98   history.blog.gov.uk/2015/05/26/a-perfect-nuisance-the-history-of-women-in-the-civil-service/, citing 'Inquiry into subsequent history of women for whom marriage bar had been waived' (1945), The National Archives T275/137, discovery.nationalarchives.gov.uk/details/r/C2190371.

99   Ibid.

100 'Women of the World review – a study of female diplomats that lacks class', www.theguardian.com/books/2014/may/25/women-world-female-diplomat-mccarthy-review.

101 Kaye Stearman, Women's Rights: Changing Attitudes 1900–2000 (Raintree Steck-Vaughn, 2000).

102 Jones, Women in British Public Life.

103 Summary from Mary Kinnear, Woman of the World: Mary McGeachy and International Cooperation, (University of Toronto Press, 2004).

104 David Langbart, 'Married women in the U.S. government, c. 1945', 28 October 2014, State and Foreign Affairs, Women's History, World War II, text-message.blogs.archives.gov/2014/10/28/married-women-in-the-u-s-government-c-1945/, citing documents in file 811.017 in the 1945–9 segment of the Central Decimal File (NAID 302021), part of RG 59: General Records of the Department of State.

105 Civil Service Marriage Bar (Abolition), HC Deb 15 October 1946 vol. 427 cc794–6 794, hansard.millbanksystems.com/commons/1946/oct/15/civil-service-marriage-bar-abolition.

106 'Marriage bar', archive.spectator.co.uk/article/23rd-august-1946/2/the-marriage-bar.

Chapter 3

1   McCarthy, Women of the World.

2   www.sis.gov.uk/our-history.html. Clare Thorp, 'The fascinating work of female spies, brought to you by Red Sparrow', Telegraph, 26 February 2018, www.telegraph.co.uk/films/red-sparrow/female-spies-through-history/. '6 Incredible Female Spies of World War II: These women risked their lives to assist the Allies' cause in World War II', exploret-hearchive.com/6-incredible-female-spies-of-world-war-ii. Christopher Andrew, Defend the Realm: The Authorized History of MI5 (New York: Alfred A. Knopf, 2009).

3   Andrew, Defend the Realm.

4   Daniel Bats, '"She used the bedroom the way James Bond used a Beretta." How seductress Betty Pack stole the secrets that helped defeat the Nazis – now Jennifer Lawrence is tapped to portray the ultimate honey trap spy', DailyMail.com, 5 July 2016, www.dailymail.co.uk/news/article-3674051/She-used-bedroom-way-James-Bond-used-Beretta-seductress-Betty-Pack-stole-secrets-helped-defeat-Nazis-Jennifer-Lawrence-tapped-portray-ultimate-honey-trap-spy.html. A great discussion of the role of women in the UK and US intelligence agencies is Elizabeth McIntosh, The Intelligence Profession Series No. 5:

The Role of Women In Intellignece (Association of Former Intelligence Officers, 1989).

5   Paddy Hayes, *Queen of Spies: Daphne Park Britain's Cold War Spy Master* (New York: Overlook Duckworth, 2016). 'Daphne Park', www. civilservant.org.uk/women-daphne_park.html.

6   hansard.millbanksystems.com/commons/1945/jun/13/foreign-service-women#S5CV0411P0_19450613_HOC_85.

7   Madeleine Herrren, 'Gender and international Relations Through the Lens of the League of Nations (1919-1945)', in Sluga and James, *Women, Diplomacy and International Politics since 1500.*

8   Foreign Service (Women's Recruitment), HC Deb 20 March 1946, vol. 420 cc1857–9, api.Parliament.uk/historic-hansard/commons/1946/ mar/20/foreign-service-womens-recruitment.

9   D.D. Dakin, 'Mrs. Monica Britton', *The Red Maids Magazine*, Women in Society No. 20, May 1980, p. 1, redmaidsschool.daisy.websds.net/ Filename.ashx?tableName=ta_publications&columnName=filename&r ecordId=24.

10 newspapers.digitalnc.org/lccn/sn84020756/1946-11-07/ed-1/seq-2/ocr. txt.

11 *The Daily Republican*, 18 October 1946, www.newspapers.com/ newspage/53428409/. 'First Woman In Br. Foreign Service', *Indian Daily Mail*, 9 October 18, 1946, eresources.nlb.gov.sg/3. www. newspapers/Digitised/Article/indiandailymail19461009-1.2.22.com/ newspage/53428409/.

12 *The Advertiser* (Adelaide, SA), 14 October 1946, trove.nla.gov.au/ newspaper/article/35761250.

13 Dickie, *The New Mandarins*, p. 24.

14 John Henshaw Britton was appointed CBE in 1972 for services to the magistracy in Bristol, Supplement to *London Gazette*, 3 June 1972, www. thegazette.co.uk/London/issue/45678/supplement/6262/data.pdf.

15 M.G. Wilson, 'Opening of the Monica Britton Exhibition Hall of Medical History', *Bristol Medical Chirurgical Journal*, 1986, p. 17, pdfs. semanticscholar.org/cfd7/aa0bdeec1d0cf0056775647fce27a252536e.pdf. 'Women in Diplomacy: The FCO, 1782–1999', 30 April 1999, issuu. com/fcohistorians/docs/history_notes_cover_hphn_6.

16 'Obituary: Lady Mayhew', *The Times*, 21 July 2016, www.thetimes. co.uk/article/lady-mayhew-chgtmfh2w.

17 Mayhew, Cicely Elizabeth (Oral History), Imperial War Museum, www. iwm.org.uk/collections/item/object/80019203.

18 Alex Barker, 'Britain's first female diplomats', *Financial Times*, 6 November 2009, www.ft.com/content/8e936c88-c9ad-11de-a071-00144feabdc0.

19   Ibid.

20   Ibid.

21   'Obituary: Lady Mayhew', *The Times*, 21 July 2016, www.thetimes.
     co.uk/article/lady-mayhew-chgtmfh2w.

22   'Dame Margaret Anstee, diplomat – obituary', *Telegraph*, 26 August
     2016, www.telegraph.co.uk/obituaries/2016/08/28/dame-margaret-
     anstee-diplomat--obituary/. 'Dame Margaret Anstee obituary', *Guardian*,
     1 September 2016, www.theguardian.com/world/2016/sep/01/
     dame-margaret-anstee-obituary.

23   Margaret Joan Anstee, *Never Learn to Type: A Woman at the United Nations*
     (Wiley, 2003). See also 'In memoriam, Dame Margaret Anstee', UN
     Women, www.unwomen.org/en/news/stories/2016/9/in-memoriam-
     dame-margaret-anstee.

24   'Patricia Hutchinson: Ambassador to Uruguay during the Falklands
     war', *The Times*, 1 January 2009, www.thetimes.co.uk/article/
     patricia-hutchinson-ambassador-to-uruguay-during-the-falklands-war-
     vzfmzhtg9d9.

25   *London Gazette*, 1 April 1980, www.thegazette.co.uk/London/
     issue/48146/page/5006/data.pdf.

26   Rosamund Benson matriculated to Sommerville College in 1942; www.
     some.ox.ac.uk/wp-content/uploads/2015/08/Somerville -College-
     Donor-Report-2011-12.pdf.

27   Letter from Rosamund Huebener née Benson to Richard Warburton,
     21 April 2017.

28   Helen McCarthy, 'Gendering Diplomatic History, Women in the
     British diplomatic service circa 1919–1972', in Sluga and James, *Women,
     Diplomacy and International Politics since 1500*.

29   Letter from Rosamund Huebener to Richard Warburton, 21 April 2017.

30   Alex Barker, 'Britain's first female diplomats', *Financial Times*,
     6 November 2009, www.ft.com/content/8e936c88-c9ad-11de-a071-
     00144feabdc0.

31   Foreign Service Regulation No. 1. His Majesty's Foreign Service:
     The Foreign Service is composed of the following five Branches.
     Members of all Branches with the exception of Branch E, are liable
     to serve in the Foreign Office or at a diplomatic or consular post
     abroad as and when required.
     1. Branch A, consisting of persons appointed, after receiving a
     certificate of qualification from the Civil Service Commissioners,
     to the Foreign Service to serve as Third Secretary or Vice-Consul
     (Grade 9, see Foreign Service (Regulation No. 2) or in any superior
     grade …

2. Branch B, consisting of persons appointed to the Foreign Service for the performance of executive and clerical duties. …

3. Branch C, consisting of persons appointed to the Foreign Service for the performance of shorthand typing and typing duties. …

4. Branch D, consisting of established King's Foreign Service Messengers.

5. Branch E, consisting of established members of the messengerial grades such as chancery servants, messengers and night.guards in diplomatic and consular posts abroad.

London Gazette, 14 January 1947, p. 280. www.thegazette.co.uk/London/issue/37852/supplement/280/data.pdf.

32 'Women in the Foreign Office: A Diplomatic Journey', speech by Dame Rosemary Spencer, given in 2018 at the Foreign and Commonwealth Office, copy provided to Richard Warburton by Dame Rosemary Spencer (personal communication).

33 Dame Veronica Sutherland, DBE, CMG, President of Lucy Cavendish College, Cambridge, interviewed by Malcolm McBain on Tuesday 19 April 2005 at Cavendish College, for the British Diplomatic Oral History Programme, www.chu.cam.ac.uk/media/uploads/files/Sutherland.pdf.

34 www.un.org/en/udhrbook/pdf/udhr_booklet_en_web.pdf.

35 www.ilo.org/legacy/english/inwork/cb-policy-guide/declarationofPhil-adelphia1944.pdf.

36 David Binder, 'Eugenie Anderson, 87, first woman to be U.S. ambassador', *New York Times*, 3 April 1997, www.nytimes.com/1997/04/03/world/eugenie-anderson-87-first-woman-to-be-us-ambassador.html?_r=0.

37 lwv.org/history.

38 *Call Me Madam* is a musical with a book by Howard Lindsay and Russel Crouse and music and lyrics by Irving Berlin. A satire on politics and foreign policy that spoofs America's penchant for lending billions of dollars to needy countries, it centres on Sally Adams, a well-meaning but ill-informed socialite widow who is appointed United States ambassador to the fictional European country of Lichtenburg. While there, she charms the local gentry, especially Cosmo Constantine, while her press attaché Kenneth Gibson falls in love with Princess Maria.

39 'A guide to the United States' history of recognition, diplomatic, and consular relations, by country, since 1776: Denmark', history.state.gov/countries/denmark.

40 www.omsd.dk/DanishOrders/en/OrderDannebrog_en.aspx.

41 www.un.org/en/sections/about-un/trusteeship-council/index.html.

42 www.un.org/en/decolonization/index.shtml. www.un.org/en/decolonization/specialcommittee.shtml

43 Homer L. Calkin, 'Women in the Department of State: Their role in American foreign affairs', Office of the Deputy Under-Secretary for Management, Department of State, 1978.

44 Kevin Theakston, 'Sharp, Evelyn Adelaide, Baroness Sharp (1903–1985)', *Oxford Dictionary of National Biography*, www. oxforddnb.com/view/10.1093/ref:odnb/9780198614128.001.0001/ odnb-9780198614128-e-31672.

Chapter 4

1 www.gov.uk/government/organisations/foreign-commonwealth-office.

2 www.gov.uk/government/organisations/department-for-international-development.

3 Vienna Convention on Diplomatic Relations, Vienna, 18 April 1961. United Nations Treaty Collection, treaties.un.org/pages/viewdetails. aspx?src=treaty&mtdsg_no=iii-3&chapter=3&lang=en.

4 Protocol and Liaison Service, Permanent Missions to the United Nations, N°306, June 2016, www.un.int/protocol/sites/www.un.int/ files/Protocol%20and%20Liaison%20Service/bb305.pdf.

Chapter 5

1 See the Report of the Committee on Representational Services Overseas Appointed by the Prime Minister Under the Chairmanship of Lord Plowden, 1962–63. The Committee on Representational Services Overseas consisted of Chairman, Lord Plowden KCB, KBE; and members Mr A.D. Bonham-Carter TD, Viscount Harcourt KCMG, OBE, the Rt Hon. Arthur Henderson QC, MP, Lord Inchyra GCMG, CVO, Sir Percivale Liesching GCMG, KCB, KCVO and Sir Charles Mott-Radclyffe MO.

2 Ibid., Miscellaneous No. 5 (1964).

3 'The FCO: Policy, People and Places, 1782–1995', 31 August 1999; this is an outline history of the Foreign and Commonwealth Office from the first mention of a king's secretary for foreign affairs in 1253 to the present day development of its policies, people and buildings, issuu.com/ fcohistorians/docs/history_notes_cover_hphn_2.

4 Betty Friedan, *The Feminine Mystique* (New York: Norton, 1963).

5   Arthur Marwick, *The Sixties, Cultural Revolution in Britain, France, Italy and the United States c.1958–c.1974* (Oxford University Press, 1998).

6   David Allyn, *Make Love Not War: The Sexual Revolution and Unfettered History* (New York: Little, Brown & Co, 2000).

7   'Mary Quant Biography, Fashion Designer (1934–)', www.biography. com/fashion-designer/mary-quant www.biography.com/fashion-designer/mary-quant.

8   Sexual Offences Act 1967, since replaced by the Sexual Offences Act 2003 in the UK. In the US Sodom was decriminalised by the US Supreme Court in 2003, Lawrence v. Texas, 539 U.S. 558 (2003).

9   Geoffrey Robertson, *The Trial of Lady Chatterley: Regina V. Penguin Books Limited: The Transcript of the Trial Paperback* (Penguin, 1991).

10   There have been many reflective personal accounts of people who lived through this time, for example Jenny Diski, *The Sixties* (New York: Picador, 2009).

11   See for example Marwick, *The Sixties*; Bernard Levin, *Run it Down the Flagpole, Britain in the Sixties* (New York: Athenaeum, 1971); Richard Avedon, *The Sixties* (New York: Random House, 1999); Robert Altman, *The Sixties* (Santa Monica Press, 2007).

12   'Women in the Foreign Office – A Diplomatic Journey', speech by Dame Rosemary Spencer.

13   Alex Barker, 'Britain's first female diplomats', *Financial Times*, 6 November 2009, www.ft.com/content/8e936c88-c9ad-11de-a071-00144feabdc0.

14   Full text of the Treaty of Rome, 25 March 1957, ec.europa.eu/romania/sites/romania/files/tratatul_de_la_roma.pdf.

15   Fiona MacCarthy, 'Dame Alix Meynell, A towering pioneer for women in the civil service and an unconventional figure in British society', *Guardian*, 1 September 1999, www.theguardian.com/news/1999/sep/02/guardianobituaries.

16   Margaret Thatcher, speech to Conservative Party conference, 10 October 1969, www.margaretthatcher.org/document/101687.

17   Equal Pay Act of 1970. Full text, www.legislation.gov.uk/ukpga/1970/41/pdfs/ukpga_19700041_en.pdf.

18   US Equal Pay Act of 1963, www.eeoc.gov/laws/statutes/epa.cfm. The original text of the law, excluding subsequent amendments, www.eeoc.gov/eeoc/history/50th/thelaw/epa.cfm.

19   Full text, www.legislation.gov.uk/ukpga/1975/65/enacted.

20   British Diplomatic Oral History Programme, Recollections of Dame Mariot Leslie DCMG at Royal Overseas League, Edinburgh, 29 March 2017, recorded and transcribed by Alasdair MacDermott, Churchill

College, Cambridge, www.chu.cam.ac.uk/media/uploads/files/Leslie.
pdf. Used with permission.

21 oasis.lib.harvard.edu/oasis/deliver/~sch00841.

22 Alison Palmer, et al., Appellants, v. James A. Baker, Iii, Secretary of
State of the United States of America, Department of State, Appellee,
Marguerite Cooper King, et al., Appellants, v. James A. Baker, Iii,
Secretary of State of the United States of America, Department of State,
Appellee, 905 F.2d 1544 (D.C. Cir. 1990), U.S. Court of Appeals for the
District of Columbia Circuit - 905 F.2d 1544 (D.C. Cir. 1990). Argued
10 April 1990, decided 11 May 1990, law.justia.com/cases/federal/
appellate-courts/F2/905/1544/176887/.
'On appeal, we reversed the district court's findings of nondiscrimination
in assignments, evaluations of female FSOs for potential, awards, and
promotions from class 5 to class 4, and remanded for further findings based
on the existing record.' Palmer v. Shultz, 815 F.2d 84, 116 (D.C. Cir. 1987).
Barbara Gamarekian, 'Women Gain, but Slowly, in the Foreign Service',
New York Times, 28 July 1989, www.nytimes.com/1989/07/28/us/
washington-talk-women-gain-but-slowly-in-the-foreign-service.html.

23 adst.org/the-palmer-case-and-the-changing-role-of-women-in-the-
foreign-service/.

24 'Past Prime Ministers: Baroness Margaret Thatcher, Conservative 1979 to
1990', www.gov.uk/government/history/past-prime-ministers/margaret-
thatcher. Charles Moore, *Margaret Thatcher: The Authorized Biography,
From Grantham to the Falklands* (New York: Alfred A. Knopf, 2013).
Charles Moore, *Margaret Thatcher: The Authorized Biography, At Her Zenith
in London, Washington and Moscow* (New York: Alfred A. Knopf, 2016).
Jonathan Aitken, *Margaret Thatcher, Power and Personality* (New York:
Bloomsbury, 2013).

25 Aitken, *Margaret Thatcher, Power and Personality*, p. 34, citing Kesteven and
Grantham Girl's School and Amy C. Old, *The History of KGGS* (KGGS,
1987), p. 7.

26 Aitken, *Margaret Thatcher, Power and Personality*, p. 34, citing *Daily Mirror*,
26 February 1975.

27 David Runciman, 'Rat-a-tat-a-tat-a-tat-a-tat', *London Review of Books*,
vol. 35, 6 June 2013, pp. 13–18; reviewing Charles Moore, *Margaret
Thatcher: The Authorized Biography. Vol. I: Not for Turning* (Allen Lane,
2013), www.lrb.co.uk/v35/n11/david-runciman/rat-a-tat-a-tat-a-tat-a-
tat.

28 Moore, *Margaret Thatcher: The Authorized Biography from Grantham to the
Falklands*, p. 117, citing an article in the *Sunday Graphic*.

29 Margaret Thatcher, speech to Conservative Party conference, 10 October
1969, www.margaretthatcher.org/document/101687.

30 Moore, *Margaret Thatcher: The Authorized Biography from Grantham to the Falklands*, p. 117.

31 Andrew S. Crines, Timothy Heppell and Peter Dorey, *The Political Rhetoric and Oratory of Margaret Thatcher* (Springer, 2016), p. 114, citing *Any Questions*, BBC, 10 June 1966.

32 Margaret Thatcher, speech to Conservative Party conference, 10 October 1969, www.margaretthatcher.org/document/101687.

33 Nicholas Wapshott, *Ronald Reagan and Margaret Thatcher, A Political Marriage* (Sentinel Penguin Group, 2007).

34 Nina Lakhani, 'Margaret Thatcher: How much did The Iron Lady do for the UK's women?' *Independent*, 8 April 2013, www.independent.co.uk/news/uk/politics/margaret-thatcher-how-much-did-the-iron-lady-do-for-the-uks-women-8564631.html.

35 Lisa Barrington, 'Britons voted Margaret Thatcher as the most influential woman of the past 200 years', Reuters, 7 February 2016, www.businessinsider.com/r-britons-vote-thatcher-most-influential-woman-of-past-200-years-2016-2.

36 Jenni Murray, 'What did Margaret Thatcher do for women?' *Guardian*, 9 April 2013, www.theguardian.com/politics/2013/apr/09/margaret-thatcher-women.

37 Louise Stewart, 'Did Margaret Thatcher help the cause of women?', BBC News, 9 April 2013, www.bbc.com/news/av/uk-politics-22084698/did-margaret-thatcher-help-the-cause-of-women.

Chapter 6

1 *Spectator*, 22 August 1946, archive.spectator.co.uk/article/23rd-august-1946/2/the-marriage-bar.

2 K. Murphy, 'A marriage bar of convenience? The BBC and married women's work 1923–39', 20th Century British History, vol. 25 (2014), pp. 533–61. Abstract, www.ncbi.nlm.nih.gov/pubmed/25608371. See also www.lloydsbankinggroup.com/our-group/our-heritage/timeline/1901-1950/ and www.archive.barclays.com/items/show/5409.

3 Marian Sawer, 'The long, slow demise of the "marriage bar"', 8 December 2016, insidestory.org.au/the-long-slow-demise-of-the-marriage-bar/. John Meagher, 'Evolution of working women in the eyes of the state', Independent.ie, 16 October 2016, www.independent.ie/life/evolution-of-working-women-in-eyes-of-state-35129127.html.

4 Hansard, HC Deb 15 October 1946, vol. 427 cc794–6, hansard.millbanksystems.com/commons/1946/oct/15/civil-service-marriage-bar-abolition.

5   McCarthy, *Women of the World*, p. 281, citing Elizabeth Adams, 'Britain's Women Diplomats', *Evening Standard*.

6   Alex Barker, 'Britain's first female diplomats', *Financial Times*, 6 November 2009, www.ft.com/content/8e936c88-c9ad-11de-a071-00144feabdc0.

7   Marriages in England and Wales 2010, www.ons.gov.uk/peoplepopulationandcommunity/birthsdeathsandmarriages/marriagecohabitationandcivilpartnerships/bulletins/marriagesinenglandandwalesprovisional/2012-02-29#marriage-rates. Marriages in England and Wales 2015, www.ons.gov.uk/peoplepopulationandcommunity/birthsdeathsandmarriages/marriagecohabitationandcivilpartnerships/bulletins/marriagesinenglandandwalesprovisional/2015.

8   *London Gazette*, 23 June 1950, www.thegazette.co.uk/London/issue/38952/page/3257/data.pdf.

9   'High Diplomatic Post For Englishwoman', *The Advertiser* (Adelaide, SA) 14 March 1951, trove.nla.gov.au/newspaper/article/45686668?searchTerm=%22barbara+salt%22. 'Young English woman wins diplomatic post', *The Courier-Mail* (Brisbane, Qld) 27 February 1951, trove.nla.gov.au/newspaper/article/50102897?searchTerm=%22barbara+salt%22.

10 'Dr Joan Macintosh, Obituary', *The Herald*, 27 June 2014, www.heraldscotland.com/opinion/obituaries/13167460.dr-joan-macintosh/.

11 'Foreign Office as matrimonial', *The Advertiser* (Adelaide, SA) 27 June 1952, trove.nla.gov.au/newspaper/article/47412500?searchTerm=%22barbara+salt%22.

12 Alex Barker, 'Britain's first female diplomats', *Financial Times*, 6 November 2009, www.ft.com/content/8e936c88-c9ad-11de-a071-00144feabdc0.

13 Email from Juliet Campbell to Richard Warburton, 22 April 2019.

14 'Women in the Foreign Office: A Diplomatic Journey', speech by Dame Rosemary Spencer.

15 McCarthy, *Women of the World*, p. 259.

16 Foreign and Commonwealth Office Historians, Freedom of Information request, 1108–18, 12 November 2018.

17 Supplement to *London Gazette*, 24 June 1946, www.thegazette.co.uk/London/issue/37617/supplement/3131/data.pdf.

18 'Women in diplomacy: The FCO, 1782–1999', *FCO Historians*, 30 April 1999, issuu.com/fcohistorians/docs/history_notes_cover_hphn_6.

19 Ibid. Grace Rolleston Gardner was born in the Wandsworth, London in 1923, the daughter of John Davy Rolleston and Mary Edith Waring. 'Frank Gardner: Who Do You Think You Are?', *The Genealogist*, 22 September 2015, www.thegenealogist.co.uk/featuredarticles/2015/who-do-you-think-you-are/frank-gardner-277/.

20 'Hutchinson, Patricia M., C.M.G. (1926–2008): Counsellor and Head of Chancery, Embassy, Sweden, 1969-1972; Counsellor, U.K. Delegation to the O.E.C.D., 1973–1975; Consul-General, Geneva, 1975-1980; Ambassador to Uruguay, 1980-1983; Consul-General, Barcelona, 1983–1986', www.gulabin.com/britishdiplomatsdirectory/pdf/british-diplomatsdirectory.pdf.

21 Sluga and James, *Women, Diplomacy and International Politics since 1500*, p. 171. Alison Shaw, 'Obituary: Dr Joan Macintosh CBE, diplomat and author', *The Scotsman*, 12 June 2014 www.scotsman.com/news/obituaries/obituary-dr-joan-macintosh-cbe-diplomat-and-author-1-3441126.

22 *The Foreign Office List and Diplomatic and Consular Year Book, Great Britain* (Foreign Office, Harrison and Sons, 1963), p. 397.

23 *The Barbados Advocate*, 6 April 1952, ufdc.ufl.edu/UF00098964/02853/6?search=katherine+du+boulay.

24 'Salt, Dame Barbara, D.B.E. (1904–1975): Counsellor, Embassy, U.S.A., 1955–1957; Counsellor and Head of Chancery, Embassy, Israel, 1957–1960; Minister, U.K. Delegation to Disarmament Conference, Geneva, 1960–1961; Minister (Economic and Social Affairs), UK Delegation to the United Nations Organization, New York, 1961–1962; designate Ambassador to Israel (did not proceed), 1962', www.gulabin.com/britishdiplomatsdirectory/pdf/britishdiplomatsdi-rectory.pdf.

25 'Graham, Kathleen M., C.B.E. (1903–19) Consul-General, Amsterdam, 1960–1963, www.gulabin.com/britishdiplomatsdirectory/pdf/britishdip-lomatsdirectory.pdf.

26 'Dame Gillian G., Brown, D.C.V.O., C.M.G. (1923–1999): Ambassador to Norway, 1981–1983'.

27 ufdcimages.uflib.ufl.edu/UF/00/09/89/64/02853/00797.pdf. *Sunday Advocate*, Barbados. 'Elizabeth Sleeman', *The International Who's Who of Women 2002* (Psychology Press, 2001).

28 'Campbell, Juliet J. d'A., C.M.G. (formerly Collins) (1935–) Counsellor (Information), Embassy, France, 1977–1980; Counsellor, Embassy, Indonesia, 1982–1983; Head of Training Department, Foreign and Commonwealth Office, 1984–1987; Ambassador to Luxemburg, 1988–1991', www.gulabin.com/britishdiplomatsdirectory/pdf/british-diplomatsdirectory.pdf.

29 Helen McCarthy, 'Gendering diplomatic history: Women in the British diplomatic service circa 1919–1972', in Sluga and James, *Women, Diplomacy and International Politics since 1500*.

30 Dame Veronica Sutherland, DBE, CMG, President of Lucy Cavendish College College, Cambridge, interviewed by Malcolm McBain on

Tuesday 19 April 2005 at Cavendish College, for the British Diplomatic Oral History Programme, www.chu.cam.ac.uk/media/uploads/files/Sutherland.pdf.

31 'Women in the Foreign Office: A Diplomatic Journey', speech by Dame Rosemary Spencer.

32 Judy Denison, 'Diplomats' wives don't cry', 29 April 1999, *The Irish Times*, www.irishtimes.com/culture/diplomats-wives-don-t-cry-1.179093.

33 Rt. Hon. Sir John Tilley and Stephen Gaselee, 'Stephen Gaselee', in *The Foreign Office* (London: G.P. Putnam's sons, 1933), p. 317.

34 Alex Barker, 'Britain's first female diplomats', *Financial Times*, 6 November 2009, www.ft.com/content/8e936c88-c9ad-11de-a071-00144feabdc0.

35 British Diplomatic Oral History Programme, Recollections of Dame Mariot Leslie DCMG at Royal Overseas League, Edinburgh, 29 March 2017, recorded and transcribed by Alasdair MacDermott, Churchill College, www.chu.cam.ac.uk/media/uploads/files/Leslie.pdf. Used with permission.

36 'Foreign Office as Matrimonial', *The Advertiser* (Adelaide, SA) 27 June 1952, trove.nla.gov.au/newspaper/article/47412500?searchTerm=%22barbara+salt%22

37 The Committee chaired by Elizabeth Kemp-Jones (1970) had the mandate to:
    Consider the employment of women in the non-industrial Home Civil Service; and in particular to examine:
    How far women might be given more part time employment in positions of responsibility;
    How it might be made easier for a married woman to combine looking after a family with a Civil Service career; and
    What retraining might be given to make it easier for women to return to Civil Service employment after a lengthy period of absence.
    'Civil Service Management Studies 3, The Employment of Women in the Civil Service', Included copy of Committee report, www.civilservant.org.uk/library/1971_kemp_jones_report.pdf.

38 McCarthy, *Women of the World*. Alex Barker, 'Britain's first female diplomats', *Financial Times*, 6 November 2009, www.ft.com/content/8e936c88-c9ad-11de-a071-00144feabdc0.

39 'Australian women in diplomacy: Australian diplomacy for women', Speech by Trevor Peacock, Australian High Commissioner to Cyprus, 7 March 2011, dfat.gov.au/news/speeches/Pages/australian-women-in-diplomacy-australian-diplomacy-for-women.aspx. Barbara Gamarekian, 'Women gain, but slowly, in the Foreign Service', *New York Times*,

28 July 1989, www.nytimes.com/1989/07/28/us/washington-talk-women-gain-but-slowly-in-the-foreign-service.html. Catherine Tsalikis, 'The making of a gender-balanced foreign service: Stories from the women driving Canada's diplomatic corps toward equality', 3 April 2018, www.opencanada.org/features/making-gender-balanced-foreign-service/. Civil Service (Employment of Married Women) Act 1973, text www.irishstatutebook.ie/eli/1973/act/17/section/2/enacted/en/html#sec2.

40 Claudia Coldin, 'Marriage bars: Discrimination against married women workers, 1920s to 1950s', University of Pennsylvania, NBER Working Paper Series, www.nber.org/papers/w2747.pdf.

Chapter 7

1 Catherine Tsalikis, 'The making of a gender-balanced foreign service: Stories from the women driving Canada's diplomatic corps toward equality', 3 April 2018, www.opencanada.org/features/making-gender-balanced-foreign-service/.

2 Alex Barker, 'Britain's first female diplomats', *Financial Times*, 6 November 2009, www.ft.com/content/8e936c88-c9ad-11de-a071-00144feabdc0.

3 Jules Chappell, 'Lessons on leadership from Britain's youngest ever ambassador', 16 March 2016, www.weforum.org/agenda/2016/03/lessons-on-leadership-from-britain-s-youngest-ambassado.

4 Event: Young Professionals in Foreign Policy's Women in Foreign Policy panel discussion #YPFP2030, Women in Foreign Policy, 11 February 2015, www.womeninforeignpolicy.org/women-in-foreign-policy-blog/2015/2/14/event-young-people-in-foreign-policys-women-in-foreign-policy-panel-discussion-ypfp2030.

5 Nahal Toosi, 'Female diplomats share secrets', *Politico*, 9 February 2014, www.politico.com/story/2014/09/diplomats-women-state-department-110506.

6 P. Richard Warburton and Elizabeth Warburton, *The Story of Britain's First Female Ambassador, Dame Anne Warburton DCVO CMG*, printed by Kindle Direct Publishing LLC, citing interview with Dame Anne Warburton by Helen McCarthy, 25 October 2010.

7 McCarthy, *Women of the World*.

8 *Women of Europe*, no. 48, 15 November 1986/15 January 1987, p. 31, aei.pitt.edu/33963/1/A443.pdf.

9 'The FCO: Policy, People and Places, 1782–1995', *FCO Historians*, 31 August 1999.

10 'Wearing the pants', *Sunday Guardian*, 10 August 2014, www.pressreader. com/india/the-sunday-guardian/20140810/282909498675713.

11 Christina Pazzanese, 'National & world affairs: Three diplomatic women', *The Harvard Gazette*, 22 April 2016, news.harvard.edu/gazette/ story/2016/04/three-diplomatic-women/.

12 Dame Veronica Sutherland, DBE, CMG, President of Lucy Cavendish College, Cambridge, interviewed by Malcolm McBain on Tuesday 19 April 2005 at Cavendish College, for the British Diplomatic Oral History Programme, www.chu.cam.ac.uk/media/uploads/files/ Sutherland.pdf.

13 Elizabeth Day, 'Interview: How Baroness Ashton's gift for consensus opened the door to Mohamed Morsi', *Guardian*, 3 August 2013, www.theguardian. com/politics/2013/aug/04/baroness-ashton-morsi-secret-meeting.

14 Roz Morris, 'Alyson Bailes obituary', *The Guardian*, 2 May 2016, www. theguardian.com/politics/2016/may/02/alyson-bailes-obituary.

15 'The Ambassador's wife is an ambassador, too', *New York Times,* 4 October 1964, www.nytimes.com/1964/10/04/archives/the-ambassadors-wife-is-an-ambassador-too.html.

16 Julia Stuart, 'Brigid Keenan: Life as an ambassador's wife', *Independent*, 13 November 2005, www.independent.co.uk/news/people/profiles/ brigid-keenan-life-as-an-ambassadors-wife-515058.html.

17 Hickman, *Daughters of Britannia*, pp. 32, 184.

18 Denison, 'Diplomats' wives don't cry'.

19 Brigid Keenan, 'Being an ambassador's wife is not all luxury compounds, gin and affairs', *Daily Telegraph,* 22 October 2013, www.telegraph.co.uk/ women/womens-life/10396893/Being-an-ambassadors-wife-is-not-all-luxury-compounds-gin-and-affairs.html.

20 Greer Fay Cashman, 'Diplomatic spouses – More than coffee and cake, wives of Australian, UK and Chilean envoys discuss life in Israel'. *Jerusalem Post*, 7 December 2014, www.jpost.com/Diplomatic-Conference/Diplomatic-spouses-more-than-coffee-and-cake-383845.

21 Stuart, 'Brigid Keenan: Life as an ambassador's wife'.

22 Barbara Crossette, 'On spouses, diplomatic; embassy Row', *New York Times*, 15 January 1982, www.nytimes.com/1982/01/15/us/ on-spouses-diplomatic-embassy-row.html. Barbara Gamarekian, 'Foreign service wives' goal: Pay', *New York Times*, 10 April 1984, www.nytimes. com/1984/04/10/us/foreign-service-wives-goal-pay.html.

23 Attachment – Policy On Wives Of Foreign Service Employees, 341. Airgram From the Department of State to All Posts, Washington, 22 January 1972, 9:05 a.m., history.state.gov/historicaldocuments/ frus1969-76v02/d341.

24 Freeman and Marks, 'Diplomacy'.

25 The Nobel Peace Prize 1905, www.nobelprize.org/prizes/peace/1905/
    summary/. Julie Anne Demel, 'Female "Diplomats" in Europe from
    1815 to the present', *Encyclopédie pour une histoire nouvelle de l'Europe*,
    ehne.fr/en/node/1122, ehne.fr/en/article/gender-and-europe/gender-
    citizenship-europe/female-diplomats-europe-1815-present.
26 'Woman, 31, is youngest ambassador', BBC News, 28 April 2009, news.
    bbc.co.uk/2/hi/uk_news/england/dorset/8023732.stm. Alex Barker,
    'Britain's first female diplomats', *Financial Times*, 6 November 2009,
    www.ft.com/content/8e936c88-c9ad-11de-a071-00144feabdc0.

Chapter 8

1   Reginald Salt was the fourth son of Thomas Salt, a banker and MP,
    and Emma Helen Mary Anderdon; he was born on 2 March 1874. On
    Barbara Salt, see Alex May, 'Salt, Dame Barbara (1904–1975)', www.
    oxforddnb.com/view/10.1093/ref:odnb/9780198614128.001.0001/
    odnb-9780198614128-e-31650;jsessionid=61C7811E9C0B252047A335
    C12CE854FA.
2   Laura grew up to become a school inspector and later worked as the
    editor of the *Oxford Junior Encyclopedia*. See Peter H. Sutcliffe, *The Oxford
    University Press: An Informal History* (Oxford University Press, 1978). She
    never married, and after a long and productive life died on 4 December
    1983 aged 82.
3   The University of Cologne was one of the great universities of Europe
    (founded in 1388), and was undergoing rapid expansion in the 1920s,
    becoming the fourth largest in Germany. Erich Meuthen, 'A Brief
    History of the University of Cologne', www.portal.uni-koeln.de/univer-
    sitaetsgeschichte.html?&L=1. Germany was then under the weak Weimar
    government and still struggling to recover from the First World War,
    alphahistory.com/weimarrepublic/great-depression/.
4   Barbara Salt: born *c*.1904, 1939–1946, TNA HS 9/1301/6.
5   Michael R.D. Foot, *SOE in France: An Account of the Work of the British
    Special Operations Executive in France 1940–1944* (Government Official
    History Series, 1966). Noreeen Riols, *The Secret Ministry of Ag. & Fish,
    My secret life in Churchill's school for spies* (Macmillan, 2013). Paddy
    Ashdown, *Game of Spies: The Secret Agent, the Traitor and the Nazi,
    Bordeaux 1942–1944* (Harper Collins, 2017).
6   Barbara Salt: born *c*.1904, 1939–1946, TNA HS 9/1301/6.
7   Nick Squires, 'The real-life James Bond', *Daily Telegraph*, 23 September
    2016, www.telegraph.co.uk/news/2016/09/22/real-life-james-bond-
    who-parachuted-behind-WWII-enemy-lines-to-be/.

8 'Tangier, Morocco', *Encyclopaedia Brittanica*, www.britannica.com/place/ Tangier-Morocco.

9 Political Warfare Executive and Foreign Office, Political Intelligence Department: Papers, discovery.nationalarchives.gov.uk/details/r/C8197.

10 Driss Maghraoui, *Revisiting the Colonial Past in Morocco* (Routledge, 2013), p. 165, citing TNA HS3/215 Venom Telgram to Mr. Gascoigne September 1st, 1942.

11 The OSS was formed on 13 June 1942, www.cia.gov/library/ publications/intelligence-history/oss/art03.htm.

12 During Operation Torch, the SOE was a junior partner, but one of its key successes was maintaining a secure radio link between Gibraltar and the Allied invasion forces at a time when the SIS communications proved to be totally inadequate and the OSS communication ran into major technical difficulties, www.cia.gov/library/publications/ intelligence-history/oss/art03.htm.

13 Nigel West, *Historical Dictionary of World War II Intelligence* (Scarecrow Press, 2007).

14 *Special Operations Executive, 1940–1946*, Series 1, 'Special Operations in Western Europe', www.ampltd.co.uk/digital_guides/special_operations_ executive_series_1_parts_1_to_5/SOE -Summary-of-Operations-in- Western-Europe.aspx. codenames.info/operation/falaise/.

15 'Edward Wharton-Tigar, 82, British agent', *New York Times*, Obituaries, 26 June 1995, www.nytimes.com/1995/06/26/obituaries/edward- wharton-tigar-82-british-agent.html.

16 Nicholas Rankin, *Defending the Rock: How Gibraltar Defeated Hitler* (Faber & Faber, 2017). The National Archives, TNA HS 6/951.

17 'The Last Sunrise, Robert Ryan, Questions and Answers', www. readingcircle.co.uk/lastsunrisea2.html.

18 Alan Ogden, *Tigers Burning Bright: SOE Heroes in the Far East* (Bene Factum Publishing, 2013).

19 Barbara Salt: born *c*.1904, 1939–1946, TNA HS 9/1301/6.

20 www.jewishvirtuallibrary.org/operation-bernhard. Emily Langer, 'Adolf Burger, survivor of Nazi counterfeiting operation, dies at 99', *Washington Post*, 8 December 2016, www.washingtonpost.com/world/ europe/adolf-burger-survivor-of-nazi-counterfeiting-operation- dies-at-99/2016/12/08/acca3698-bd5a-11e6-91ee-1adddfe36cbe_story. html. Wharton-Tigar was later posted to the Balkans, and was replaced in Tangier by Lt. J.B. Wilson (code name GB7000). Wilson was later posted to SOE's F Section (France) in early 1944 and Barbara Salt became head of the Tangier operations and remained there until November 1946. Maghraoui, *Revisiting the Colonial Past in Morocco*, p. 164.

21 Barbara Salt: born *c*.1904, 1939–1946, TNA HS 9/1301/6.

22 Miss Barbara Salt, Civil Assistant, War Office. Supplement to *London Gazette*, 9 January 1946, www.thegazette.co.uk/London/issue/37412/supplement/303/data.pdf.

23 www.encyclopedia.com/women/encyclopedias-almanacs-transcripts-and-maps/salt-barbara-1904-1975.

24 Sluga and James, *Women, Diplomacy and International Politics since 1500*, p. 171.

25 *The Times*, 11 January 1973.

26 Alfred William Brian Simpson, *Human Rights and the End of Empire: Britain and the Genesis of the European Convention* (Oxford University Press, 2004), p. 807, footnote 8.

27 The proposals on the table were parity for the five major powers, and the universality of application for the 1 per cent, i.e. a 1-million-man limitation on effectives. The original United Kingdom proposal was for a 3-million-man limitation on the forces of the US–UK–France and of the USSR–Communist China. Foreign Relations of the United States, 1951, National Security Affairs; Foreign Economic Policy, Volume, PPS Files, Lot 64 D 563, Memorandum of Conversation, by Mr Howard Meyers of the Office of United Nations Political and Security Affairs top secret, [Washington,] 5 October 1951. Working Papers Advancing Disarmament Proposals on the Basis of NSC 112, history.state.gov/historicaldocuments/frus1951v01/d144.

28 Foreign Relations of the United States, 1952–54, United Nations Affairs, Volume III, Hickerson–Murphy–Key files, lot 58 D 33, 'US–UK Talks—September 1952' United States Informal Minutes of Meeting Between the United States and United Kingdom Groups (Fourth Session), Washington, 24 September 1952, secret. Office of the Historian, US Department of State, history.state.gov/historicaldocuments/frus1952-54v03/d12.

29 *London Gazette*, 4 February 1958, www.thegazette.co.uk/London/issue/41303/page/783/data.pdf.

30 Simpson, *Human Rights and the End of Empire*, p. 530.

31 Foreign Relations of the United States, 1952–54, United Nations Affairs, Volume III, 310.2/6–1352, Memorandum of Conversation, by Paul W. Jones of the Office of United Nations Political and Security Affairs, secret, [Washington] 13 June 1952, history.state.gov/historical-documents/frus1952-54v03/d569.
    Foreign Relations of the United States, 1952–1954, United Nations Affairs, Volume III, 310.2/8–2753, Memorandum of Conversation, by the Officer in Charge of General Assembly Affairs (Taylor), confidential, [Washington] 27 August 1953, history.state.gov/historicaldocuments/frus1952-54v03/d650,.

32 Foreign Relations of the United States, 1955–57, Soviet Union, Eastern Mediterranean, Volume XXIV 197. Memorandum of a Conversation, Department of State, Washington, 26 September 1956, Washington, history.state.gov/historicaldocuments/frus1955-57v24/d197.

33 www.history.com/this-day-in-history/soviets-put-brutal-end-to-hungarian-revolution. As Arnold Hadwin said in a BBC report: 'I detected a certain bitterness towards the West. They had heard reports on Western radio stations promising help for Hungary. But there was no help; it was just words. The words were misleading because this was a Cold War stand-off. We knew it, the Russians knew it. The Hungarians didn't.' Arnold Hadwin, 'Eyewitness: The Hungarian Uprising of 1956', Sunday 22 October 2006, news.bbc.co.uk/2/hi/uk_news/6069582.stm.

34 Notes on the 59th Meeting of the Special Committee on Soviet and Related Problems, Washington, 4 January 1957, history.state.gov/historicaldocuments/frus1955-57v25/d221.

35 Jonathan Dean was born in 1924 in New York. He attended Harvard College and Columbia University and served in the Canadian and US Armies in the Second World War. His foreign service career took him to Germany, in which he was very much involved, Czechoslovakia, and Katanga. He was interviewed by Charles Stuart Kennedy in 1997, adst. org/wp-content/uploads/2012/09/US-AND-USSR-RELATIONS.pdf.

36 Memorandum by Robert Matteson of conversation with Barbara Salt, Salt, Counsellor, British Embassy, 6 February 1957, White House Office Files, Special Assistant for Disarmament Files, Box 34, f. Bilateral Conferences-United Kingdom 1957–58 (3), DDEL., cited in Jack Cunningham, *Nuclear Sharing And Nuclear Crises: A Study In Anglo-American Relations, 1957–1963*, PhD thesis, University of Toronto, 2010, tspace.library.utoronto.ca/bitstream/1807/24467/1/Cunningham_Jack_201003_PhD_thesis.pdf.pdf.

37 Foreign Office, 2 December 1957. 'The Queen has been graciously pleased to appoint, with effect from the dates respectively indicated: Miss Barbara Salt, M.B.E., to be Her Majesty's Consul-General for the State of Israel, with the exception of the Northern and Haifa districts and the New City of Jerusalem, to reside at Tel Aviv (30th July, 1957)'. *London Gazette*, 3 December 1957, www.thegazette.co.uk/London/issue/41244/page/7057/data.pdf.

38 Central Chancery Of The Orders Of Knighthood; St. James's Palace, London S.W.I.; 'The Queen has been graciously pleased to give orders for the following promotions in, and appointments to, the Most Excellent Order of the British Empire: To be an Ordinary Knight Grand Cross of the Civil Division of the said Most Excellent Order : [...] Miss.Barbara Salt, M.B.E., Counsellor, Her Majesty's Embassy, Tel Aviv.'

Supplement to *London Gazette*, 1 January 1959, www.thegazette.co.uk/London/issue/41589/supplement/20/data.pdf.

39   archivo.cepal.org/pdfs/1962/S6200035.pdf.

40   Recollections of Sir Nicholas Bayne KCMG, Recorded and Transcribed By Abbey Wright. AW: 2 March 2016 Interview with Bayne. BDOHP – British Diplomatic Oral History Programme – Churchill College, www.chu.cam.ac.uk/media/uploads/files/Bayne.pdf.

41   'Britain appoints first woman ambassador as envoy to Israel', *Jewish Telegraphic Agency*, 5 November 1962. 'Britain yesterday appointed as its new Ambassador to Israel Miss Barbara Salt, 58. Miss Salt, who becomes England's first woman ambassador, served as counselor at the British Embassy in Tel Aviv from 1957 to 1960. She succeeds Ambassador Patrick Hancock. Miss Salt, who has most recently served as British representative on the United Nations Economic and Social Council, has held British diplomatic posts in Washington and Moscow.' www.jta.org/1962/11/05/archive/britain-appoints-first-woman-ambassador-as-envoy-to-israel.

42   www.encyclopedia.com/women/encyclopedias-almanacs-transcripts-and-maps/salt-barbara-1904-1975.

43   Central Chancery of the Orders Of Knighthood St. James's Palace, London S.W.I. 'The Queen has been graciously pleased, on the occasion of the Celebration of Her Majesty's Birthday, to give orders for the following promotions in, and appointments to, the Most Excellent Order of the British Empire: To be an Ordinary Dame Commander of the Civil Division of the said Most Excellent Order: Miss Barbara Salt, C.B.E., lately Minister, United Kingdom Mission to the United Nations, New York.' Supplement to *London Gazette*, 5 June 1963, www.thegazette.co.uk/London/issue/43010/supplement/4812/data.pdf.

44   www.encyclopedia.com/women/encyclopedias-almanacs-transcripts-and-maps/salt-barbara-1904-1975.

45   Ibid.; *The Times*, 11 January 1973.

46   Treaty Series No. 53 (1965), Exchanges of Notes between the Government of the United Kingdom of Great Britain and Northern Ireland and the Government of Israel on the Settlement of outstanding Financial Matters London, 15 April, 1965. Presented to Parliament by the Secretary of State for Foreign Affairs by Command of Her Majesty, July 1965 (London, Her Majesty's Stationery Office, 1965).

47   hansard.millbanksystems.com/written_answers/1964/may/07/council-for-volunteers-overseas#S5LV0257P0_19640507_LWA_4. hansard.millbanksystems.com/commons/1964/may/07/the-council-for-volunteers-overseas#S5CV0694P0_19640507_HOC_49.

48 www.encyclopedia.com/women/encyclopedias-almanacs-transcripts-and-maps/salt-barbara-1904-1975.

49 While some of the advice is amusing, much of it is eminently practical, such as that regarding women's hats: 'It is always best to err on the side of caution. Too little formality can cause offence; too much can be easily dispelled by laughter.'

Another gem of Sir Marcus's wisdom is:

> If ever you fail to penetrate a man's personal attitude towards yourself or towards the business that you have in hand, the following tactic will often give results; say your farewells, and then, at the last moment before you are to vanish from his sight – at that very last instant before the door closes upon you – cast one rapid glance back. The expression which you will catch on the face of the man with whom you have been conversing is sometimes absolutely devastating.

> Mr. Cheke's book is not to be published, if for no other reason because of the fun which it sometimes pokes at foreign mentality. This fun is good-natured enough but it might not always be understood. In consequence, this text-book has been marked 'Confidential,' and care should be treated as such. It should not for instance be circulated, even 'confidentially' amongst the *chers collègues* of the Diplomatic Corps.['Guidance for Foreign Service' Circular 02 from O.G. Seargent to Foreign Office 20 January 1949. Enclosed with copy of 'Guidance on foreign usages and ceremony, and other matters, for a Member of His Majesty's Foreign Service on his first appointment to a Post Abroad' by Marcus Cheke, January 1949. Available in British Library.]

Guidance on foreign usages and ceremony, and other matters, for a member of His Majesty's Foreign Service on his first appointment to a post abroad, by Marcus Cheke; Publ. [London] : [Diplomatic Corps], 1949. Candida Slater ['Good Manners and Bad Behaviour, the Unofficial Rules of Diplomacy, Candida Slater, (2008).] accurately described Sir Marcus Cheke's guidance as an hilariously idiosyncratic account, far removed from the dry tome that preceded it, namely the Guide to Diplomatic Practice by Sir Ernest Satow (1917 – updated several times by distinguished diplomats, notably Lord Gore-Booth).

50 Barbara Salt, Diplomatic Administration Office Guidance to Diplomatic Service and other Officers, and Wives, posted to Diplomatic Service missions overseas Or 'Some 'do's' and 'don'ts' of Diplomatic Etiquette and other relevant matters, 1965.

51 Christopher R. Moran, *Classified: Secrecy and the State in Modern Britain* (Cambridge University Press, 2013), p. 308, citing B. Salt, 'Study of the

Pros and Cons of Publication of Further Histories of the SOE', July 1969, TNA CAB 103/570.

52 Brian Gordon Lett, *Ian Fleming and SOE's Operation Postmaster: The Top Secret Story Behind 007* (Grub Street Publishers, 2012).

53 *The Times*, 11 January 1973.

54 Will of Salt, Dame Barbara of Flat 178 Montagu Sq. London W1, died 28 December 1975. Probate London 3 February £51,348, 760100117c, probatesearch.service.gov.uk/Calendar?surname=salt&yearOfDeath=1976&page=1#calendar.

55 *The Times*, 11 January 1973.

56 Will of Salt, Dame Barbara of Flat 178 Montagu Sq. London W1, died 28 December 1975. Probate London 3 February £51,348, 760100117c, probatesearch.service.gov.uk/Calendar?surname=salt&yearOfDeath=1976&page=1#calendar.

57 CPRS 'Review Of Overseas Representation', HL Deb 23 November 1977 vol. 387 cc852–1016. hansard.millbanksystems.com/lords/1977/nov/23/cprs-review-of-overseas-representation.

58 'Obituary for Eleanor Emery', *Daily Telegraph*, 17 July 2007, www.telegraph.co.uk/news/obituaries/1557632/Eleanor Emery.html. 'Eleanor Emery Obituary', *The Times*, 10 July 2007. *The Guardian*, 9 May 1973, www.newspapers.com/image/259770549.

59 Nellie and Eleanor returned to Glasgow for a holiday in April 1923, returning a month later on the Canadian Pacific ship *Metagama May*, www.ancestry.com/family-tree/person/tree/1310700/person/-1525497839/facts.

60 'Obituary for Eleanor Emery', *Daily Telegraph*, 17 July 2007, www.telegraph.co.uk/news/obituaries/1557632/Eleanor -Emery.html.

61 'Three golden rules for diplomats', *The Canberra Times*, 17 April 1973, trove.nla.gov.au/newspaper/article/136970852?searchTerm=%22barbara+salt%22.

62 Joyce Zachariah (Eleanor emery's sister), Email to Richard Warburton, 15 April 2018.

63 *Nanaimo Daily News* (Nanaimo, British Columbia, Canada), 5 April 1973, www.newspapers.com/image/324659547.

64 *The Guardian*, 9 May 1973, www.newspapers.com/image/259770549.

65 *Nanaimo Daily News* (Nanaimo, British Columbia, Canada), 5 April 1973, www.newspapers.com/image/324659547.

66 *Guardian*, 9 May 1973, www.newspapers.com/image/259770549.

67 'Obituary for Eleanor Emery', *Daily Telegraph*, 17 July 2007, www.telegraph.co.uk/news/obituaries/1557632/Eleanor Emery.html.

68 CHAR 20/197B/236, Typescript note from John Peck [Prime Minister's Private Secretary] to Miss Eleanor Emery [Assistant

Private Secretary] (Dominions Office) marked 'immediate' asking her to convey a message to Admiral Lord Keyes [see CHAR 20/197B/235 &238], and stating that he does not know where he is, but believes that he was in a hospital in Adelaide [Australia]. Churchill Archive, www.churchillarchive.com/explore/page?id=CHAR%20 20%2F197B%2F236#image=0.

69   CHAR 20/197B/239, 12 February 1945. Letter from Eleanor Emery [Assistant Private Secretary] (Dominions Office) to John Peck [Prime Minister's Private Secretary] enclosing a copy of a telegram from the Governor of South Australia about the health of Admiral Lord Keyes [see CHAR 20/197B/238] and informing him that in addition to this information Keyes is suffering from 'cardiac failure', the doctors have forbidden him to fly home, the remainder of his tour is being cancelled and arrangements are being made for Lord and Lady Keyes to return home. She also states that she has taken the liberty of passing this information to Lady Gough, Lord Keyes' sister. Churchill Archive, www.churchillarchive.com/explore/page?id=CHAR%20 20%2F197B%2F239#image=0.

70   CHAR 20/229B/189 Letter from 'J R C' [John Colville, Prime Minister's Private Secretary] to Eleanor Emery [Assistant Private Secretary to the Secretary of State for the Dominions] (Dominions Office) on forwarding a letter to Captain Ejnar Mikkelsen, a Danish official in Greenland, through the Canadian Council in Godthab [Greenland]. [Carbon copy]. 30 May 1945. Churchill Archive, www-archives.chu.cam.ac.uk/perl/node?a=a;reference=CHAR%20 20%2F229A-C.

71   CHAR 20/229C/204 Letter from 'J H P' [John Peck, Prime Minister's Private Secretary] to Eleanor Emery [Assistant Private Secretary to the Secretary of State for the Dominions] (Dominions Office) on acknowledging a letter from Sir Cyril Newall [Governor General of New Zealand]. [Carbon copy]. 1 June 1945. Churchill Archive, www-archives.chu.cam.ac.uk/perl/node?a=a;reference=CHAR%20 20%2F229A-C.

72   CHAR 20/229C/244 Letter from Anthony Bevir [Prime Minister's Private Secretary] to Eleanor Emery [Assistant Private Secretary to the Secretary of State for the Dominions] (Dominions Office) enclosing a letter to [Major-General] Sir Charles Rosenthal [Administrator of Norfolk Island, Australia]. [Carbon copy]. 16 June 1945. Churchill Archive, www-archives.chu.cam.ac.uk/perl/ node?a=a;reference=CHAR%2020%2F229A-C.

73   CHAR 20/229C/246 Letter from Eleanor Emery [Assistant Private Secretary to the Secretary of State for the Dominions] (Dominions

Office) to [Anthony] Bevir [Prime Minister's Private Secretary] on acknowledging a letter from Major-General Sir Charles Rosenthal [Administrator of Norfolk Island, Australia to WSC. [signed; annotated by WSC's Private Office]. 14 June 1945. Churchill Archive, www-archives.chu.cam.ac.uk/perl/node?a=a;reference=CHAR%20 20%2F229A-C.

74 On 24 May 1945 Eleanor sent a letter to John Peck, the Prime Minister's private secretary, enclosing a telegram from the Governor of Victoria [Australia, Major-General Sir Winston Dugan] conveying a message for WSC and the King [George VI] and Queen [Elizabeth] from the Honorary Justices Association of Victoria. [signed; annotated by Peck]. Official: Prime Minister: victory messages from Dominion and Colonial Governments. Date: 3 May 1945–18 July 1945, www-archives. chu.cam.ac.uk/perl/node?a=a;reference=CHAR%2020%2F226.

75 *Nanaimo Daily News* (Nanaimo, British Columbia, Canada), 5 April 1973, www.newspapers.com/image/324659547.

76 *The Ottawa Journal*, 10 December 1947, www.newspapers.com/ image/49376217.

77 University of Botswana History Department, Bechuanaland Colonial Administrators *c*.1884–*c*.1965, www.thuto.org/ubh/bw/colad/coloff. htm.

78 'Eleanor Emery Obituary', *The Times*, 10 July 2007.

79 *The Ottawa Journal*, 11 July 1950, www.newspapers.com/ image/50141812.

80 University of Botswana History Department, Bechuanaland Colonial Administrators *c*.1884–*c*.1965, www.thuto.org/ubh/bw/colad/coloff. htm.

81 'How the father of Botswana got his country back: Hugh Massingberd reviews *Colour Bar: the Triumph of Seretse Khama and his Nation* by Susan Williams', *Telegraph*, 2 July 2006, www.telegraph.co.uk/culture/ books/3653555/How-the-father-of-Botswana-got-his-country-back. html.

82 Robert I. Rotberg, *Transformative Political Leadership, Making a Difference in the Developing World* (University of Chicago Press, 2012), p. 73.

83 'Obituary of Lady Ruth Khama', *Guardian*, 29 May 2002, www. theguardian.com/news/2002/may/29/guardianobituaries. 'Suffered racial discrimination and years of British hypocrisy', *Irish Times*, 8 June 2002, www.irishtimes.com/news/suffered-racial-discrimination-and-years- of-british-hypocrisy-1.1060003.

84 Susan Williams, *Colour Bar, The Triumph of Seretse Khama and his Nation* (Penguin Books, 2006). 'Obituary for Eleanor Emery', *Daily Telegraph*,

17 July 2007, www.telegraph.co.uk/news/obituaries/1557632/Eleanor Emery.html.

85 Margaret West, *Catching the Bag, Who'd be a Woman Diplomat* (Edinburgh: Pentland Press, 2000) mentions staying with Eleanor in Pretoria (p. 250).

86 www.dirco.gov.za/foreign/bilateral/uk.html.

87 Bill Keller, 'Nelson Mandela, South Africa's liberator as prisoner and President, dies at 95', *New York Times*, 5 December 2013, www.nytimes.com/2013/12/06/world/africa/nelson-mandela_obit.html. David Beresford, 'Nelson Mandela obituary', *Guardian*, 5 December 2013, www.theguardian.com/world/2013/dec/05/nelson-mandela-obituary.

88 W. David McIntyre, *Winding up the British Empire in the Pacific Islands* (Oxford University Press, 2016).

89 Godwin Ligo, 'How Independence was celebrated in 1980', *Daily Post*, 29 July 2017, dailypost.vu/news/how-independence-was-celebrated-in/article_6f0d540a-2f26-5431-8c52-782e5fea62ad.html. Ron Adams and Sophie Foster, 'Vanuatu', *Encyclopedia Britannica*, www.britannica.com/place/Vanuatu.

90 The University of London Institute of Commonwealth Studies has compiled a more detailed description of these negotiations and the associated documents. University of London Institute of Commonwealth Studies, HM Stationery Office, 2006, books.google.com/books?id=Z2R3Nk3jUlsC&dq=%22india%22+%22eleanor+emery%22&source=gbs_navlinks_s. The resulting constitution offered universal suffrage, with guarantees for Fijian land rights; and the Fijian chiefs, through their dominance of the Senate, had in effect a veto on constitutional change. Fiji became independent on 10 October 1970, thecommonwealth.org/our-member-countries/fiji/history.

91 Kevin Shillington, *Albert René: The Father of Modern Seychelles: A Biography* (Apollo Books, 2014), p. 130.

92 Ibid., citing an Emery memo of 13 June 1969.

93 Sharon Ernesta and Tony Mathiot, 'France Albert Rene, former President of Seychelles, dies at age 83', *Seychelles News Agency*, 27 February 2019, www.seychellesnewsagency.com/articles/10572/France+Albert+Rene%2C+former+President+of+Seychelles%2C+dies+at+age+.

94 'Obituary for Eleanor Emery', *Daily Telegraph*, 17 July 2007, www.telegraph.co.uk/news/obituaries/1557632/Eleanor Emery.html.

95 www.britannica.com/place/Canada /Quebec-separatism.

96 *The Ottawa Journal*, 13 November 1964, www.newspapers.com. 'Eleanor Emery Obituary', *The Times*, 10 July 2007.

97 *East of Suez and the Commonwealth 1964–1971: Europe, Rhodesia, Commonwealth, Part 2* (University of London Institute of

Commonwealth Studies, HM Stationery Office, 2004), p. 354, citing DO 193/79, no. 7, 1 December 1966.

98 Interview of Sir Wynn Hugh-Jones by Malcolm McBain on 15 August 2005, www.chu.cam.ac.uk/media/uploads/files/Hugh-Jones.pdf.

99 David Vine, *Island of Shame: The Secret History of the US Military Base on Diego Garcia* (Princeton University Press, 2009).

100 United Nations, Treaty Series, vol. 603, p. 273, and annex A in volume 866; full text docs.google.com/viewer?a=v&pid=sites&srcid=Z-GVmYXVsdGRvbWFpbnx0aGVjaGFnb3NhcmNoaXBlbGFnb2ZhY3 RzfGd4OjY0ZTAzZjJkNGM2MTU2YTc.

101 Vine, *Island of Shame*, p 104, citing K.R. Whitnall, letter to Mr, Matthews, Miss Emery, 7 May 1969, UKTB:6-755.

102 biot.gov.io/about/history/.

103 The archipelago and the islands of Aldabra, Farquhar and Desroches formed the newly made BIOT, but since then all but the Chagos Islands have been returned to the Seychelles, so that the BIOT now only comprises the Chagos Archipelago. The territory is currently administered from London, with a commissioner appointed by the queen, biot.gov.io/about/history/.

104 publications.Parliament.uk/pa/cm200001/cmhansrd/vo010109/halltext /10109h03.htm.

105 'General Assembly adopts resolution seeking International Court's advisory opinion on pre-independence separation of Chagos Archipelago from Mauritius', 22 June 2017, www.un.org/press/ en/2017/ga11924.doc.htm.

106 Owen Boycott, 'Mauritius takes UK to court over Chagos Islands sovereignty', *Guardian*, 3 September 2018, www.theguardian.com/ world/2018/sep/03/mauritius-takes-uk-to-court-over-chagos-islands-sovereignty. 'Legal consequences of the separation of the Chagos Archipelago from Mauritius In 1965', 25 February 2019, advisory opinion, International Court of Justice, www.icj-cij.org/files/ case-related/169/169-20190225-01-00-EN.pdf.

107 'General Assembly welcomes International Court of Justice opinion on Chagos Archipelago, adopts text calling for Mauritius' complete decolonization,, 22 May 2019, www.un.org/press/en/2019/ga12146. doc.htm.

108 Rick Gladstone, 'Britain dealt defeat at U.N. over its control of Chagos Islands', *New York Times*, 22 May 2019, www.nytimes.com/2019/05/22/ world/africa/britain-chagos-mauritius.html.

109 www.bbc.com/news/uk-36659976. The FCO apparently knew at some point that there was an indigenous population on the islands but is not clear whether they were apprised of that fact when the original

agreement was signed with the US in 1966. However, the current BIOT website's description of the population states that the residents were always transitory and/or temporary. As for the population of the islands, after emancipation some slaves became contract employees; the population changed over time by import of contract labour from Mauritius and, in the 1950s, from Seychelles, so that by the late 1960s, those living on the islands were contract employees of the copra plantations. Neither they, nor those permitted by the plantation owners to remain, owned land or houses. They had licences to reside there at the discretion of the owners and moved from island to island as work required, biot.gov.io/about/history/.

110 'Stealing a Nation', a special report by John Pilger, ITV (2004), www.bullfrogfilms.com/guides/stealguide.pdf.

111 House of Commons debate regarding the British Indian Ocean Territory, 9 January 2001, publications.Parliament.uk/pa/cm200001/cmhansrd/vo010109/halltext/10109h03.htm.

112 'Obituary for Eleanor Emery', *Daily Telegraph*, 17 July 2007, www.telegraph.co.uk/news/obituaries/1557632/Eleanor -Emery.html.

113 *Nanaimo Daily News* (Nanaimo, British Columbia, Canada), 3 April 1973, www.newspapers.com/image/324658209. *The Ottawa Journal*, 4 April 1973, www.newspapers.com/image/45747179.

114 *Nanaimo Daily News* (Nanaimo, British Columbia, Canada), 5 April 1973, www.newspapers.com/image/32465954.

115 'Three golden rules for diplomats', *The Canberra Times*, 17 April 1973, trove.nla.gov.au/newspaper/article/136970852?searchTerm=%22barbara+salt%22.

116 'Eleanor Emery Obituary', *The Times*, 10 July 2007.

117 HL Deb 9 May 1973 vol. 342 cc437–503, hansard.millbank-systems.com/lords/1973/may/09/commonwealth-consultation-1#S5LV0342P0_19730509_HOL_143.

118 HL Deb 09 May 1973 vol. 342 cc410–28, hansard.millbanksystems.com/lords/1973/may/09/commonwealth-consultation.

119 HC Deb 02 April 1973 vol. 854 cc23–4, hansard.millbank-systems.com/commons/1973/apr/02/employment-of-women-report#S5CV0854P0_19730402_HOC_150.

120 *The Ottawa Journal*, 4 April 1973, www.newspapers.com/newspage/45747179/. *The Ottawa Journal*, 5 April 1973, www.newspapers.com/image/45750062. *Nanaimo Daily News* (Nanaimo, British Columbia, Canada), 5 April 1973, www.newspapers.com/image/324659547. *Guardian*, 4 April 1973, www.newspapers.com/image/259741639.

121 'Three golden rules for diplomats', *The Canberra Times*, 17 April 1973, trove.nla.gov.au/newspaper/article/136970852?searchTerm=%22barbara+salt%22.

122 *Nanaimo Daily News* (Nanaimo, British Columbia, Canada), 5 April 1973, www.newspapers.com/image/324659547.

123 Interview with Terry Coleman, *Guardian*, 9 May 1973, www.newspapers.com/image/259770549.

124 Ibid.

125 'Three golden rules for diplomats', *The Canberra Times*, 17 April 1973, trove.nla.gov.au/newspaper/article/136970852?searchTerm=%22barbara+salt%22.

126 *Nanaimo Daily News* (Nanaimo, British Columbia, Canada), 5 April 1973, www.newspapers.com/image/324659547.

127 'Obituary for Eleanor Emery', *Daily Telegraph*, 17 July 2007, www.telegraph.co.uk/news/obituaries/1557632/Eleanor Emery.html. 'Eleanor Emery Obituary', *The Times*, 10 July 2007. The hospital was built in 1933–34 by the United Free Church of Scotland and was officially launched on 3 September 1934 with twenty beds. The hospital is now a government-run state-of-the-art hospital, www.webcitation.org/6HLlxKBgq.

128 Southern Rhodesia was a self-governing British crown colony from 1923 until its unilateral declaration of independence in 1965, forming the unrecognised state of Rhodesia, ruled by the white-minority government led by Ian Smith. Britain attempted to resolve the issue diplomatically and the UN imposed sanctions against Rhodesia. Rhodesia declared itself a 'republic' in 1970 and a civil war ensued between the government and two main resistance groups, Joshua Nkomo's Zimbabwe African People's Union (ZAPU) and Robert Mugabe's Zimbabwe African National Union (ZANU) organisations, supported by assistance from the governments of Zambia and Mozambique. *Nanaimo Daily News* (Nanaimo, British Columbia, Canada), 5 April 1973, www.newspapers.com/image/324659547.

129 For example, when in January 1973 James Callahan, then foreign secretary, visited Botswana to meet President Khama as the telegram from the US Embassy in Gaborone illustrates, Emery met with the Americans and other interested parties to negotiate positions, wikileaks.org/plusd/cables/1975GABORO00031_b.html. With the 1976 election of Jimmy Carter as President, the US and UK worked hard to apply additional pressure (sanctions were already in place) on the Rhodesian government to persuade them to relinquish power. Memorandum From Secretary of State Vance to President Carter, Washington, 12 September 1977, history.state.gov/historicaldocuments/frus1977-80v16/d167.

130 Jay Ross, 'Zimbabwe gains independence', *Washington Post*, 18 April 1980, www.washingtonpost.com/archive/politics/1980/04/18/ zimbabwe-gains-independence/185c3573-e9e4-4d3a-9dce- 5fe89bf04605/. Alan Cowell, 'Robert Mugabe, strongman who cried, "Zimbabwe Is Mine", dies at 95', *New York Times*, 6 September 2019, www.nytimes.com/2019/09/06/obituaries/robert-mugabe-dead.html.

131 'Eleanor Emery Obituary', *The Times*, 10 July 2007.

132 Joyce Zachariah, email to Richard Warburton, 15 April 2018.

133 'Eleanor Emery Obituary', *The Times*, 10 July 2007.

134 *The Observer*, 27 July 1980, www.newspapers.com/image/258380296.

135 www.findagrave.com/memorial/20121402.

136 www.gla.ac.uk/news/archiveofnews/2009/may/headline_117817_ en.html.

137 Warburton and Warburton, *The Story of Britain's First Female Ambassador*.

138 In 1994 Somerville College voted to accept men for the first time, www.some.ox.ac.uk/about-somerville/history/.

139 www.independent.co.uk/news/people/dame-anne-warburton- britains-first-female-ambassador-who-later-became-an-inspirational- President-of-10330078.html.

140 Foreign Service Regulation No. 1, *London* Gazette, 14 January 1947, www.thegazette.co.uk/London/issue/37852/supplement/280/data.pdf.

141 *The Advertiser* (Adelaide, SA) 14 October 1946, trove.nla.gov.au/ newspaper/article/35761250.

142 *London Gazette*, 5 April 1960, www.thegazette.co.uk/London/ issue/42001/page/2467/data.pdf.

143 'Queen Elizabeth at 90: The Story of Britain's Longest Reigning Monarch', *LIFE*, 1 April 2016.

144 *London Gazette*, 22 June 1965, p. 5981.

145 research.omicsgroup.org/index.php/Anne _Warburton. *London Gazette*, 24 June 1976.

146 McCarthy, *Women of the World*, p. 297, citing Shirley Harrison, 'The not so diplomatic wives', *Homes & Gardens* February 1978, pp. 80–2.

147 www.independent.co.uk/news/people/dame-anne-warburton- britains-first-female-ambassador-who-later-became-an-inspirational- President-of-10330078.html. *Financial Times*, 7/8 November 2009. www. west-info.eu/warburton-became-britains-first-female-ambassador- presenting-her-credentials-to-the-danish-court-in-1976/.

148 Interview with Sir Michael Palliser by Helen McCarthy, 4 October 2011, cited in McCarthy, *Women of the World*, p. 297.

149 Ibid.

150 Interview with Lord Ashdown of Norton-sub-Hamdon by Richard Warburton, 4 July 2017.

151 Correspondence with Elizabeth Warburton, 3 April 2017.

152 *London Gazette*, Supplement, 11 June 1977.

153 Anne Warburton, *Signposts to Denmark* (Hernov, 1992).

154 Anne Warburton interview notes, *c.*1995, interviewer unknown, provided by Beth Butler.

155 *London Gazette*, 8 June 1979.

156 Interview by Jonathan Gregson with Dame Anne Warburton, President of Lucy Cavendish College, Cambridge, Cambridge Alumni Magazine, *c.*1992.

157 www.anglo-danishsociety.org.uk/uploads/images/file/ADS-Sep-2015. pdf.

158 Address: H.E. Dame Anne Warburton D.C.V.O., C.M,G., Ambassador, Permanent Mission of the United Kingdom, 37–39, rue de Vermont, 1211 Genève 20, Switzerland, idl-bnc.idrc.ca/dspace/ bitstream/10625/9595/1/WCED_v43_doc1-14.pdf.
GATT Office Circular No. 270/Corr.l, List Of Liaison Officers And Representatives, Corrigendum, United Kingdom (E). H.E. Dame Anne Warburton D.C.V.O., C.M.G.★, Ambassador, Permanent Representative of the United Kingdom to the Office of the United Nations and other international organizations at Geneva, 22 January 1985, docs.wto.org/ gattdocs/s/.%5CGG%5CGATTOFFCIR%5C270C1.pdf.

159 Nigel Watson, *The Opportunity to Be Myself: A History of Lucy Cavendish College, Cambridge* (London: James & James, 2002).

160 *Guardian*, 15 June 2015, www.theguardian.com/politics/2015/jun/15/ dame-anne-warburton.

161 EC Investigative Mission Into The Treatment Of Muslim Women In The Former Yugoslavia: Report To EC Foreign Ministers, Released February 1993 By Udenrigsministeriat, Ministry Of Foreign Affairs Copenhagen [Section 10].

162 European Political Cooperation Documentation Bulletin, 1993 Vol. 9; 93/035. Statement on the follow-up to the Warburton Mission, Date of issue: 1 February 1993, Place of issue: Brussels, Copenhagen, Country of Presidency: Denmark, Status of document: Press statement, aei.pitt. edu/36868/1/A2877.pdf.

163 Paul Lewis, *New York Times*, 3 June 1994 on final report of a United Nations commission set up to collect evidence of war crimes in the former Yugoslavia, www.nytimes.com/1994/06/03/world/un-report-accuses-serbs-of-crimes-against-humanity.html.

164 Interview with Lord Ashdown of Norton-sub-Hamdon by Richard Warbuton, 4 July 2017.

165 The Situation of Human Rights in the Territory of the Former Yugoslavia. Report A/48/92, S/25341, 26 February 1993, repository.

un.org/bitstream/handle/11176/51391/A_48_92%3bS_25341-EN. pdf?sequence=21&isAllowed=y. Paul Lewis, *New York Times*, 3 June 1994 on final report of a United Nations commission set up to collect evidence of war crimes in the former Yugoslavia, www.nytimes. com/1994/06/03/world/un-report-accuses-serbs-of-crimes-against-humanity.html. 'Rape was weapon of Serbs, UN Says', *New York Times*, 20 October 1993, page 1. 'Bosnia-Herzegovina: Rape and sexual abuse by armed forces, Amnesty International, 21 January 1993, Index number: EUR 63/001/1993, www.amnesty.org/en/documents/eur63/001/1993/ en/. 'War crimes in Bosnia-Hercegovina (Volume I)', August 1992, www.hrw.org/report/1992/08/01/war-crimes-bosnia-hercegovina-volume-i. 'War Crimes in Bosnia-Hercegovina (Volume II)', April 1993, www.hrw.org/report/1993/04/01/war-crimes-bosnia-hercegovina-volume-ii.

166 GB 141 BODA – The Balkan Odyssey Digital Archive, University of Liverpool, sca-arch.liv.ac.uk/ead/html/gb141boda-p12.shtml#boda.05. Hansard Columns 782 & 783, www.publications.Parliament.uk/pa/ cm199293/cmhansrd/1993-02-23/Debate-3.html. hansard.millbank-systems.com/commons/1993/feb/23/international-peacekeeping.

167 Commission On Human Rights Forty-Ninth Session, Situation Of Human Rights In The Territory Of The Former Yugoslavia, 17 February 1993, documents-dds-ny.un.org/doc/UNDOC/LTD/G93/108/15/ pdf/G9310815.pdf?OpenElement. Commission On Human Rights, Forty-Ninth Session, Situation Of Human Rights In The Territory Of The Former Yugoslavia, 22 February 1993, documents-dds-ny.un.org/ doc/UNDOC/LTD/G93/109/81/pdf/G9310981.pdf?OpenElement.

168 www.un.org/en/ga/search/view_doc.asp?symbol=S/RES/808(1993).

169 'Chapter VII: Action With Respect To Threats To The Peace, Breaches Of The Peace, And Acts Of Aggression', www.un.org/en/sections/ un-charter/chapter-vii/index.html.

170 Rachel Kerr, *The International Criminal Tribunal for the Former Yugoslavia, An Exercise in Law, Politics and Diplomacy* (Oxford University Press, 2004). Further detailed description of the establishment and history of the International Criminal Tribunal for the Former Yugoslavia may be found in Serge Brammertz and Michelle Jarvis, eds., *Prosecuting Conflict-Related Sexual Violence at the ICTY* (Oxford University Press, 2016).

171 www.icc-cpi.int/about.

172 Dame Rosemary Spencer, e-mail to Richard Warburton, 20 September 2019.

Chapter 9

1   Caroline Wilson, 'Women leading British diplomacy across
    Europe', 8 March 2017, blogs.fco.gov.uk/fcoeditorial/2017/03/08/
    women-leading-british-diplomacy-across-europe/. Ben C. Fletcher,
    'What your clothes might be saying about you', 20 April 2013, www.
    psychologytoday.com/us/blog/do-something-different/201304/
    what-your-clothes-might-be-saying-about-you. Janine Willis and
    Alexander Todorov, 'First impressions: Making up your mind After a
    100-Ms exposure to a face', *Psychological Science*, vol. 17 (2006), p. 17.
    Jaynine Howard, 'In 2018, professional women are still judged by
    their appearances', 23 February 2018, www.recruiter.com/i/in-2018-
    professional-women-are-still-judged-by-their-appearances/.

2   Anna Gawel, '"Diplomacy by design" examines what clothes
    say about us', *The Washington Diplomat*, 29 November 2016,
    washdiplomat.com/index.php?option=com_content&view=article&
    id=14511:diplomacy-by-design-examines-what-clothes-say-about-
    us&catid=1551&Itemid=428.

3   Laura E. Kirkpatrick, 'Call me Dame Karen: UK's ambassador
    dashes style with diplomacy', PassBlue, 12 June 2019, www.passblue.
    com/2019/06/12/call-me-dame-karen-uks-ambassador-dashes-style-
    with-diplomacy/.

4   *PassBlue* is an independent, women-led journalism site that is considered
    the most influential media source covering the US-UN relationship,
    women's issues, human rights, peacekeeping and other urgent global
    matters playing out in the UN, www.passblue.com/about-us/.

5   Wilson, 'Women leading British diplomacy across Europe'.

6   Ibid.

7   Dame Denise Holt, interview with Richard Warburton, 14 October
    2019.

8   Kate Wills, 'The secret world of ambassadors: what do they actually
    do?', *Evening Standard*, 24 July 2019, www.standard.co.uk/lifestyle/
    esmagazine/ambassador-diplomats-kim-darroch-a4195186.html.

9   Catherine Arnold, 'What's it like being the UK Ambassador in
    Mongolia?, *Civil Service World*, 28 August 2015, www.civilserviceworld.
    com/articles/opinion/what%E2%80%99s-it-being-uk-ambassador-
    mongolia.

10 Christopher White and Inés San Martín, 'Female envoys to Vatican say
    it's past time for Church to empower women', 25 September 2017,
    Crux, cruxnow.com/vatican/2017/09/25/female-envoys-vatican-say-
    past-time-church-empower-women/.

11   Freeman and Marks, 'Diplomacy'.

12   'House of Beaufort meets Jules Chapell OBE, the UK's youngest Ambassador', 18 May 2017, www.houseofbeaufort.com/2017/05/18/house-of-beaufort-meets-jules-chapell-obe-the-uks-youngest-ambassador/.

13   Julie Chappell, 'The future of activism in a pussy-grabbing world', TEDxLSE, 8 May 2017, www.youtube.com/watch?v=vq92--p9sbk.

14   Toosi, 'Female diplomats share secrets'.

15   Data from Colin Mackie, *A Directory of British Diplomats*, 2016.

16   Dame Denise Holt, interview with Richard Warburton, 14 October 2019.

17   Regina Respondent and R. Appellant, House of Lords, the Law Reports (Appeal Cases)[1992] 1 AC 599, 1 July 1991; Oct. 23, www.bailii.org/uk/cases/UKHL/1991/12.html.

18   Hilaire Barnett, *Britain Unwrapped: Government and Constitution Explained* (Penguin, 2002), p. 168. *Historia Placitorum Coronæ: The History of the Pleas of the Crown*, Part 2, Section 629, 1736, full text lawlibrary.wm.edu/wythepedia/library/HaleHistoryOfThePleasOfTheCrown1736Vol2.pdf.

19   Convention on the Elimination of All Forms of Discrimination against Women, New York, 18 December 1979, treaties.un.org/Pages/ViewDetails.aspx?src=TREATY&mtdsg_no=IV-8&chapter=4&clang=_en.

20   Wilson, 'Women leading British diplomacy across Europe'.

21   Dickie, *The New Mandarins*, p. 24.

22   McCarthy, *Women of the World*, p. 291.

23   Working for FCO, www.gov.uk/government/organisations/foreign-commonwealth-office/about/recruitment.

24   www.yourdanishlife.dk/meet-the-british-ambassador/.

25   'Women in foreign policy, interview/diplomacy, Vivien Life, British ambassador To Denmark', www.womeninforeignpolicy.org/diplomacy/2016/7/6/vivien-life.

26   Alex Barker, 'Britain's first female diplomats', *Financial Times*, 6 November 2009, www.ft.com/content/8e936c88-c9ad-11de-a071-00144feabdc0.

27   'Women in the Foreign Office: A Diplomatic Journey', speech by Dame Rosemary Spencer.

28   Dame Denise Holt, interview with Richard Warburton, 14 October 2019.

29   Helen Pidd, 'Mr and Mrs Ambassador', 1 August 2008, *Guardian*, www.theguardian.com/world/2008/aug/02/zambia.

30 'Change of Her Majesty's Ambassadors to Armenia', FCO news story, 15 August 2011, www.gov.uk/government/news/change-of-her-majestys-ambassadors-to-armenia.

31 Kathy Leach, 'The ambassadorial job share', *Our Civil Service*, 3 March 2014, civilservice.blog.gov.uk/2014/03/03/the-ambassadorial-job-share/.

32 The Equality Act of 2010. Full text is www.legislation.gov.uk/ukpga/2010/15/contents.

33 Foreign and Commonwealth Office (FCO) Diversity and Equality Report 2016–17 in response to the Equality Act 2010, assets.publishing. service.gov.uk/government/uploads/system/uploads/attachment_data/file/672480/FCO_Diversity_and_Equality_Report_2016-2017.pdf.

34 'Women in diplomacy: An assessment of British female ambassadors in overcoming gender hierarchy, 1990–2010', *American Diplomacy*, April 2010, www.unc.edu/depts/diplomat/item/2011/0104/comm/rahman_women.html#note72.

35 Interview with Menna Rawlings, 18 August, 2016, www.lowyinstitute. org/the-interpreter/women-diplomacy-look-how-far-weve-come.

36 'Women in the Foreign Office: A Diplomatic Journey', Speech by Dame Rosemary Spencer, given in 2018 at the Foreign and Commonwealth Office, copy provided to RW by Dame Rosemary Spencer via email 16 September 2019.

37 'The Foreign Office has traditionally been a place for eccentric males', *Guardian*, 18 June 2014, www.theguardian.com/public-leaders-network/2014/jun/18/foreign-office-eccentric-males-women-pay-gap.

38 www.gov.uk/government/people/joanna-roper.

39 Speech by Barbara Woodward, 15 April 2016, www.gov.uk/government/speeches/british-ambassadors-speech-at-the-her-village-forum-on-inspiring.

40 Matthew Mercer, 'Doing well abroad: Britain's youngest ever ambassador on delivering diplomacy', Center for Public Impact, 27 February 2017, www.centreforpublicimpact.org/britains-youngest-ever-ambassador-diplomacy/.

41 Ibid.

42 Wills, 'The secret world of ambassadors'.

43 *The Times*, 1 January 2009.

44 'BBC On this day 1950–2005', news.bbc.co.uk/onthisday/hi/dates/stories/september/9/newsid_3634000/3634352.stm.

45 Interview with Sir Michael Palliser by Helen McCarthy, 4 October 2011, cited in McCarthy, *Women of the World*, p. 299.

46 Cameron, 'Why British women need a diplomatic coup'.

47　Global Peace Index Report 2017, visionofhumanity.org/app/ uploads/2017/06/GPI17-Report.pdf. www.atlasandboots.com/ most-dangerous-countries-in-the-world-ranked/.

48　A list of heads of mission is available for 2014, www.gov.uk/ government/publications/foi-release-list-of-uk-heads-of-mission.

49　www.gov.uk/government/people/nicholas-kay.

50　www.gov.uk/government/people/alison-blackburne.

51　Wilson, 'Women leading British diplomacy across Europe'. Cameron, 'Why British women need a diplomatic coup'.

52　'Karen Pierce becomes first female UK ambassador to the UN', *Guardian*, 27 November 2017, www.theguardian.com/world/2017/ nov/27/karen-pierce-first-female-uk-ambassador-to-un.

53　Helen Crane, 'Foreign Office is now more accessible to women, says former ambassador', *Guardian*, 10 December 2013, www.theguardian. com/public-leaders-network/women-leadership-blog/2013/dec/10/ foreign-office-accessible-women-julie-chappell.

54　www.afsa.org/female-us-ambassadors.

55　Lisa Feierman, 'Where are all the female diplomats?', *Kennedy School Review*, 6 November 2016, ksr.hkspublications.org/2016/11/06/where- are-all-the-female-diplomats/.

56　Ann Towns and Birgitta Niklasson, 'Gender, international status, and ambassador appointments', *Foreign Policy Analysis*, vol. (2017), pp. 521–40, academic.oup.com/fpa/article/13/3/521/2625550.

57　James Southern, 'Black skin, Whitehall: Race and the Foreign Office 1945–2018', *FCO History Notes* 21, assets.publishing.service.gov.uk/ government/uploads/system/uploads/attachment_data/file/745663/ Race_and_FCO_History_Note.pdf, citing Percival Waterfield, 'Memorandum by the Civil Service Commissioners for the Information and Guidance of all Chairmen of Selection Boards: Coloured British Candidates', 3 January 1951, TNA/DO/35/2593.

58　Southern, 'Black skin, Whitehall'.

59　Mr. Bradshaw, State for Foreign and Commonwealth Affairs, *Hansard*, 11 May 2001, vol. 374, hansard.Parliament.uk/commons/2001-05-11/ debates/62a0501a-b164-429a-b6e6-a4d451eaa649/ Ambassadors(EthnicOrigin).

60　US Department of State, Office of the Historian, Ebenezer Don Carlos Bassett (1833–1908), history.state.gov/departmenthistory/people/ bassett-ebenezer-don-carlos.

61　US Department of State, Office of the Historian, Edward Richard Dudley (1911–2005), history.state.gov/departmenthistory/people/ dudley-edward-richard.

62 US Department of State, Office of the Historian, Patricia Roberts Harris (1924–1985), history.state.gov/departmenthistory/people/harris-patricia-roberts.

63 Robin Cook, *Hansard*, HC Deb, 11 May 1999, vol. 331 c118W, 11 May 1999, api.Parliament.uk/historic-hansard/written-answers/1999/may/11/minority-ethnic-liaison-officer#S6CV0331P0_19990511_CWA_269.

64 FCO diversity and equality report 2018, 5 November 2018, www.gov.uk/government/publications/fco-diversity-and-equality-report-2018.

65 BAME stands for black, Asian and minority ethnic, i.e. government shorthand for 'not white'.

66 Nicola Slawson, 'First black female UK career diplomat appointed High Commissioner', *Guardian*, 22 March 2018, www.theguardian.com/politics/2018/mar/22/first-black-female-high-commissioner-appointed-by-foreign-office-nnenne-iwuji-eme.

67 *The Morning Post*, issue 20273, p. 4, 1835, British Library Collection, www.bl.uk/collection-items/the-execution-of-james-pratt-and-john-smith.

68 Report of the Departmental Committee on Homosexual Offences and Prostitution, chaired by Sir John Wolfenden. *International Congress On Clinical Chemistry*, *British Medical Journal*, 14 September 1957, p. 639, www.ncbi.nlm.nih.gov/pmc/articles/PMC1962139/pdf/brmedj03120-0059.pdf.

69 Criminal Justice and Public Order Act 1994; Sexual Offences (Amendment) Act 2000; Sexual Offences Act 2003.

70 Tracy McVeigh, 'Heckled but happy: the graceful star of gay marriage debate', *Guardian*, 25 May 2013, www.theguardian.com/society/2013/may/26/margot-james-heckled-but-happy?CMP=share_btn_tw.

71 Denis Campbell, 'The pioneer who changed gay lives: By coming out Chris Smith transformed attitudes', *Guardian*, 30 January 2005, www.theguardian.com/politics/2005/jan/30/uk.aids.

72 David Shariatmadari, 'The quiet revolution: why Britain has more gay MPs than anywhere else', *Guardian*, 13 May 2015, www.theguardian.com/world/2015/may/13/quiet-revolution-britain-more-gay-mps-than-anywhere-else-lgbt. In 2017, 2 per cent of adults identified as lesbian, gay or bisexual, as did 4.2 per cent of people aged 16 to 24. Sexual orientation, UK: 2017, Office of National Statistics, www.ons.gov.uk/peoplepopulationandcommunity/culturalidentity/sexuality/bulletins/sexualidentityuk/2017.

73 Jon Kelly, 'The era when gay spies were feared', *BBC News Magazine*, 20 January 2016, www.bbc.com/news/magazine-35360172.

74　James Southern, 'Homosexuality at the Foreign Office 1967–1991', *History Notes* 19.

75　Patrick Strudwick, 'This is what it's like being an ambassador to an anti-gay country when you're a lesbian', *Buzzfeed*, 19 March 2016, www.buzzfeednews.com/article/patrickstrudwick/this-is-what-its-like-being-an-ambassador-to-an-anti-gay-cou.

76　The Prime Minister announced the changes for security clearances for government departments including the FCO. Prime Minister responding to question from Sir John Wheeler, *Hansard* Security Vetting, HC Deb 23 July 1991, vol. 195 c474W, api.Parliament.uk/historic-hansard/written-answers/1991/jul/23/security-vetting.

77　Annika Savill, 'Inside file: Gay diplomats are safer in the closet', *Independent*, 17 March 1994, www.independent.co.uk/news/world/europe/inside-file-gay-diplomats-are-safer-in-the-closet-1429599.html.

78　James Southern, 'Homosexuality at the Foreign Office 1967–1991', *History Notes* 19.

79　Richard Norton-Taylor, 'Forces ban on gays is lifted', *Guardian*, 12 January 2000, www.theguardian.com/uk/2000/jan/13/richardnortontaylor.

80　Helen Pidd, 'Mr and Mrs Ambassador', 1 August 2008, *Guardian*, www.theguardian.com/world/2008/aug/02/zambia.

81　Civil Partnership Act 2004; The Marriage (Same Sex Couples) Act 2013.

82　Ben Blanchard, 'China's Parliament rules out allowing same-sex marriage', *Reuters*, 21 August 2019, www.reuters.com/article/us-china-lgbt-marriage/china-Parliament-rules-out-allowing-same-sex-marriage-idUSKCN1VB09E.

83　Philip Sherwell, 'British diplomat Brian Davidson promotes LGBTI understanding just by living his life', *Newsweek*, 16 May 2107, www.newsweek.com/british-diplomat-brian-davidson-lbgti-tolerance-living-life-610347.

84　'UK embassy performs first gay marriage in Dominican Republic', *Associated Press*, 31 December 2014, www.foxnews.com/world/uk-embassy-performs-first-gay-marriage-in-dominican-republic,.

85　Patrick Strudwick, 'This is what it's like being an ambassador to an anti-gay country when you're a lesbian', *Buzzfeed*, 19 March 2016, www.buzzfeednews.com/article/patrickstrudwick/this-is-what-its-like-being-an-ambassador-to-an-anti-gay-cou.

86　Foreign and Commonwealth Office (FCO) Diversity and Equality Report 2017–18 in response to the Equality Act 2010.

87　Jane Merrick, 'Barbara Woodward: Britain's first female ambassador to China intends to forge strong links with the growing economic superpower', *Independent*, 1 March 2015, www.independent.co.uk/news/

people/barbara-woodward-britains-first-female-ambassador-to-china-intends-to-forge-strong-links-with-the-10077676.html.

88 Speech by Barbara Woodward, 15 April 2016, www.gov.uk/government/speeches/british-ambassadors-speech-at-the-her-village-forum-on-inspiring.

89 Dame Denise Holt, interview with Richard Warburton, 14 October 2019.

Chapter 10

1 www.gov.uk/government/organisations/foreign-commonwealth-office/about/our-governance.

2 British Diplomatic Oral History Programme, Recollections of Dame Mariot Leslie DCMG at Royal Overseas League, Edinburgh, 29 March 2017, recorded and transcribed by Alasdair MacDermott, Churchill College, Cambridge, www.chu.cam.ac.uk/media/uploads/files/Leslie.pdf. Used with permission.

3 *London Gazette* (Supplement), No. 50948, 13 June 1987, www.thegazette.co.uk/London/issue/50948/supplement/3.

4 *London Gazette* (Supplement), No. 54255, 29 December 1995, www.thegazette.co.uk/London/issue/54255/supplement/3.

5 'Who is Dame Pauline Neville-Jones?', *Guardian*, 2 September 2003, www.theguardian.com/media/2003/sep/02/davidkelly.hutton3.

6 Polly Toynbee, 'A very undiplomatic incident', *Independent*, 6 February 1996, www.independent.co.uk/news/uk/a-very-undiplomatic-incident-1317584.html.

7 www.Parliament.uk/biographies/lords/baroness-neville-jones/3840.

8 www.gov.uk/government/publications/foreign-and-commonwealth-office-directors/fco-directors.

9 The list of current ministers at the FCO can be found at www.gov.uk/government/organisations/foreign-commonwealth-office or www.gov.uk/government/ministers.

10 Lena Jeger, 'Obituary for Baroness White of Rhymney', *Guardian*, 27 December 1999, www.theguardian.com/news/1999/dec/27/guardianobituaries. Jane Merrick, 'Eirene White', in The *Honourable Ladies: Volume I: Profiles of Women MPs 1918–1996*, ed. Iain Dale and Jacqui Smith (Biteback Publishing, 2018).

11 Dame Anne Begg, 'Priscilla Buchan, Lady Tweedsmuir', in *The Honourable Ladies: Volume I*, ed. Dale and Smith.

12 Lena Jeger, 'Baroness White of Rhymney', *Guardian*, 27 December 1999, www.theguardian.com/news/1999/dec/27/guardianobituaries.

13 Elizabeth L. Ewan, Sue Innes, Sian Reynolds and Rose Pipes, eds.,
   Biographical Dictionary of Scottish Women (Edinburgh University Press,
   2007), p. 51.
14 www.thepeerage.com/p5854.htm#i58532.
15 www.geni.com/people/Priscilla-Tweedsmuir/6000000006339029109.
16 James Buchan, 'Obituary: Lord Tweedsmuir', *Independent*, 22 June
   1996, www.independent.co.uk/news/people/obituary-lord-
   tweedsmuir-1338173.html.
17 Rosemary Spears, 'Lady Tweedsmuir puts on mother-in-law's mink',
   Winipeg Free Press, 14 December 1966, newspaperarchive.com/winnipeg-
   free-press-dec-14-1966-p-22/.
18 www.theqe2story.com/forum/index.php?topic=7394.0. Anne Wealleans,
   Designing Liners: A History of Interior Design Afloat (Routledge, 2006),
   p. 159.
19 *London Gazette*, 3 July 1970, www.thegazette.co.uk/London/
   issue/45142/page/7377. api.Parliament.uk/historic-hansard/lords/1970/
   jul/01/baroness-tweedsmuir-of-belhelvie.
20 *The Honourable Ladies: Volume I*, ed. Dale and Smith.
21 Bahamas Independence Bill, HL Deb 7 June 1973, vol. 343 cc214–38,
   api.Parliament.uk/historic-hansard/lords/1973/jun/07/bahamas-
   independence-bill. Visit of Lady Tweedsmuir, Minister of State for
   Foreign and Commonwealth Affairs, to West Africa, 16–31 January
   1973, TNA FCO 65/1274. Visit by Foreign and Commonwealth
   Office Minister of State, Lady Tweedsmuir, from UK to Zambia,
   14–18 October 1972, TNA FCO 45/1158. Visit of Lady Tweedsmuir,
   Minister of State, to United Nations, November 1972, TNA FCO
   58/708.
22 P. Ward, *Unionism in the United Kingdom, 1918–1974* (Springer, 2005),
   p. 69, citing *Evening Standard*, 11 July 1972.
23 Ibid., citing *Daily Mail*, 5 December 1972.
24 *London Gazette* (Supplement), No. 46254, 2 April 1974.
25 Tributes To The Late Lady Tweedsmuir Of Belhelvie, HL Deb 13 March
   1978 vol. 389 cc1035–41 1035. The Lord Privy Seal (Lord Peart). api.
   Parliament.uk/historic-hansard/lords/1978/mar/13/tributes-to-the-
   late-lady-tweedsmuir-of.
26 Tam Dalyell, 'Obituary: Baroness Lestor of Eccles', *Independent*, 30 March
   1998, www.independent.co.uk/news/obituaries/obituary-baroness-
   lestor-of-eccles-1153447.html.
27 Anne Perkins, 'How Barbara Castle broke the glass ceiling of politics',
   BBC Radio 4, 3 September 2010, www.bbc.com/news/uk-politics-
   11149803. Anne Perkins, 'Barbara Castle: Obituary', *Guardian*, 3 May

2002, www.theguardian.com/politics/2002/may/03/obituaries.
anneperkins.

28 J.R.T. Wood, *A Matter of Weeks Rather Than Months: The Impasse Between
    Harold Wilson and Ian Smith Sanctions, Aborted Settlements and War
    1965–1969* (Trafford Publishing, 2012), chapter 8.

29 'Judith Hart, 67, dies; Labor cabinet minister', *The Associated Press*,
    9 December 1991, www.nytimes.com/1991/12/09/obituaries/judith-
    hart-67-dies-labor-cabinet-minister.html.

30 *London Gazette* (Supplement), No. 47868, 14 June 1979, *London Gazette*.
    No. 51238, 11 February 1988.

31 Data from Women in the House of Commons, House of Commons
    Information Office Factsheet M4, Appendix C, Women MPs who
    have held Ministerial office, www.Parliament.uk/documents/
    commons-information-office/m04c.pdf.

32 Guida M. Jackson, *Women Leaders of Europe and the Western Hemisphere:
    A Biographical Reference* (Xlibris Corporation, 2009), p. 40. Andrew
    Mitchell, 'Biography of Margaret Beckett', *Biographical Dictionary of
    European Labor Leaders, Volume 1*, ed. A. T. Lane (Greenwood Publishing,
    1995), p. 67.

33 Isabel Hilton, *Independent*, 19 May 1994, www.independent.co.uk/
    life-style/so-why-not-margaret-amid-all-the-speculation-about-who-
    will-be-the-next-leader-of-the-labour-party-1437025.html.

34 Mandy Rhodes, 'Nothing like a dame: interview with Dame Margaret
    Beckett', *Hollyrood Magazine*, 14 March 2018, www.holyrood.com/
    articles/inside-politics/nothing-dame-interview-dame-margaret-
    beckett.

35 www.ndhs.org.uk. The school was originally operated by the Sisters of
    Notre Dame de Namur, but since 1979 it has been run by the Diocese
    of East Anglia.

36 'Margaret Beckett: Leader of the House', BBC News, 27 February
    2001, news.bbc.co.uk/news/vote2001/hi/english/key_people/
    newsid_1179000/1179262.stm.

37 'Margaret Beckett: You ask the questions', *Independent*, 30 October 2006,
    www.independent.co.uk/news/people/profiles/margaret-beckett-you-
    ask-the-questions-5331100.html.

38 'Margaret Beckett: Leader of the House', BBC News, 27 February
    2001, news.bbc.co.uk/news/vote2001/hi/english/key_people/
    newsid_1179000/1179262.stm. SEM is scanning electron microscopy
    – a microscope method that uses electrons instead of light and can
    produce images with micrometer resolution.

39 Margaret Beckett, 'This is what I've learned as Britain's longest-serving
    female MP', *Independent*, 12 November 2018, www.independent.

co.uk/voices/women-politics-vote-female-mps-westminster-bullying-harassment-margaret-beckett-a8629676.html.

40   Mary Riddell and John Kampfner, 'Interview with Margaret Beckett', *New Statesman*, 18 December 2006, www.newstatesman.com/node/195686.

41   Fred Barbash, 'New Labor Cabinet is unusually diverse lot' *Pittsburgh Post Gazette*, 14 May 1997, p. A-3.

42   'EU still opposes airlines' alliance', *Pittsburgh Post Gazette*, 21 May 1997, p. B-13, citing the *Financial Times*. 'British government blocks beer merger over fear of monopoly, *The Spokesman Review*, 13 July 1997, Associated Press, www.spokesman.com/stories/1997/jul/13/british-government-blocks-beer-merger-over-fear/.

43   David Hencke, 'Profile: Margaret Beckett', *Guardian*, 3 October 2008, www.theguardian.com/politics/2008/oct/03/labour.gordonbrown2.

44   Arthur Max, '165 countries approve rules on global warming', *Pittsburgh Post-Gazette*, 11 November 2001, p A-3.

45   '"Fuck, I'm stunned," new foreign secretary told Blair', *Guardian*, 28 June 2006, www.theguardian.com/politics/2006/jun/28/labour.uk.

46   'Margaret Beckett: You ask the questions'.

47   Margaret Beckett interviewed by Nicola Hughes and Catherine Haddon, 12 July 2016, www.instituteforgovernment.org.uk/ministers-reflect/person/margaret-beckett/.

48   Andrew Anthony, 'Six former foreign secretaries on Brexit, Britain… and Boris', *Guardian*, 4 March 2018, www.theguardian.com/politics/2018/mar/04/britain-brexit-boris-johnson-six-former-foreign-secretaries-speak.

49   Riddell and Kampfner, 'Interview with Margaret Beckett'.

50   www.britannica.com/topic/ministerial-responsibility.

51   'UK foreign policy emphasises disarmament while MoD presses ahead with renewing Trident', *Disarmament Diplomacy*, Issue No. 86, Autumn 2007, UK news and key policy documents, www.acronym.org.uk/old/archive/dd/dd86/86uk.htm#beckett.

52   George P. Schultz, William J. Perry, Henry A. Kissinger and Sam Nunn, 'Toward a nuclear-free world', *Wall Street Journal*, 15 January 2008, p. A13.

53   'Margaret Beckett: You ask the questions'.

54   Ibid.

55   Matthew Parris, 'Freedom of information killed ambassadors' valedictory dispatches. Could blogging bring them back?', *Spectator*, 22 August 2015, www.spectator.co.uk/2015/08/freedom-of-information-killed-ambassadors-valedictory-dispatches-could-blogging-bring-them-back/.

56 On 24 March 2017, Dame Margaret Beckett MP became the longest-serving female MP, serving for thirty-eight years and 128 days, in two separate periods, overtaking Gwyneth Dunwoody as the female MP with longest total service since women were first elected to the House of Commons in 1918. ukvote100.org/2017/03/27/another-record-breaker-margaret-beckett-longest-serving-woman-mp/.

57 Rhodes, 'Nothing like a dame'.

58 Gillian Merron, 'Dame Margaret Beckett', in *The Honourable Ladies: Volume I*, ed. Dale and Smith.

59 *London Gazette*, 29 December 2012, Supplement No. 1, www.thegazette. co.uk/London/issue/60367/supplement/6/data.pdf. 'New Year Honours: Margaret Beckett and Richard Shepherd on list', BBC News, 29 December 2012, www.bbc.com/news/uk-politics-20858556.

60 Beckett, 'This is what I've learned'.

61 'Talking of gender issues, does she think the next deputy leader should be a woman? "No. I think it should go to the best person."' Riddell and Kampfner, 'Interview with Margaret Beckett'.

62 'Would you favour quotas or positive discrimination to help women get on in politics? … I supported women-only shortlists as a way of redressing the under-representation of women in the House of Commons.' 'Margaret Beckett: You ask the questions'.

63 Angela Rayner: 'Women must be at the forefront of unifying our divided party', Labour List, 24 September 2016, labourlist.org/2016/09/women-who-must-be-at-the-forefront-of-unifying-our-divided-party-angela-rayners-speech/.

64 'In praise of… Margaret Beckett', *Guardian*, 10 November 2005, www.theguardian.com/politics/2005/nov/11/women.labour.

65 labourlist.org/2017/03/margaret-beckett-becomes-longest-serving-woman-mp-in-history/. www.Parliament.uk/about/art-in-Parliament/news/2017/march/monthly-artwork-beckett/.

66 www.derby.ac.uk/online/news/honorary-awards-list-announced-university-derby-nov2017.

67 Data from Former Women Ministers in UK Governments, Center for Advancement of Women in Politics, www.qub.ac.uk/cawp/UKhtmls/UKministers2.htm.

Chapter 11

1 Margaret Coker, 'How guardianship laws still control Saudi women', *New York Times*, 22 June 2018, www.nytimes.com/2018/06/22/world/middleeast/saudi-women-guardianship.html?module=inline. Megan

Specia, 'Saudi Arabia granted women the right to drive. A year on, it's still complicated', *New York Times*, 24 June 2019, www.nytimes.com/2019/06/24/world/middleeast/saudi-driving-ban-anniversary.html. Aileen Torres-Bennett and Anna Gawel, 'Female ambassadors to U.S. make strides, although progress uneven', *The Washington Diplomat*, 29 March 2019, www.washdiplomat.com/index.php?option=com_content&view=article&id=19366:female-ambassadors-to-us-make-strides-although-progress-uneven&catid=1582&Itemid=428.

2   Data from First Female Ambassadors, Worldwide Guide to Women in Leadership, compiled by Martin Iversen Christensen (with some information supplied by Mart Martin), guide2womenleaders.com/Ambassadors_F-I.htm.

3   Towns and Niklasson, 'Gender, international status, and ambassador appointments'.

4   Foreign and Commonwealth Office (FCO) Diversity and Equality Report 2017–18 in response to the Equality Act 2010. Wilson, 'Women leading British diplomacy across Europe'. FOI release: list of UK heads of mission, 5 December 2014, www.gov.uk/government/publications/foi-release-list-of-uk-heads-of-mission.

5   Foreign and Commonwealth Office (FCO) Diversity and Equality Report 2017–18 in response to the Equality Act 2010.

6   Torres-Bennett and Gawel, 'Female ambassadors to U.S. make strides'.

7   Joyce Hackel, 'Madeleine Albright: "Many of the best diplomats are women"', *The World*, Public Radio International, 25 January 2018, www.pri.org/stories/2018-01-25/madeleine-albright-many-best-diplomats-are-women.

8   Madeleine Albright, 'Madeleine Albright: My undiplomatic moment', *New York Times*, 12 February 2016, www.nytimes.com/2016/02/13/opinion/madeleine-albright-my-undiplomatic-moment.html.

9   Ray Strachey, *The Cause: A Short History of the Women's Movement in Great Britain* (Kennikat Press, 1969), p. 392.

10   Amanda Wills, Jacque Smith and Casey Hicks, 'All the countries that had a woman leader before the U.S.', *CNN*, 28 January 2019, www.cnn.com/interactive/2016/06/politics/women-world-leaders/.

11   'Facts and figures: Leadership and political participation', UN Women, June 2019, www.unwomen.org/en/what-we-do/leadership-and-political-participation/facts-and-figures.

12   www.ethnicity-facts-figures.service.gov.uk/british-population/demographics/male-and-female-populations/latest.

13   www.cawp.rutgers.edu/women-us-congress-2018.

14 'Facts and figures: Leadership and political participation', UN Women, June 2019, www.unwomen.org/en/what-we-do/leadership-and-political-participation/facts-and-figures.

15 www.theguardian.com/business/2016/apr/27/women-uk-board-positions-gender-equality-europe.

16 www.bloomberg.com/quicktake/women-boards. Rachel Feintzeig, 'Women's share of board seats rises to 20%', *Wall Street Journal*, www.wsj.com/articles/womens-share-of-board-seats-rises-to-20-11568194200.

17 nces.ed.gov/fastfacts/display.asp?id=98.

18 www.theguardian.com/education/datablog/2013/jan/29/how-many-men-and-women-are-studying-at-my-university.

19 www.computerscience.org/resources/women-in-computer-science/.

20 newsroom.ucla.edu/stories/cracking-the-code:-why-aren-t-more-women-majoring-in-computer-science.

21 ngcproject.org/statistics.

22 news.aamc.org/press-releases/article/applicant-enrollment-2016/. www.bmj.com/bmj/section-pdf/959692?path=/bmj/360/8138/Careers.full.pdf.

23 Sheryl Sandberg with Nell Scovell, *Lean In: Women, Work and the Will to Lead* (New York: Alfred A. Knopf, 2013).

24 Ibid., citing McKinsey & Company, 'Unlocking the full potential of women at work', April 2012, www.mckinsey.com/careers/women/~/media/Reports/Women/2012%20WSJ%20Women%20in%twentiethe%20Economy%20white%20paper%20FINAL.ashx.

25 quotefancy.com/quote/14867/Joseph-Campbell-If-the-path-before-you-is-clear-you-re-probably-on-someone-else-s.

26 www.ellevatenetwork.com/articles/7604-quotes-about-being-a-pioneer.

INDEX